Shattering Silence

*

A tender and protective madonna looks over the beginning of Falls Road. Republican black taxis busy themselves up and down the road. On the far right a brick wall traces the peace line.

Shattering Silence

WOMEN, NATIONALISM, AND POLITICAL
SUBJECTIVITY IN NORTHERN IRELAND

*

BEGOÑA ARETXAGA

PRINCETON UNIVERSITY PRESS

PRINCETON, NEW JERSEY

Library of Congress Cataloging-in-Publication Data
Aretxaga, Begoña.
Shattering silence : women, nationalism, and political
subjectivity in Northern Ireland / Begoña Aretxaga.
p. cm.
Includes bibliographical references and index.
ISBN 0-691-03755-8 (cloth : alk. paper). — ISBN 0-691-03754-X
(pbk. : alk. paper)
1. Women—Northern Ireland—Belfast—Political activity. 2. Women
political activists—Northern Ireland—Belfast. 3. Nationalism—
Northern Ireland. 4. Northern Ireland—Politics and
government—1960–1994. 5. Belfast (Northern Ireland)—Politics and
government. I. Title.
HQ1236.5.G7A74 1997   97-4176
306.2'082—dc21   CIP

This book has been composed in Baskerville

The poem "Punishment" by Seamus Heaney that appears on
page 152 is reprinted from Seamus Heaney, *North* (London:
Faber and Faber Ltd., 1975), with permission of the publisher.

A portion of the poem "Easter 1991" by Máighréad Medbh that appears on
page 168 is reprinted from *Feminist Review* 44 (Summer 1993),
Nationalism and National Identities, with permission of the author.

http://pup.princeton.edu

Printed in the United States of America

10 9 8 7 6 5 4 3 2 1

10 9 8 7 6 5 4 3 2
(Pbk.)

A MI MADRE, MERTXE SANTOS
Y MI ABUELA, MERCEDES GONZALEZ
Y PARA KOLDO, ARANTXA Y AMAIA

*

* Contents *

* Preface *

W HEN I arrived in Belfast for the first time in the summer of 1987, I went to the Falls Road, the main street of the larger Catholic area, which would become my home for more than fifteen months the following year. This was the stronghold of the IRA, and I had been warned by a professor at Queens University to stay clear of it. Siobhan, a native of Belfast and then fellow graduate student at Princeton University, kindly offered to come with me on that first visit to The Falls. As we walked up the hill, I became both slightly apprehensive and bemused by the murals and graffiti that greeted us with the images of a political culture yet unknown to me. The encouragement I received from one such writing on the wall, which, like a tourist's guide, stated "Welcome to Provo Land" (provo being a derivation of Provisionals, the name given to the current IRA after the organization split in 1972), seemed to take an ironic tone in the face of the menacing presence of military troops who, fully equipped and armed, moved watchfully up and down the street. It was a sunny day, however, and, as I would soon learn, this alone gave the district a cheerful aspect. Roses were in bloom in the tiny backyards; children played on the streets; people were smiling and joking with each other.

I had gone to Falls Road to talk about my research with Con, whose name I had been given by a colleague as someone who knew about "nationalist women." It was my first conversation with one of the locals. When I mentioned to her that I was interested in writing a book about nationalist women, she said forcefully: "Women are the backbone of the struggle; they are the ones carrying the war here and they are not receiving the recognition they deserve." There was nothing exceptional about this statement; it is well known that the participation of women in revolutionary struggles and wars of liberation is often observed as much in scholarship of political life as in the unfolding political practice. Yet her words remained in the back of my mind, unobtrusive but unfading, for the duration of my research. What exactly did unrecognized mean? The previous day a representative of the Women's Center in the neutral area of downtown Belfast had strongly emphasized to me that women, both Catholic and Protestant, were the real victims of the violent conflict. Now, Con was telling me that women were carrying the war. What did she mean? And what did it mean to say that women were the backbone of the struggle? Did she imply that women were the pillars of radical nationalism or that the republican struggle was being fought on the backs of women, or both? By talking about women as the "backbone"—a metaphor that I would hear now and again—Con could also imply that women formed a sort of rearguard, an invisible, if not necessarily passive, support structure. If this were so, then why after almost twenty years had women not become part of the visible body of the struggle? And if they had become visible, then why were they still politically unrecognized?

This book is an ethnography of nationalist, working-class women, who are both unrecognized and misrecognized. It is not, however, about "setting the record straight"; it is about the gender structure of politics and the political structuring of gender. It is about the processes that make nationalist women in Northern Ireland political subjects of a particular kind, differentiated among themselves and different from men. The politics within which I locate the political subjectivity of nationalist women are those of the state, republican nationalism, and feminism. As this book is concerned with the formation of gendered political subjects, its central question is about the possibilities and limits of feminist change within the constraints of social and political relations of power. Foremost among these relations of power are the interlocking systems of inequality of colonialism, class, and gender.

My research was conducted in Catholic West Belfast, a district of approximately one hundred thousand inhabitants, largely working class, with a high percentage of unemployment. The electoral ward of West Belfast includes the hardcore Protestant area of Shankill Road, which is separated from the Catholic area by a wall called "the peace line." In this book I follow local custom of using simply West Belfast to refer to Catholic West Belfast, the larger part of the district. I lived for fifteen months in Springfield-Beechmount, a tightly knit area that grows off Falls Road at the heart of West Belfast. This is not, however, a community study. Given the high level of military surveillance, a small community study would have been extremely difficult and inappropriate, as local people rightly feel that the gathering of detailed information on their everyday lives may contribute to military intelligence. Legitimate research is not discouraged, however. One goal of my prospective visit to Belfast during the summer of 1986 was to determine the feasibility of conducting research about the relation of women to nationalism. The community activists and Sinn Fein members with whom I consulted on this respect were enthusiastic about the research and eager to provide helpful information. They also encouraged me to live in a nationalist area while conducting the research so I could see for myself what life was like there.

Nationalist women were often more self-conscious of security and more reluctant to speak about their political experience than men, who in my experience had little trouble recounting their tales. In good part for this reason I decided to focus my research on past events that took place during the first decade of the conflict. This decision made sense on a number of levels. It was simply less risky for people to talk about the past. Former prisoners, for example, could be candid about their political involvement because they had already served sentence for it. Current militants could not afford the same openness. On a few occasions I had to face women who simply did not wish to speak to me about their political histories, who refused to become subjects of study, as Kamala Visweswaran has recently put it (1994, 60). A prominent member of the Relatives Action Committees that I discuss in chapter 5 was at the time of my fieldwork "tired of telling her life." An energetic member of Sinn Fein wanted to arrange for me an interview with a couple of elderly nationalist women, former members of Cumman na mBan (the female branch of the IRA). These women kept postponing the date for an interview until I was finally told that they were concerned about how their words might be used and did not want to go through with the interview. In addition to an awareness of the power of knowledge produced by living in a community subjected to constant surveillance—a community that has experienced the imprisonment of people solely on the word of informers—women shared a skepticism about the uses of representation. Although journalism was most often the object of critique for misrepresenting the social realities of Northern Ireland, scholarly representations were not totally beyond reproach either. Many women, of course, spoke freely and forcefully about themselves and the politics of Northern Ireland; otherwise, this book would not have been written. However, situating the terrain of inquiry in the past helped dispel reticence and made it possible to articulate present dilemmas in a safe way.

My initial idea, however, was to research the relation of nationalism to gender structures as they manifested themselves at the time of my fieldwork. Yet, in talking about their contemporary experience of politics, women of different feminist and nationalist persuasions kept alluding, both implicitly and explicitly to a previous political history. I became convinced that only by researching their history could I understand the present dilemmas defining the relation between nationalism and feminism. This historical perspective also seemed appropriate for assessing processes of social change. But this is not a book about what happened to women during the 1970s; rather, it is about processes and mechanisms of transformation—cultural, personal, sociopolitical—about the way they do and do not work. This is a crucial question for those who find themselves in a socially subordinated position, more so for those whose subordinate position is multiplied by the confluence of class, gender, race, ethnicity, religion, and so on. I have tried to look at how transformation both occurs and is limited through what Sally Moore (1987) called "diagnostic events" and Venna Das (1995) more recently has named "critical events." In either case these are events capable of producing a change in the way people think about things, events that contain in their complexity the intertwined, often contradictory threads of social experience and are thus particularly rich and illuminating fields of enquiry. The events through which I develop my reflections on transformation unfolded during the 1970s and beginning of the 1980s. I do not think that I could have understood and analyzed them in the way that I have done without the knowledge gained by living for fifteen months in West Belfast. I think now that my writing bears a peculiar relation to history: the past could not have been interpreted without my fieldwork in the present, nor could the present be understood without knowledge of the past. For this reason, this book neither dispenses with chronology, nor does it follow a continued chronological narrative; it moves back and forth as it explores themes articulated in nodal events.

Following sociological and anthropological scholarship on Northern Ireland, I use the labels "Catholic" and "nationalist" interchangeably to refer to an ethnic identity rather than a religious or strictly political one. Not all Catholics are nationalists, nor are all nationalists Catholic. But both terms commonly designate an "imagined community" in the sense of Benedict Anderson (1983) that defines itself as Irish rather than British and prefers the political frame of a united Ireland rather than that of the United Kingdom. In this sense my use of "community," like the sense used by the people of Belfast, refers to a shared identity, general culture, and historical experience, rather than to an internally homogeneous group (if indeed homogeneity is ever anything more than imagined in any community). Important political differences within the nationalist community of West Belfast have led to bitter disputes and on various occasions to violent feuds. Yet these differences do not override for people a sense of shared experience and identity.

This book deals primarily with the republican sector of the national-ist community, that is, radical nationalists committed to achieving a united Irish republic. Its core consists of the IRA and the political party Sinn Fein. However, a number of other smaller republican parties, born from a history of IRA splits, also operate in the community. In addition, there is a multiplicity of grass-roots community organizations whose members might loosely share a republican ideology but do not form part of any defined political party or paramilitary group. As a movement, republicanism is highly fluid. As other researchers have pointed out (Burton 1978; Sluka 1989), republicanism springs from the wider na-tionalist culture of Catholic working-class areas and surpasses any spe-cific organization.

Most women with whom I worked ranged in age from twenty to fifty years. Some were older, some younger. I have used pseudonyms throughout the book to conceal the identity of the people with whom I worked, except for those who gave me explicit permission to use their names. For the same reason I have also avoided other details that might contribute to their identification.

Many people have made this book possible. Without the generosity and support of people in Belfast the research would never have gotten off the ground. I thank especially Joe, Eileen M., Roisin, Marie, Una, Catherine, Mairead, Chrissie, Jennifer, Marguerite, Mary B., Geraldine, Tish, Ruth, Brenda, Eileen L., Mary E., Rita, Lili, Emma, Bid, Carol, Ann Mary, Briege, Barbara, Fran. In Derry I thank Daisy, Martha, Bernie, Louise. I withhold their surnames to protect their identity, but they know who they are. Their words traverse the pages of this book under disguised names. Renee and John Kilfeather were like family to me from the very beginning, providing endless warmth, hot meals, hot toddies, and always interesting stories. Joe and Eileen also became family through the travails of close life in West Belfast; I learned much from their generosity and courage. Thanks to the department of anthropol-ogy at Queen's University, especially May McCann for her support of my project and help with gaining access to the university library and ser-vices. I am deeply indebted to Robert Bell, former director of the polit-ical collection of the Linen Hall Library; he and the library staff at the political collection went out of their way to help me with sources and to accommodate my working through boxes and stacks of papers in the midst of their cataloguing in the tiny space they shared with me. Thanks also to the Belfast Public Library, The Women's Center in Donegal Street, The Falls Women's Center, Women's News, Falls Road Community Center, Sinn Fein Women's Department, Sinn Fein Advice Center (Falls Road), Connolly House, Derry Sinn Fein Center.

In the United States I received the support and intellectual challenge of the faculty and graduate students of the anthropology department at Princeton University, where I wrote the first draft of this book as a doctoral dissertation. I am indebted to Gananath Obeyesekere, James Fernandez, Kay Warren, and Joan Scott, for much support, inspiration, and good advice in the writing of this book. William Christian, Kamala Visweswaran, and Joan Vincent read the whole manuscript in earlier and/or later versions and improved it with their suggestions, comments, and articulations of what was inchoate in it. Hildreed Geertz, Ernestine Friedl, Jim Boon, and John Kelly helped in different ways. My colleagues at Harvard have been an ongoing source of intellectual stimulation and collegial support. Mary Steedly, Kenneth George, and Mary-Jo DelVecchio Good read parts of the manuscript and helped with titles and remaining obscurities. Stanley Tambiah and Michael Herzfeld have been terrific interlocutors with whom I have sharpened ideas during innumerable conversations. Many thanks to them all.

Mary Murrell has been an unfailingly supportive editor, and I am grateful for her guidance in navigating this mysterious world of book production. Sara Bush fought valiantly against bureaucratic rules and regulations to obtain the photograph of a Belfast map hidden in Firestone Library. Jane Huber went beyond duty and friendship in editing the manuscript before it went to the Press and making sure all its pieces were in the right place. She also composed the index. I'll be eternally grateful. Andrew Gossen helped with bits and pieces, and was invaluable in tracking down references. Lisa Jerry, the copy editor, improved the manuscript in a sensible and sensitive manner. Stever Burger did a wonderful job developing black and white photographs out of color negatives.

The research for this book was funded by the Institute of Intercultural Studies, a joint grant by the Social Sciences Research Council and the American Council of Learned Societies, the MacArthur Foundation, and a Milton grant for faculty research from Harvard University.

Shattering Silence

*

CHAPTER 1

Opening the Space of Interpretation

I READ the headlines of the *New York Times* on September 1, 1994, with joyful surprise: "IRA declares cease-fire seeing new opportunity to negotiate Irish peace." The photograph in the front page of the newspaper depicted two girls happily waving little nationalist flags through the window of a passing car in West Belfast. For once the news was good. Not long after the IRA's declaration, Protestant paramilitaries called a cease-fire, too. The war in Northern Ireland was apparently over. In the whirlwind of political statements and diplomatic activities that followed, Gerry Adams, president of Sinn Fein—the political wing of the IRA— swiftly changed from terrorist to emerging statesman in yet another demonstration of how fluid such categories can be. There were a lot of questions in my mind. I was writing this book about the politics of nationalist women during the violent conflict that followed the rise of the civil rights movement in Northern Ireland in 1968. Now the war seemed to have come to an end. What were these women thinking? What were they doing? How would they participate in the newly opened peace process? There was no mention of women in the multiple declarations and news reports about the peace. I telephoned Marie, a republican community activist I had come to know well during my fieldwork research in 1988–1989. She was full of news but also apprehensive. Contrary to my unqualified excitement Marie sounded skeptical: "There is no peace yet," she said, "only deals being made by male politicians behind closed doors; it's all very confusing." Marie, a republican feminist, was critical of the fact that a decision so profoundly affecting the lives of everybody in Northern Ireland had been made so unilaterally, without consultation to different sectors of the communities. Her skepticism was shared by other republican feminists with whom I spoke in Belfast three months later. Not all republican women had the same opinion, of course; some were unconditionally supporting Sinn Fein policy. Nevertheless, there were enough critics to cause a stir among the ranks of the well-disciplined republican movement. At first I could not understand why these women were so critical. In the face of such a major breakthrough in the politics of Northern Ireland their concerns appeared petty. It seemed logical to me that in a context dominated by the secrecy

3

of military organizations, a decision so politically delicate as a cease-fire would not have been openly discussed. And yet this was precisely the point. For republican feminists a lasting peace could only coalesce through an open process of discussion that involved all parts in the different communities. At stake for these women was not just the cessation of bombings and killings, but the future that they had envisioned through twenty-five years of struggle, a future that appeared in danger of being hijacked by the secret negotiations of a male leadership.

At a time of international complacency with the cease-fire in Northern Ireland, the critical attitude of republican feminists seem to run against the grain of the cherished stereotypes that so often have associated women with peace and men with war, as if these less than straightforward notions—peace and war—were a matter of hormone secretion. Despite the growing documentation of women's involvement in guerrilla movements and wars of liberation, the popular perception of women as the "non-combatant many" (Elshtain 1987, 163) continues to be dominant. Indeed representations of the conflict in Northern Ireland have been saturated with images of violent men and victimized women.[1] This simplistic genderized polarization is profoundly disrupted by the reality of the heterogeneous and contraposed political positions taken by women. Because these positions escape easy categorization, the politics of women further disturbs and complicates all major representational narratives of the conflict that have been organized around sets of demarcated binarisms like British/Irish, nationalist/loyalist, Catholic/Protestant. Precisely because of their anomalous and subversive character within established definitions of the political, the politics of nationalist women has been eclipsed in the accounts of Northern Ireland conflict. Women have been left out not because analysts have recognized their subversive potential but because, by not fitting existing discourses, they have not been recognized at all as socially relevant. If this is the case for nationalist women in general, then it is more so when it comes to republican women, whose political involvement often runs against the grain of the two major political fields in which it operates: nationalism and feminism. The critical attitude of republican women toward the peace process is both an example and a result of their specific, uneasy positioning within Northern Ireland's politics.

Republican women like Marie do, of course, want peace. That is not the issue. The question for them is what exactly does peace mean? Defining peace, like defining war, means delineating the terms for a particular kind of society and a particular political structure. Peace and war are not so much two opposed states of being as they are multifaceted, ambiguous, mutually imbricated arenas of struggle. Peace does not necessarily entail the end of violent conflict; indeed, it can often heighten it, as recent developments in South Africa and Palestine, for example, illustrate.

When I visited Belfast in January 1995, republican feminists—some members of Sinn Fein, others not, most of them community activists— were worried and angered by the invisibility of women in the political process opened by the cease-fire. Their concern was shared by other women's organizations that were organizing themselves to have an input in the process.[2] To ensure that their voices would not be ignored in the new political conjuncture republican women had formed an organization Clar na mBan (Women's Agenda) whose main goal was to formulate and advance a "women's agenda for peace" that would be at once republican and feminist. With that purpose in mind, Clar na mBan held a conference in Belfast. More than 150 women from different community organizations gathered to discuss the peace process. The published report of the conference was an attempt to articulate the positions of republican feminists at a time when their voice was marginalized as much by republican discourse as by moderate mainstream feminism. The report declared at the outset the importance for women of "asserting our differences as well as our common ground."[3] The recognition and negotiation of difference was a salient theme of the conference. The other central issue was the implementation of democratic mechanisms that could ensure political participation of all social groups. This might seem a reasonable demand, but in a place marked by the scars of systematic ethnic and gender discrimination, the call for democracy as the sine qua non condition for peace was radical. The call was also a lucid reminder that political exclusion and violence are profoundly linked in the history of Ireland. Indeed, the inability to include Sinn Fein in all party talks— that is, to recognize republicans as subjects of political discourse in their own right—lead in February 1996 to the breakdown of the cease-fire and the crisis of the peace process.

Marginal as it might be within the intricate political landscape of Northern Ireland, the formation of Clar na mBan is important as an interpellation to historical narratives, nationalist or otherwise, that have excluded women from their records. I use interpellation here in its strict sense rather than in the sense Althusser uses it to describe the functioning of ideology. The *Oxford English Dictionary* defines the action of interpellation as "to appeal, to interrupt in speaking, to break in on or to disturb." I see Clar na mBan, and the political practices that I describe in this book, as constituting precisely such irruptions in political discourse, disturbing presences that break the order of authorized historical narratives and in so doing raise questions about the nature of such order.

Clar na mBan is a preemptive move to the familiar dismissal of women: "the war is over; your services are no longer required." By this deadly sentence Irish women, like so many others, were gradually forced back into the restrictive domesticity of postcolonial Ireland. It emerged thus as an affirmation of historical agency by nationalist women, at a moment when such agency ran the risk of being reified into oblivion, the way the inconvenient history of the "unmanageable revolutionaries" (Ward 1983) of preindependence Ireland was left to dust on the old shelves of archives, airing it now and then to pay lip service at the occasional commemoration. This is the irony of history: it is written not to be forgotten, and yet, once it is written it can be forgotten.

The breakdown of the cease-fire has again shifted women's political perspectives in Northern Ireland. For republican nationalist women questions of historical agency are likely to be framed in yet another context. But just what kind of agency is it? Through what discourses and practices has it been constituted? What political subjectivities has it engendered? What social effects has it produced? To answer these questions I turn now to the field of war.

CONSTRUCTING GENDERED IDENTITIES

During the 1970s, women in the Catholic/nationalist districts of Belfast organized popular forms of resistance against the violence deployed by the Northern Ireland police and the British army in those areas of the city. Yet in the abundant social science literature on the conflict the political practices of nationalist women have either passed virtually unnoticed or been considered anecdotal to the *real politics* of the conflict.[4] I intend to show that, far from being politically irrelevant, these "invisible" practices were crucial to the local configuration of the conflict with important effects on the organization of nationalist culture and the refiguration of women's identities. Furthermore nationalist women's political practices illuminate the complex mechanisms by which political processes in general and Irish nationalism in particular are en-gendered. Moreover, because they operate in the interstices of political life the politics of nationalist women offer a unique perspective from which to examine the possibilities and limits of social transformation.

Despite the general absence of research about Northern Ireland women, a number of articles, pamphlets, and a few books have emerged during the last fifteen years.[5] Most of them have been written by local feminist activists. They reflect ongoing debates among Irish feminists and articulate the variety of political positions taken by feminist women (Devaney et al. 1989; Evason 1991; Loughran 1986; Ward 1983, 1987, 1991).[6] Common to these pieces is the ineludible tension of difference within Irish feminism. The attempt to come to terms with the impossibility of a feminist practice based on a common identity as women was the object of an important feminist conference held in Belfast in 1983, a decade after second-wave feminism began its first steps in Northern Ireland. Coming to terms with difference was not an easy task. Its difficulty was reflected in the telling title of the published report of the conference, *A Difficult, Dangerous Honesty: Ten Years of Feminism in Northern Ireland*, edited by Margaret Ward. As in other parts of the world, the feminist movement in Northern Ireland had initially hoped to foster a unitary women's identity that could transcend the polarized ethnic divide between Catholic and Protestants, nationalists and loyalists. The prison protests of the late 1970s made evident that feminism could not exist outside prevailing structures of power, which in Northern Ireland were inescapably defined by ethnicity and class (Loughran 1986). In 1989 a pamphlet significantly titled *Unfinished Revolution* (Devaney et al. 1989) went a step further, from the recognition to the articulation of political difference. The authors of this text—republican women, lesbians, Irish language activists—proposed new forms of feminism in which their voices, hitherto silenced by mainstream feminism, could be represented. The arguments filtering through these feminist writings provide an important window into the complexities, ambiguities, and instabilities that permeate the politics of identity in Northern Ireland. For all its ambiguity, the politics of identity have shaped the political experience of women, leading them to take different and often contraposed positions in the not less ambiguous arena of feminism. Women frequently refer to their different social experience to reinforce their diverse political positions. Nationalist women, for example, say that experiencing anti-Catholic violence taught them the meaning of second-class citizenship or that living under military occupation committed them to fight against the injustice of colonialism. Thus, nationalist women ex-

7

plicitly blend their lived experience into a political view of social relations, into what I call a political experience, the experience of an engagement to change the world in which they live from a particular social position. Yet the complex processes that have constituted such political experience—their contradictions, ambiguities, limits, and possibilities—have been seldom examined. Those processes are precisely my concern in this book.

Joan Scott (1991) has warned historians about the perils of taking experience as unproblematic evidence of social processes. The warning does also apply to anthropologists. Yet not only scholars, but also historical actors, may take experience for granted. The appeal to experience, to different experiences, is what legitimizes different feminist positions in Northern Ireland. When the experience of women from subordinate groups (nationalist women, lesbian women, working-class women, loyalist women) is what is obscured, denied, excluded from public discourse, to foreground experience might indeed be a necessary political act. Much of this book is therefore about the political experience of nationalist women, an experience that I and they acutely feel has been socially unrecognized, rendered invisible as much by the dominant discourse within feminism as by that of nationalism. In foregrounding experience, however, one runs the risk of leaving unquestioned the conditions that enable it, that make this particular political experience historically possible. How then can we write about experience in a way that foregrounds it yet does not take it for granted? While discourse theorists tend to focus on the linguistic construction of experience rather than on the meaning of lived experience, phenomenologically oriented scholars are often unconcerned with the political histories of its construction. It is as if attention to discourse would preclude attention to experience, and yet it seems to me that neither can exist without the other. For political agency—the capacity of people to become historical subjects deliberately intervening in the making and changing of their worlds—is the product of a movement that goes back and forth from discursive possibility to experience to change in the conditions of possibility. Political agency thus presupposes a degree of consciousness and intentionality as the Comaroffs (1991) have observed, but it is anchored in a cultural repository of largely unconscious discourses and images, modes of thinking and feeling. Whether we think of this cultural repository as the Foucaudian "episteme," Bourdieu's "habitus," Gramsci's "hegemony," or the Lacanian "imaginary," an account of political experience that seeks to elucidate the possibilities of social transformation cannot afford to ig-

political agency

8

nore it. It cannot because, as Obeyesekere (1990) has argued, the transformation of culture entails the change of meanings and affects that are deeply rooted in the personal and social imaginary of particular people. For Drucilla Cornell we must pay attention to how this collective imaginary works because "part of the political struggle is to shift reality through shifting the meaning of our shared symbols. Politics is not just about power but also about the very basis of what can become 'real' and thus accessible to consciousness and change" (1993, 194). An account of political agency must go beyond, not beside, the narratives of political experience as told by specific individuals to inquire about the formation of political subjectivity. This means asking how political subjects come to be formed, and (to echo Clifford Geertz) not just formed in abstract, general ways but within systems of ethnic, gender, and sexual difference that are particularly configured within local places. Thus, in this book I am concerned with the political subjectivity of working-class nationalist women, the mechanisms through which it is constituted and transformed, and the effects that such subjectivity can produce on a political culture and on a gendered universe.

REPRESENTATIONS

Nationalist women's political activism has been interpreted in the scant available literature as either an extension of a domestic role without broader transformative implications or as cooptation in a male-led war (Buckley and Lonergan 1984; Edgerton 1986; Fairweather et al. 1984; Shannon 1989). These works tend to portray women as victims of a violent conflict over which they have little control. This victimization of women is also a feature of popular fiction written about the North. When women are not represented as passive victims, as is the case with members of the IRA, they appear as viragos (Rolston 1989), out-of-place women who are "hovering in the marginal interstices of cultural life" (Elshtain 1987, 170). Northern Ireland women writers also tend to represent women as trapped victims. The Catholic women in Anne Devlin's plays, for example, are pawns in men's fights with each other. The female characters of contemporary Irish novels written by women on the subject of Northern Ireland are overwhelmed by impotence in the face of a meaningless violence (Weekes 1995). When women struggle to establish an independent existence within a male-dominated universe of violence, they are either defeated as in Jennifer Johnston's *Shadows on*

women as victims

Our Skin (1978), or their defiance is composed of solitary and self-contained gestures, as in Mary Beckett's stories *A Belfast Woman* (1980), where women are left to an aimless use of what James Scott has called "weapons of the weak" (1985).[7] A notable exception to this pervasive representation of women is Nell McCafferty's *Peggy Deery* (1981), the biography of an "ordinary" nationalist woman that depicts with sharpness, wit, and insight the complexity of women's lives within the violent political context of the city of Derry.

By judging from these representations nationalist women seemingly have no choice and little agency. But then, what are we going to make of the women who walked the streets of their neighborhoods at night to prevent their menfolk from military detention, organized marches to protest arbitrary arrests, took arms against the state, defied the penal system by smearing their prison cells with feces and menstrual blood, clad themselves in blankets and traveled the world to break the silence on state violence, or argued to assert a distinctive feminist voice within male-dominated organizations? These women, their history, and their complex social practices challenge the assumption that women are the passive bystanders of a war between male factions. Nationalist women who have taken sides in the war become anomalies within representations of the conflict, co-opted into either defending male interests or acting like men, that is, being not quite women. This narrow representation of nationalist women assumes that women's first interests reside in an unquestioned gender identity and ignores, as Coulter has noted, the links between women and their communities (1993, 54).

It is precisely the confining limits of representations of femininity that produce, for Drucilla Cornell, the experience of silencing for actual women. Thus, for her, feminism cannot be separated from the attempt to articulate "the experience of being pushed against the limit of meaning as an actual woman struggling with and against the restrictive femininity imposed by the gender hierarchy" (1993, 77). The story of the women who are protagonists in this book is a story of pushing against the limits of cultural meaning. Excluded from the discourses of war and from the discourse of feminism, marginal to the arena of dominant political practices, the actions of nationalist women emerge, however, as the locus of a political subjectivity that explodes the limits of gender and nationalist representations in Northern Ireland.

The limits of gender identity as the axis of feminist politics have been, of course, amply noted by a long list of feminist scholars and activists all over the world. Feminists in postcolonial societies and women of color,

often grouped under the rubric of "minority women," a misnomer because they are the majority in the world, have repeatedly pointed out that
the struggle against gender inequality has concealed other inequalities in
the feminist movement. Feminist theorists have increasingly recognized
that gendered subjects are constructed in an inextricable relation with
positions of class, race, ethnicity, which are historically articulated
through contested social structures and cultural representations (Scott
1988). As political subjects, nationalist women in Northern Ireland must
also be situated in relation to, and in the context of the gendered organization of nationalist politics, the history of Anglo-Irish colonial relations, and historically situated cultural representations. From this view,
the politics of nationalist women affects not only the sphere of gender
relations, representations, and symbols, but also historical narratives, nationalist discourse, and colonial practices.

The question that must be posed is not about the relation between
two different terms women and nationalism, or women and colonialism;
the question is about the mechanisms by which colonial and nationalist
discourses and practices are en-gendered and the process by which gendered subjects may change them via practice. Thus posed this question
entails an interrogation of the mechanisms of social and political
change. The leading question of this book is how does this process of
transformation work in a nationalist ghetto of Belfast from what Donna
Haraway (1991, 191) has called a "subjugated standpoint," that of nationalist women? Phrased in another way the question I pursue becomes: what are the possibilities of feminist transformation within the
context of a colonial and nationalist history that has used gender as a
symbolic terrain wherein to formulate arguments of domination and resistance? Answering this question entails, as Mohanty has argued in relation to women's history in postcolonial societies, reading against the
grain of a number of intersecting discourses: nationalist, feminist, colonialist, capitalist (Mohanty et al. 1991, 4). I situate political subjectivity
at the intersection of these discourses and the practices they engender
in particular localities such as Belfast.

THE AMBIGUITIES OF COLONIALISM

Reading against the grain of colonial and nationalist discourses is to ask
how does gender function as signifying form. The scholarship on colonialism has shown that gender cannot be extricated from constructions

11

of sexuality and race in enabling hierarchical definitions of "self" and "other" (Bhabha 1994; Comaroff and Comaroff 1991; Fanon 1967; Nandy 1983; Said 1978; Suleri 1992b), organizing political debates (Kelly 1991), designing colonial policies (Stoler 1991), and constructing national identities (Chatterjee 1986, 1993; Mani 1990). Ireland does not escape these interrelations. In fact the status of Ireland as a colony continues to be, as David Lloyd has recently noted, a vexing question that has raised continued debate among Irish historians and literary critics and generated a good deal of public polemic.[8] The partition of the island in 1921 and the continuation of Northern Ireland under British dominion has contributed in no small measure to the uncertainty that permeates representations of Ireland.

In many ways the peculiarities and complexities of the Anglo-Irish colonial relation complicate the very categories of colonial and postcolonial often used interchangeably with that of the Third World. The concept of postcolonialism is not in itself devoid of ambiguities. Postcolonialism indicates the formal decolonization of the world and the rise of new nations, but, as Dirks has reminded us, such formal discontinuity with the colonial political systems of the past barely disguises the continuation of relations of exploitation in the new world order of transnational capital and international division of labor (1992, 5). In this sense the notion of postcolonialism, like all post-something, while signaling a new arena of relationships, retains and for its meaning depends on both the old colonial situation and contemporary readings of it.

Colonialism and postcolonialism, however, like its accompanying term postmodernism, have been frequently dislodged in the various intellectual discourses from their historical specificities to variously allegorize an ensemble of different things: a cultural field, a situation of oppression, a condition of being (as in "the postcolonial condition"), or an alter to Western subjectivity. Sara Suleri has pointedly argued that, although this usage of the notion of the postcolonial is helpful in opening the space to new theoretical articulations around issues of migrancy and transnationalism, at the same time "the metaphorization of postcolonialism threatens to become so amorphous as to repudiate any locality for cultural thickness" (1992b, 759). The risk of displacing thick cultural analysis in favor of conceptual clichés has also been the central point of Sherry Ortner's (1995) critique of the way resistance is treated in ethnographic writing.

The danger of intellectual cliché emerges with pointed clarity when it comes to feminism. Within feminist discourse the category of "Third World women" or the seemingly identical designation of "postcolonial women" has brought to the surface the unacknowledged differences of power among women, yet it has also posited an identity that has obscured the complexities of power confronting women in specific postcolonial settings. The categorical demarcation between Western and non-Western that the category of postcolonial women entails runs the risk of reinstating old colonial binarisms that grouped together people of different societies and cultures into a native "other." But it also articulates a political voice by women hitherto marginalized in mainstream feminism. This double edge has provoked much debate among feminist critics.

Chandra Mohanty, for example, has critiqued the deployment of the category of Third World women in the writing of Western feminists. For her, such category has been anchored in notions of victimhood that occlude the historical agency of Third World women and thus effectively function as a form of reification. Such critique does not impede Mohanty to affirm the analytical validity of the category, that, becomes helpful when used by Third World women, the only ones who for her, can accurately represent their own histories. For Mohanty, foregrounding the category of Third World women advantageously emphasizes the links between their histories and struggles by suggesting "an imagined community of Third World oppositional struggles. A community that is not homogeneous and in which gender is not defined in a transhistorical way" (Mohanty et al. 1991, 4). The idea of an "imagined community" of Third World women has indeed political advantages, not the least of which is the ability to contextualize particular struggles within a broader internationalist context, allowing thus exchange of information, contacts, and political alliances. Movements of national liberation, for example, were not solely shaped by their specific histories; their struggles did not develop in isolation from each other but in the context of mutual influence and political support. The struggle for Irish independence during the first two decades of the twentieth century was followed with great interest by Asian and African nationalists, many of whom made a point of visiting Ireland (Brasted 1980; Davis 1986). This was also the case for women, involved in these movements, whose demands for emancipation were shaped by not only the example of women in other revolutionary movements but also feminists struggles in Europe, as Jayawardena has

13

documented (1986, 10–14). Republican/nationalist women often represent themselves alongside Palestinian and South African women in an international revolutionary scape.

Beyond the vagaries of political representation, however, Mohanty's main argument is epistemological in character. For her only Third World women can know and accurately represent the reality of women's lives in postcolonial societies. Thus Mohanty endows the idea of an "imagined community" with an epistemological foundation that authenticates or disavows the production of knowledge on the basis of origin. This argument is of course problematic. As Suleri (1992b) has noted, it reduces the complexities and enormous differences between women's lives in the Third World to the questionable idea of shared experience and common purpose. Although such an idea can perhaps operate as advantageous political tactic in some particular contexts it cannot serve as epistemological foundation.

The critic Gayatry Spivak (1988) has eloquently argued that the notion of subaltern women accessible to and representable by disinterested Third World intellectuals cannot be sustained. On the one hand, such a notion assumes the idea of a consciousness already existing in some authentic form that can be heard if only one listens carefully. The problem, Spivak has argued, is that such consciousness already has a history (the gendering history of colonialism, of anticolonial resistance, of local patriarchal authority) that has constructed it in contradictory forms. The scholar then is able to represent not the authentic consciousness of subaltern woman but a historical form of it (see, e.g., Pathak and Rajan 1992). On the other hand, the idea of a disinterested postcolonial intellectual who, by virtue of an assumed common position as a Third World person, can represent the experience of subaltern people is, for Spivak, disingenuous. It masks the fact that any representation is necessarily a construction made from a political and epistemological position, which already differs from that of the subaltern subject the postcolonial intellectual seeks to represent. To rephrase Spivak's critique we could say that Third World feminists do not escape ideology any more than Western feminists do. Not to recognize this fact might be to fall prey to a pernicious kind of false consciousness, that is, to reproduce in an inverted form the imperialist illusion of an unproblematic knowing subject.

The problems noted above are particularly highlighted by the "Anomalous State of Ireland" (Lloyd 1993). Caught between colonialism, postcoloniality and Europeaness, Ireland, to evoke Luce Irigaray, is *that nation that is not one.* It is not one not only because it is literally divided in what it seems irreconciliable parts but because as a national reality Ireland is constituted by a lack that exceeds and escapes dominant representation. The 1921 treaty between England and the leaders of the Irish war of independence that gave Ireland home rule (a status of partial independence) also left the country divided in two parts, and irreconcilably split in a war among protreaty and antitreaty factions. Partition—the exclusion of the six counties that became Northern Ireland from the national project—was, in fact, the price paid by Ireland to achieve the status of nationhood within the world order. The violence of this exclusion, iconized in the civil war that followed the division of the country, became the great silence upon which Irish national identity was constructed. Postcolonial nationalism was not built on the imagery of fraternity that Benedict Anderson (1983) attributes to nationalism, but on the silent facts of fratricide—not on the affirmation of territorial sovereignty, but on the certainty of territorial fragmentation. Precisely for this reason Northern Ireland functioned as a reminder of the precarious identity of Ireland as a nation. In the postcolonial process of constructing the Irish nation-state, Northern Ireland became the jettisoned other against which the government of the independent Ireland erected a powerful barrier of information censorship. In the mirroring play of identity, Northern Ireland became both the unaltered "other" of Britain and the suppressed internal "other" of Ireland. This silenced internal alterity was shattered by the political violence that has constituted a permanent feature of Northern Ireland since 1969. "The troubles" materialized Northern Ireland as phantasmatic and negated "other" of Britain and Ireland and constituted it as a place out of place on which the hegemonic nationalist order of Britain and Ireland hinged and by which violent excess it was threatened.

If the status of Ireland as postcolonial nation is anomalous, then this anomaly is compounded by the fact that Ireland is not only the oldest British colony but also an undeniably European country. Although it shares with other postcolonial countries a legacy of British colonial administration and a subjection to the dictates of dominant states in the global economic order, Ireland also benefits from the subsidies that the European Union offers to its members. Thus the dualism between the West and the postcolonial world, between the West and the Third World, which so predominates colonial and postcolonial studies, emerges as particularly problematic from the optic of Ireland, a country that is literally betwixt and between these categories (Coulter 1990).

The limitations of dualist thinking extend as well to the status of

Ireland as a colony

15

women in Ireland. For if we deploy the dominant categories of what has been called postcolonial feminism in Ireland we would have to categorize women in Ireland as postcolonial and Western. Women in Northern Ireland would occupy a variety of positions. Catholic women could be colonized and Western; their Protestant counterparts could be colonizer and Western. But the status of this Protestant colonizer-Western woman in Northern Ireland would be different from the status of the Western woman in England who would undoubtedly form part of the metropolitan colonizer. In its turn, the status of the colonized woman in Northern Ireland would not be the same as that of the Irish women of preindependence Ireland. And furthermore all these categories can be traversed by class and racialized ethnicity. It is clear from this brief exercise that the categories of postcolonial or Third World women set in opposition to the West are all too simple to understand the complexity of women's realities in Ireland.

This complexity also delineates the ambiguous and conflictive site of feminism in Ireland. Nationalist women in Northern Ireland have often positioned themselves alongside Third World women and/or women of color in opposition to British and Irish feminists. Feminists in the Republic of Ireland while often in conflict with British feminists have also distanced themselves from nationalist women. Non-nationalist feminism in Northern Ireland, however, has tried to form an autonomous space of women based on a politics of gender identity that sidesteps the pending issues of coloniality, postcoloniality, and nationalism. The politics of feminism in Ireland, as I show in chapter 6, has been marked by complicities, ambivalence, and exclusions. In this context to speak about the political experience of women appears as a particularly complicated enterprise that necessarily exceeds the limits of gender or colonial binarism. The question then is the delimitation of a theoretical framework that would permit the exploration of the agency of women as political subjects without reifying it within rigid categories.

EXPERIENCE, SUBJECTIVITY, AND SEXUAL DIFFERENCE

Since the late 1970s an important number of feminist anthropologists have been concerned with the historical processes through which women resist, manipulate, and contest social structures and cultural representations. This interest in studying the agency of women was part of a renewed anthropological interest in the mechanisms of cultural change triggered by processes of decolonization and the realization that the societies studied traditionally by anthropologists had already been substantially changed by colonialism (Ortner 1984). The necessity of accounting for change in anthropology led to a considerable reflection on the relation between social-cultural structures and historical processes and an exploration of the relation between anthropology and history. While the early work of feminist anthropologist of colonialism stressed the need to consider colonized women as historical agents and not merely passive victims or repositories of change (Etienne and Leacock 1980; Silverblatt 1987), others insisted in the agency of women as gender relations were changed by the interface of global and local economies (Bourque and Warren 1981; Fernández-Kelly 1983; Nash and Fernández-Kelly 1983; Ong 1983).

Concern with agency also sparked a renewed concern with issues of experience and subjectivity. If the different positions of power occupied by women in the social world rendered the notion of a unifying women's experience problematic within the feminist movement, then no less problematic appeared the relation between the feminist ethnographer and the women she studied. The difficulties of such relation were articulated in a number of articles and ethnographies.[9] Conscious of issues of power and problems of representation some ethnographers have opted for a hands-off narrative approach that allows women to tell their stories in their own words. Yet it seems to me that an engagement with the transformation of relations of power—and this includes feminist transformation—must go beyond recounting suppressed forms of experience to account for how this experience is constituted by the very power relations one seeks to illuminate. In my view, such account entails an interpretative exercise that might require getting one's hands muddied; taking the risk of interpreting other peoples' interpretations of the world might be the only way to establish a dialogue with them as well as with a community of colleagues. This seems a necessary premise for critical thinking and still a valid task for a critical anthropology.

I conceptualize experience as an ongoing construction always placed within the arena of existing discursive fields and social practices. By saying this I do not mean that experience is a fleeting reality always in flux. The experience of poverty or military harassment that I witnessed in the working-class neighborhoods of Belfast had a consistency and permanence that would be difficult to bypass. Neither do I mean that the narrative of experience is unimportant, nor do I negate the capacity of conscious experience to constitute a social force capable of transforming

17

personal lives and cultural representations. Rather I mean to say that, as Mary Steedly has noted in her ethnography of narrative experience of Karo people, "experience is that which is at once most necessary and most in need of examination" (1993, 25). This double dimension of experience is intimately entangled with the central political conundrum of feminism, that of identity and difference. For Drucilla Cornell,

> If there is to be feminism at all, we must rely on a feminine "voice" and a feminine "reality" that can be identified as such and correlated with the lives of actual women; and yet at the same time all accounts of the feminine seem to reset the trap of rigid gender identities, deny the real differences between women and reflect the history of oppression and discrimination rather than an ideal or an ethical positioning to the other to which we can aspire. (1991, 3)

Any positing of identity entails a claim to political space, just as any account of experience is a claim to existential recognition and presence. How can we then pose some form of identity that can occupy a political space without erasing difference? How can we construct a critical account of political experience that neither forgets the experience in the attempt of telling it nor reifies it? Experience is inextricably linked with subjectivity, but to locate subjectivity solely in conscious experience is to take subjectivity for granted rather than to examine the mechanisms through which it is historically constituted. For Lacan, subjectivity is always grounded in history, a history that is as much personal as collective, a history that includes not only conscious narratives but also forgotten episodes and hidden discourses (1977, 50–52). This conception of subjectivity is critical for the cultural analysis of politics because it leads our attention to what it is either obscured or taken for granted in relations of power. It allows us to go, as Joan Scott (1991) has suggested, beyond what is consciously experienced by the individual to analyze the discourses, practices, and motivations that configure particular subjectivities. To take such a view of subjectivity does not entail to bypass experience as it is narrated by concrete individuals. On the contrary, such narrativized experience remains crucial to the interpretative exercise because it shows how personal and social realities are endowed with meaning and power. Narratives of experience provide a critical point of entry into the history that conforms those realities. Without the narratives of experience we cannot ask how experience works in a social universe configured by unequal relationships. In this sense I depart from Foucault's view of subjectivity.

Foucault has argued that subjectivity is formed by the intersection of a set of dominant discourses (particularly the humanistic discourses of Enlightenment that enabled the emergence of the human sciences) and a set of nonverbal practices—disciplinary procedures, routines, technologies, tactics—that form what he calls a microphysics of power.[10] Foucault's insight was to show that scientific discourses are not the neutral representations of reality they purport to be but that they are intimately linked to practices of power. This combination of power/knowledge, he argues, difuminates through the social body by creating particular forms of thinking, feeling, and desiring—that is, particular subjectivities. What Foucault did not elaborate is the mechanisms by which discourses and practices are in turn transformed by the very subjectivities they enable. Foucault has shown how subjectivity has a social history but has not provided a convincing account of how that history moves. A privileged site for the exploration of such transformation, its possibilities and limits, can reside in what de Certeau (1984) has called "oppositional practices of everyday life." These practices flourish in the interstices of institutional technologies and dominant discourses. For de Certeau, these practices may or may not give rise to specific discursive configurations, but they are often accompanied by disruptions and gaps in dominant discourses that open the space for subtle transformations in social and personal meanings. De Certeau's notion of everyday practices is close to James Scott's "everyday forms of resistance," yet I find the former's much more illuminating than the latter's. For while Scott is invested in demonstrating that marginal practices of oppressed people constitute forms of resistance to hegemonic social orders, he emphasizes not the theoretical status and social meaning of resistance but the assertion of agency. It is agency, not resistance, that interests Scott. Thus his analysis has limited theoretical value because it does not go beyond the general identification of heterogeneous practices as resistance; precisely this limitation is in good part responsible for the "ethnographic refusal" (Ortner 1995) that characterizes many studies of resistance and the "romance of resistance" (Abu-Lughod 1991), now fading, that has infused such reprisal. De Certeau, on the contrary, is less interested in demonstrating agency in everyday practices than in analyzing them as spaces of social transformation. The workings of transformation, the openings and foreclosures of social space for political intervention, the subtle changes of meaning in dominant discourses, is what concerns de Certeau, and what I find important for an ethnography of resistance. Republican nationalist women in Belfast occupy exactly the complex space of these marginal

19

oppositional practices. In this book I explore the configuration and experience of such particular praxis, its conditions of possibility as well as its transformative capacity.

The question that remains to be formulated is how does this transformation occur within a hierarchical system of gender and sexual difference? To ask this question is to ask how gendered subjectivities are formed within a context already marked by the hierarchical meanings of ethnic and class difference. It is also to ponder the possibilities and limits of feminist transformation.

Influenced in different manners by Lacan, poststructuralist feminists have linked the formation of subjectivity to the acquisition of language. Subjects are constituted as such by their incorporation into a symbolic order (the order of culture and social relations) that is marked with the meanings of male dominance. Thus, women become subjects in a position of dependence to men, the reality of women's lives masked by a universe of patriarchal representations. As subject—that is, as beings capable of discourse—women can only speak through a language that excludes them or through the very disruption of language, through gaps that point to what is suppressed in dominant male representations. The question that has vexed feminists, then, is how within this context can transformation occur? This question is particularly pertinent in the context of colonial-postcolonial Ireland so overdetermined by gendered discourses that have excluded women.

One answer may lie in the very iterability of language. This is the position that feminist theorists like Judith Butler and Drucilla Cornell have taken. Transformation can occur because meaning, inasmuch as it is established in a chain of signifiers, can always slide, thereby producing new meanings in the process (Cornell 1993, 184). In the following pages, I attempt an ethnographic analysis of how this movement is accomplished in political practice. I show how nationalist women in Northern Ireland disrupt dominant representations through signifying practices. Such practices signify precisely because they are deployed within a shared universe of meaning, but, in so doing they are capable of provoking a sliding of signifiers and thereby triggering new forms of representation and knowledge.

A second form of transformation can be triggered by the transgression of taboo and the eruption of a feminine experience that is suppressed in language, that is, by what Kristeva (1982, 71) has called the abject of sexual difference. In chapter 5, for example, I examine how the political visibility of menstrual blood during the prison protest under-

20

taken by IRA women in 1980 acted as transgressive symbol of a femininity excluded, jettisoned from existing fields of discourse, thus forcing an opening in representation. I argue that the suppressed femininity of which the body of these prisoners speak is not universal but already marked by the racialized meanings of colonialism, the meanings of nationalism and the exclusions of feminism.

STORYTELLING

Ultimately this book is an exercise in ethnographic interpretation. In attempting to make sense of the political experience of Belfast nationalist women I feel that I, too, have been wrestling in some kind of interstitial space between and betwixt, around and across, the contours of social theories and disciplinary boundaries. I often found myself battling to open a space of interpretation from which to assess a reality that appeared fragmented, pushed out of social representations and academic discourses. The result has followed the narrative path of a story. It might be, as de Certeau (1986, 192) has suggested that narrative is indissociable from any theory of practice. Or it might be that I was first attuned to the subtleties of politics through the murmur of stories and the telling silences of stories untold. The Irish have a well-deserved reputation for storytelling, and it is tempting to say that the stories I encountered in the field shaped the narrative of this book. That shedding of authorial responsibility would, however, be neither fair nor accurate. Ethnography is after all a dialogical enterprise, as Clifford (1988) reminded us, to which all bring their own baggage. In as much as it might situate the ethnographic narrative let me say something about mine.

My concern with issues of gender and political violence is as much existential as it is intellectual. I was born in the Basque Country, a place divided between the French and Spanish states, embattled then to assert its suppressed identity and struggling now to come to terms with competing versions of that identity. I grew up in the midst of a dictatorship— which is to say in a country grappling with violence and silence. Early in life I became the daughter of a single mother, who was in turn the daughter of a single mother. My grandfather was killed after the Civil War that devastated the country, leaving my grandmother to wrestle alone with six children in the impoverished social world of rural Spain. My mother separated from her husband at a time when such an act was sure to attract social ostracism and economic difficulties. To be a poor woman and a single parent in Francoist Spain was slightly better in the 1960s than it had been in the 1940s, but it was difficult nevertheless.

My mother and grandmother were by necessity strong women. They both raised large families in a social system that closed the doors of work to women and condemned single mothers to the margins in the name of Family, Religion, and Fatherland. They represent two generations of women whose struggle to survive with dignity was rendered invisible and whose pain was articulated more often in dense silences than public discourses, in gestures rather than words, in humor more often than tears. There is little doubt in my mind that my interest in marginal social practices and nonverbal cultural expressions springs from the necessity of reading between lines and beyond words those personal and political realities that were, in Francoist Spain, unspeakable. My mother and grandmother, like the Irish women of this book, know more about social contradictions than we, feminists critics and social scientists, have cared to acknowledge. This book stems from the desire to unravel that implicit knowledge and its significance in social practice.

Problems too close to home have been frequently explored through the mirror of some "other." Yet any close look at otherness reflects back hidden images of ourselves. The Belfast I encountered during my fieldwork had a family resemblance with the Basque society of the late 1960s and early 1970s in which I grew up. The upsurge of Irish political violence differed from that of Basque violence, yet they shared similar features. At home that history had faded smoothly into the background. It was so present in myriad familiar vestiges that it became invisible. In Belfast, I could not escape that forgotten history, full of silences, gaps, gestures, and repressed memories, at once personal and collective. I could not because the people I worked with were trying to make sense of their own history, and to understand them, I had to make sense of my own. The story of this book is the product of that—sometimes confusing, sometimes insightful—dialogue.

In Northern Ireland, as perhaps in all places, writing does not escape the arena of hotly contested political claims. I learned that long before I went to Belfast by way of the multiple and even opposed interpretations that my book about Basque nationalism had triggered in the Basque Country. It would be disingenuous for me, therefore, to pretend that there is a neutral space for academic writing. As any narrative, this one is, no doubt, written from a particular point of view and subject to its own exclusions. As Weber (1949) observed long ago, partiality is the inevitable predicament of the social sciences. I could not possibly have discussed the experiences of all women, nor did I have a desire to do so. Nor do I claim to speak for the subjects of the ethnography. My account is based on their narratives, the evidence I could find in the archives, and that invaluable source that Malinowski (1961[1922]) called "the imponderabilia of everyday life" in West Belfast. Ultimately the interpretation is mine. Thus, it risks pleasing nobody, and it is likely to play into the lines of current conflicts. I have no control about the latter, but I must assume full responsibility for the authorship of the story that I am about to tell.

Catholic West Belfast: A Sense of Place

IN NORTHERN Ireland place is not a simple matter. In its different dimensions of landscape, space, or territory, place is overwhelmingly present in the minds and social interactions of people as it is in the fiction and poetry of writers (Foster 1991) and academic analyses of geographers, sociologists, and anthropologists. To a large extent this is because place is inextricably linked to the formation and re-creation of ethnic identities in Northern Ireland, which in turn are inseparable from the avatars of plantation settlements, land surveys, and forced displacement that characterized British colonization in Ireland, particularly the northeast. Place is thus in Northern Ireland both the product of relations of power and the material through which such relations are culturally articulated, challenged, and reproduced. From the vantage point of West Belfast, place is also a way of being-in-the-world, a space at once material and symbolic in and through which people construct personal histories and deploy historical action.

My goal in this chapter is not to provide an account of the history and sociology of Belfast, even when I necessarily refer to them. Not only is the history of Belfast already well documented, but the complexity of such history would make the attempt to compress it into a chapter either defeating or deceptively general—in either case, futile. Nor is this an analysis of the relations among territoriality, ethnic identity, and political violence, well studied by geographers and anthropologists, although aspects of those relations form part of the chapter. Rather, I aim to provide the reader with a sense of place that highlights the gendering of social and cultural space and that in so doing brings to attention those spaces from which women become historical actors. The gendering of social and cultural space has remained invisible in the different accounts of the meaning of locality and space in Belfast. This stark invisibility has lead me to search for clues and connections in pieces of evidence often disregarded by other analysts. On this I follow the lead of feminist geographers, who have sought to trace the spatial contours of women's activities, emphasizing the multiple ways in which constructions of masculinity and femininity are constituted over space and located in particular places (Bondi 1990; Gregory 1994, 124–27; Nash 1993).

1. This graffiti announces IRA territory. Written alongside the peace line
fence at the beginning of Falls Road it leaves no doubt about the
side you are entering.

I realize that the meandering path my search for women's space has
taken closely resembles the narrative conventions through which I was
told about the place, often during walks, always listening to the stories
frequently evoked by inscriptions in the urban facades. Knowledge of
place was deeply constructed through the senses—moving, seeing, listening, evoking smell—which endowed spatial images with emotional
moods—nostalgia, rage, bitterness, hope, mocking distance, longing—
to convey a sense of place, a place that was at once object of knowledge
and object of feeling. This chapter foregrounds those connections that
lie at the heart of constructions of local and ethnic identity, attempting
to locate the actors, actions, and themes that occupy the rest of book.
The practices of *location* through which anthropologists have traditionally circumscribed their subjects have been the object of much necessary
critique (Appadurai 1986, 1988; Ferguson and Gupta 1992). Such containment of culture within fixed borders reifies culture and people,
making them appear as bounded, homogenous entities isolated from
transnational processes and immune to internal differences. I fear, however, that the critique of location has often led to emphasize transnational space as the unproblematic side of what risks becoming yet an-

other binarism. If Appadurai is right in saying that anthropologists have often imprisoned natives through their narrow constructions of place, we may not forget either that anthropologists are not the only ones who construct local places; *natives* do, too. People construct their own sense of locality and place, most of the time quite independently of anthropologists' constructions, and do give meaning to their actions within localized places. Although no place escapes heterogeneity and the avatars of transnational movements and politics, it would be a mistake to assume that the meaning of locality has become irrelevant to cultural analysis. Inevitably this narrative of place is the result of the interaction between my own sense of Catholic West Belfast and that of the people there with whom I lived. Ultimately, as Strathern (1986) has pointed out, all anthropological locations are the product of such displaced interactions.

BELFAST AND WEST BELFAST

Belfast was built on tidal land at a ford across the river Lagan. The city's name, derived from the Irish Beal Feirsde, literally meant the mouth of the sand banks. In 1553 the English Lord Chancellor Cusacke described Belfast as woods and bogs for the greatest part (Wilson 1967, 18). To the English lord, the place appeared wild and empty in spite of the presence of a castle inhabited by the aristocratic Ulster family, the O'Neills of Tyrone. Belfast was an insignificant nucleus of population until the seventeenth century. It was in the hands of Gaelic chiefs until the end of the sixteenth century when the Elizabethan administration gave the castle and harbor of Belfast to a succession of royal retainers. In 1613 James I granted the town the status of corporate borough. The new status qualified Belfast to send representatives to the Irish parliament. In fact, the foundation of the town of Belfast was part of a colonial strategy to anglicize Ireland by ensuring a Protestant majority in the Irish parliament, dominated until then by Catholic Anglo-Normans who had come to Ireland in the twelfth century (Beckett and Glasscock 1967, 183). To this purpose forty towns were created in Ireland between 1610 and 1613 (Budge and O'Leary 1973, 2). During the seventeenth century Belfast enjoyed steady development, rapidly becoming a center for Scottish Presbyterians and English settlers. Its population doubled in two decades, and by the end of the century Belfast was the fourth most important port of Ireland and the principal commercial center of Ireland's

Phillips' map of 1685, reproduced as part of "Plans of the principal towns and forts and harbours in Ireland; for Mr. Tindal's continuation of Mr. Rapin's history. 1785." Note the line of houses outside the city walls. (From Collection of Historic Maps. Visual Materials Division. Department of Rare Books and Special Collections. Princeton University Library. Reproduced with permission.)

northeast (Beckett and Glasscock 1967). At the end of the eighteenth century, Belfast was a Presbyterian town with only one Catholic church, St. Mary's, located in Chapel Lane, an obscure and marginal alley.

Belfast is a city whose conflicted history is inscribed in its physical layout, its internal distribution, its landscape, the names of its streets, and the images stamped on its facades. Castle Street, for example, derives its name from the castle built there by Sir Arthur Chichester in 1611. It leads to Falls Road, the central artery of the main Catholic area, in the city's southwest. The concentration of Belfast Catholics in this area has an old history. What is today Castle Street appears on Phillips's map of 1685 as a line of houses outside the town walls, as a continuation of the main thoroughfare, High Street (see map). These extramural houses were little more than thatched cabins inhabited by Catholic Irish suggesting, according to geographer Emyrs Jones (1956:167–89), a pattern

27

of segregation already established in the seventeenth century. Evidence of the number and social position of the Irish at this time is scarce. According to the counts of the High Constable, there were no more than 150 Catholics in the area of Belfast in 1708 (Bardon 1982, 28). The number of Belfast Catholics rose to 556 by 1756 and 1,092 by 1784 representing 8 percent of the total population (Budge and O'Leary 1973; Bardon 1982; Jones 1956). Perhaps given their small numbers, as Bardon (1982, 50) has suggested, and their low status, Belfast Catholics enjoyed during the eighteenth century a higher degree of tolerance than Catholics in other parts of Ireland.

By 1800, with approximately twenty thousand inhabitants, Belfast was the fifth largest town in Ireland. With Belfast's industrial growth, the proportion of Catholics rose sharply in the first half of the nineteenth century. The industrial expansion of the northeast of Ireland concentrated on linen production and shipbuilding, two areas not totally dominated by British production that had subordinated the economic development of Ireland to the needs of British markets. The development of the wet-spinning process in 1825 hastened the development of the linen industry in Belfast. In the 1700s linen production had been a cottage industry based in Ulster towns scattered throughout the countryside. A market of brown (unbleached) linen was organized in Belfast in 1720, and by 1757 the market had begun to develop an industrial base. While linen production remained primarily a cottage industry, cotton production was established on a factory basis in the 1780s. By 1806 two thousand people—out of a population of twenty-two thousand—were employed weaving cotton. In 1840 there were eighteen flax mills and six cotton mills in Belfast; by 1852 there were twenty-four flax mills; by 1861 the number had increased to thirty-two. And in the second half of the nineteenth century the city, attaining maximum growth, became the world's primary producer and exporter of linen.

In addition to the industrialization of linen production, the textile and marine engineering industries grew enormously, and Belfast's harbor developed to accommodate the extensive trade and growing shipbuilding industry. By 1858 the firm Harland and Wolff had transformed their small iron shipbuilding industry into one of the largest shipbuilding centers in the world, and its work force was almost exclusively Protestant.

During the first half of the nineteenth century, most Belfast immigrants were rural Catholics who were escaping high tenant rents and famine. They settled in the overcrowded working-class district of what is now called the Lower Falls. Women and children found work in the surrounding linen mills. The highly unstable male employment was mostly in unskilled jobs. As was common in the working districts of Victorian industrial centers, long hours, exhausting working conditions, inadequate diet, scarcity of water, and lack of proper sanitation led to a high incidence of health problems and high mortality rate (Armstrong 1951, 235–69). Over the course of three generations the population of Belfast increased sixfold, reaching 119,000 in 1871 and nearly tripling in the next generation. The proportion of Catholics also rose with the growth of the city reaching a high point after the famine of the 1840s. In 1834 Catholics comprised 32 percent of the 19,712 inhabitants. By 1859 they reached 34 percent of a total population of 41,406. After that high point the proportion of Catholics dropped to 23 percent and remained fairly stable from 1881 until the middle of the twentieth century (Budge and O'Leary 1973, 32). Most immigrants after the 1850s were Protestant, who settled predominantly in East Belfast, an area that was expanding with the shipbuilding industry. At the turn of the century, the height of industrialization, work discrimination was well ingrained in Belfast. The 1911 census shows that 85 percent of Belfast Catholics lived in West Belfast. While women worked in the textile industry, the largest category of men who were employed worked as unskilled laborers, a small 7 percent worked in the building trade, and a few more in the transport business, as carters and haulers. Conversely Protestant working men were overrepresented in the areas of engineering and shipbuilding (Rolston and Tomlinson 1988, 26).

After World War II the traditional industries of the North entered into an acute crisis. Between 1950 and 1976, when employment in the linen industry fell from 61,000 to 19,000, 70 percent of the jobs in Catholic West Belfast disappeared. The crisis strongly affected women, whose employment dropped from 46,000 to 13,000, a 72 percent decrease (Rolston and Tomlinson 1988, 27). Protestant workers also experienced the drastic decline of 60 percent of the jobs in the shipbuilding and engineering industry. The jobs, created with the help of the government to palliate the situation were located in Protestant towns outside Belfast, thus outside the reach of Catholics. As the Obeir Report on Unemployment in West Belfast puts it, "as the Catholic women in West Belfast lost their jobs in the mills, the replacement jobs were occupied by Protestant men" (Rolston and Tomlinson 1988, 28).

The development of the public sector has deterred the total economic debacle of West Belfast. The Royal Victoria Hospital in the Falls Road has provided the main source of employment for women, but these are part-time jobs at the low scale of the hierarchy (O'Dowd 1987). Since the 1970s unemployment has risen enormously owing to the cuts in public expending and the more profitable labor markets in other parts of the world.

THE TROUBLES: SOME NOTES

The current conflict in Northern Ireland, or, as the locals call it, "the troubles," began in 1968 with the campaign for Catholic civil rights. The conflict is grounded, however, in the very formation of Northern Ireland. The alliance during the nineteenth century of the Conservative party in Britain with Ulster Unionists fostered the growth of the latter and set in place the political conditions that led to the partition of Ireland in 1921. The boundaries of Northern Ireland were drawn to include six of the traditional nine counties of Ulster, ensuring a religious cleavage of 820,000 Protestants (most of whom supported the British connection) and 430,000 Catholics (most of whom opposed it) (Darby 1983). The result was an inherently unstable state, riddled with discrimination and political violence.

Northern Ireland was born amid bloodshed and social disturbance. The formal opening of its parliament on June 1921 was accompanied by riots and reprisals. Of the 93,000 Catholics in Belfast during this time, 11,000 were fired or intimidated into leaving their jobs, and 23,000 were driven from their homes by police forces and Protestant mobs (Farrell 1976). Political and economic discrimination against the Catholic minority was institutionalized in the structure of the Northern Ireland state. In 1922 the existing electoral system of proportional representation, which hitherto had given nationalists certain control in local government, was abolished. Simultaneously, electoral boundaries were redrawn to ensure a Unionist majority, even in the councils of nationalist enclaves such as the city of Derry. The government of Northern Ireland also restricted the nationalist franchise by excluding nonratepayers, the poorest of the working class, from voting.[1] Because the Unionist councils actively discriminated against Catholics in housing allocation and public employment and encouraged discrimination in the private sector as well, Catholics were twice as likely as Protestants to be poor and therefore to be excluded from electoral politics. As a result, a quarter of the

30

adult population of the new state was disenfranchised—the majority of whom were Catholics (Cameron Report 1969).

The structure of Northern Ireland was sustained by a heavy security apparatus (Flackes and Elliott 1989). The regular police force, the Royal Ulster Constabulary (RUC), was overwhelmingly Protestant and the part-time voluntary force (known as B Specials) was exclusively Protestant and known for its anti-Catholic practices. Repressive legislation gave wide ranging powers to the police. The Civil Authorities (Special Powers) Act of 1922, most frequently enacted against the Catholic population, gave police the authority to take actions that represented a practical abrogation of civil and legal rights: arrests and internment without trials, house searches without warrants, and censorship (Hillyard 1983). This legislation also introduced the death penalty for possession of explosives and gave the minister of Home Affairs power to examine citizens' bank accounts and to seize their money (Rowthorn and Wayne 1988). Similarly, the judiciary afforded Catholics little confidence. The majority of judges appointed since 1922 in Northern Ireland have been associated with the Unionist party and, therefore, openly antinationalist.[2]

Influenced by the civil rights movement in America and student agitation in Europe, a group of students at Queen's University (Belfast) formed the Northern Ireland Civil Rights Association (NICRA) in 1967 to campaign against housing and job discrimination and for universal franchise. This movement, composed largely of the first generation of working-class Catholics to receive a college education, quickly attracted general support within the Catholic population.

The government response to the civil rights movement pleased nobody. Its social reforms were too tame to appease Catholic discontent, yet strong enough to disgruntle and embitter important sectors of the Protestant political spectrum. Political confrontations intensified. Social tension reached a breaking point in August 1969 when Protestant mobs and local police attacked and burned houses in the Catholic Bogside district of Derry and the Catholic Lower Falls area of Belfast. On August 14, the day after the attack on the Lower Falls and two days after that in Derry, the British government sent the army into Northern Ireland. To date, the British government has been unable to achieve a military resolution of the conflict. Its continuing presence, contributing to the high toll of violence, has created a lore of bitter memories among working-class, ghettoized Catholics.[3]

A Sense of Place

Falls is the anglicized word for the Gaelic *fals* meaning "edges." It is a revelatory irony that Fals was the name given to a district that originated in the displacements and replacements of the colonial encounter. In the seventeenth century the Falls was literally the edge of Belfast: the space beyond the walls that surrounded the town. The wall itself delineated more than the physical limits of the expanding town. Built after the Irish rebellion of 1641, the wall was constructed to provide Belfast with protection against the treachery of the natives. But it also symbolized an iconic act of exclusion from the new corporation. After the rebellion was defeated, the few native Irish inhabiting Belfast were expelled. The irony inherent in the descriptive literality of the word *fals* is exceeded by the fact that such physical eccentricity has perdured into actual forms of ghettoization that edge the inhabitants of the Falls out of the social and political center. Such urban marginality functioned as a sign that the locals were incapable of doing better, giving rise at some point to a discourse whereby people were assigned to specific places, "put in their place," through practices of routinized violence such as paramilitary raids and policing or collective displacements like those accompanying the riots of 1969. Through the discourse of place, the topography of Belfast often acquires a fantastic quality, with some places existing only as the object of projected fantasies and fears. In response to a question about the location of the Falls district a middle-aged woman who had given me a ride to Queen's University, and who turned out to be a faculty member, answered with apprehension: "The Falls is on the other side of the city, but I wouldn't go there. It's not safe; something may happened to you. I wouldn't go to the Shankill [the loyalist Protestant district in West Belfast] either." And she concluded, "You are quite safe in Belfast if you don't go the Falls or the Shankill." This woman had never set foot in West Belfast, yet its reputation as a threatening place—a reputation created repeatedly by the local evening news, local newspapers, and above all social rumor—allowed her a feeling of security predicated on the construction of a safe geography. There is in Belfast a multiplicity of invisible yet tangible geographical distinctions. There are good and bad, safe and unsafe, clean and dirty, peaceful and violent places. As geographers and anthropologists have repeatedly noted (Boal et al. 1976; Boal and Douglas 1982; Feldman 1991; Kenney 1991; O'Dowd

1987), the lines that demarcate these territories are deeply interlocked with social class positions and ethnic distinctions. These distinctions constitute a body of unwritten local knowledge, an implicit code of social relations that organizes the movement of people through urban space, determining some routes, discarding others. This implicit knowledge reproduces as much as expresses ethnic and class distinctions.

Implicit Knowledge

When I first visited Belfast, during the summer of 1987, Castle Street was jammed, as it generally is, with street vendors, shoppers, and a line of collective taxis in constant motion. They are commonly known as the "black taxis" because of their color. They have a capacity for six customers, although they accommodate greater numbers if children are among the passengers. Several men stationed on the street asked incoming people their destination and directed them to the appropriate taxi, according to prefixed routes. The stops themselves are not fixed, but are indicated by knocking on the plastic panel that separates the driver from the back seat passengers. One may also hail a taxi at any point on its route. The use of black taxis requires good knowledge of local geography and of the implicit cultural conventions of riding because they not only operate in nationalist areas but also in the loyalist neighborhoods of the Shankill and North Belfast. Although they look exactly the same, the geographic routes of nationalists taxis are different from loyalist taxis; so, too, are the conventional routines that structure the ride such as stopping and paying. Loyalist taxis, for example, have fixed stops; knocking the plastic panel in one of them would be an indication of familiarity with nationalist conventions and ignorance of loyalist ones, which would betray outsidedness and arouse suspicion. Although outsidedness may not be problematic when it comes to foreigners, it can be highly dangerous for locals who avoid as much as they can being "out of place."

In the absence of physical marks of ethnicity, territory and a myriad of other signs become crucial diacritics of identity. The fear and anxiety, sometimes also the exhilaration, produced by inhabiting even if temporarily an unfamiliar territory emerge frequently in conversations. Perhaps the best example comes from Rebecca, an outgoing Protestant woman in her late twenties. In the course of a conversation one afternoon Rebecca suddenly asked, "How do you stop a black taxi in the Falls?" Somewhat embarrassed, she explained that she had recently been in the Falls attending a feminist lecture held on occasion of International Women's Day at the Conway Mill community center. This was the first time she was in the Falls.

> I am used to the loyalist murals, but the republican ones were completely new. I was looking to one place and another around me. It was like being in a different world. I felt also very self-conscious, as if I had a tag in my forehead saying "Protestant," and everybody was seeing it. When I was coming down the Falls in my way home I didn't feel like walking, and I thought about taking a black taxi. Then I realized I didn't know how to stop one. I was already apprehensive and I didn't want to be conspicuous, so I ended up walking.

Nationalist black taxis are managed by the West Belfast Taxi Association and their drivers are frequently former prisoners. This is not an indication of complicity with the IRA, as the British government has often purported, given that in nationalist working-class areas a large percentage of men have been in jail for political reasons at one time or another during the last twenty years. The taxis were organized at the height of the 1969 rioting when city bus service was often suspended and sometimes not reinstated for days. Black taxis provided a more reliable form of transportation than buses. After some time, loyalists started their own taxi service. Black taxis are no longer located in Castle Street. The growth of their service led them to occupy an empty lot at the end of the street. Black taxis are widely used in nationalist areas because of their flexibility and cheaper price. They are especially used by women with children who can stack the pram in the trunk and travel more comfortably. Women were thus particularly affected by the attacks of loyalist paramilitaries on black taxis in nationalist areas during the early 1990s.

At the end of Castle Street an iron fence indicates the edge of the city center and the beginning of the ghetto. The fence, built just at the very spot were the town wall stood in the seventeenth century, is closed to traffic at night allowing people to pass in, but not out, through a noisy revolving door of corrugated iron. This iron barrier was erected as part of a larger project that encircled the city center, separating it from the immediately surrounding districts. It was built at the beginning of the 1970s as part of the counterinsurgency designed to combat terrorism (Faligot 1983). During the day guards check people and vehicles going in and out. Beyond Castle Street the road rises up the Falls, tracing a hill that was, until the development of the linen industry, a series of meadows through which the Farset River flowed.

Parallel to Falls Road runs Shankill Road, the apex of working-class Protestant loyalists. The Falls constitutes the stronghold of Irish republicanism, Shankill that of Ulster loyalism. Before 1969 a web of little streets connected both areas. These streets housed a mixed population, with Catholics and Protestants living side by side. After the riots of 1969, when houses in this mixed zone were attacked and burned out, a wall was erected between the Falls and the Shankill, at the precise place where rioting had been reoccurring since 1913 (Boal et al. 1976). The city authorities called it "the peace line." The people living on either side regarded it, however, as the war line—a space of uncertainty in which skirmishes and attacks continue to occur frequently.

Springfield is one of the few roads running through West Belfast that connects nationalist and loyalist neighborhoods. This fact makes it at once an ambiguous, dangerous, and, in some stretches, deserted area. Springfield Road rises up the hill from Falls Road to the depressed housing estate of Ballymurphy at the very base of the Black Mountain, once a popular place of recreation, now a strategic military space. An army observation post in the mountainside above the upperside of Springfield Road monitored life in the Catholic ghettos of Ballymurphy and Turf Lodge, where male unemployment reaches 80 percent. Some yards below, between Catholic Ballymurphy and loyalist Springmartin, there is another army station. In 1970 a pitched battle took place there that signaled in local folk history the beginning of the hostilities between the local people and the then-recently arrived British army.

Places and Names

Places have encoded meaning in Belfast. One's address or name is pregnant with sociopolitical significance. Class position, religion, and national identity can be guessed, or imputed, through one's name and the area in which one lives. Interlocutors unfamiliar with each other often observe elaborate rituals to locate the other on the sociopolitical map. Burton (1978) has called this practice "telling." He defines "telling" as "the pattern of signs and cues by which religious ascription is arrived at in the everyday interactions of Protestant and Catholics" (Burton 1978, 38). Telling is based on the social significance of name, face, area of residence, school attended, linguistic use, color, and so forth. Because of the high degree of ambiguity and inmateriality of these signs of identity, the process of telling is always open to negotiation. Indirect questions are frequently answered with ambiguous responses. Questions and answers, constructed to demarcate the terrain of interactive possibilities, avoid any "sensitive" topic in order to display one strategy or another. Roisin, a young woman not yet in her twenties, told me how she and her friends went once to the swimming pool on the loyalist Shankill Road, purportedly the best of Belfast. Because "Roisin" was too obviously a Catholic name she pretended to be called Roberta to disguise her identity, yet she said, "I was afraid that they could tell all the time."

"Where are you staying?" meaning "Where do you live?" was always, when introduced, one of the first questions I was asked. My answer delineated the rest of the conversation, and therefore I, too, learned quickly to choose my response. I lived at one edge of a republican area called Beechmount, off Springfield. Across the road, on the other side, was another republican area called Clonard. Beechmount and Clonard were unequivocally nationalist. Springfield, however, was more ambiguous. When talking with a nationalist I answered precisely; if I did not know my interlocutor, I answered ambiguously. Burton too had observed the use of ambiguous territorial referents in possible mixed situation in the Belfast community that he studied in the early 1970s (1978, 57). Evasion and ambiguity are the flip side of the practice of telling. They function as a defense mechanism against the potential danger that might derive from having one's identity *told*, imputed, in situations of nondominance.

Borders

The stretch of Springfield Road that abuts Clonard is a borderzone or as geographers of Belfast have called it an "interface." Cupar Street, at the edge of the neighborhood, is guarded by the "peace line" beyond which lies "Indian territory," as the local people, borrowing an image from the myth of the American frontier, call the Shankill, where they rarely venture. The territorial limits of nationalist and loyalist districts are signaled on curbstones and lightposts painted with the colors of either the Irish or the British flag, as well as with partisan murals and graffiti. A couple of blocks of burned and wrecked houses stood until 1990 on the Springfield Road as a transitional landmark between republican and loyalist areas, a material reminder of past clashes and actual danger. Only a Chinese take-out stood amidst the ruins of the battle line, a neutral spot where people from both sides went to buy the occasional fast dinner. In 1989, at the time of my fieldwork the door man of a local pub was killed in this borderzone. The body—still lying on the pavement when my local friends and I passed through the street—served as a chilling reminder that the spatial ethnic divisions in Belfast were also divisions between life and death. Feldman, elaborating on the "interface," has identified this border violence as a ritual colonization of community space (1991, 30).

During my time in Belfast some of the wrecked houses were razed to build new ones, but my neighbors wondered who would risk living there. Risk, however, is a relative perception. I have often heard people living farther from the "peace line" in the Upper Falls puzzle about how anybody could live in such dangerous area as Clonard. Yet people in Clonard could not imagine living in the small Catholic enclaves of North Belfast or the Short Strand. I witnessed several conversations in which the merits, demerits, and degrees of risk were endlessly debated among friends living in different Catholic areas of Belfast. The results were always inconclusive.

Spatial Mnemonics and Historical Memory

Cormac and Anne were from the Clonard side of Springfield. Like other people, they had moved several times since "the troubles" began, never relocating far from the area. They were in their late thirties. Cormac had been imprisoned for republican activities several times, and both were well-known and liked in the area. As we all lived close to Clonard, I visited that area with them frequently. Walking through the streets of his neighborhood Cormac often reminisced about events that marked the local experience of "the troubles." In his stories history and memory were crafted through landscape inscriptions.

"See that door?" he said pointing to one of the undifferentiated tiny terrace houses. "The Brits were at the opposite corner of the street—where we are now—and shots were being fired at them, and they couldn't figure out where they came from. There was nobody in the street. And the shots came from the mailbox attached to the front door, you see?" He and his friends laughed at the situation that had been stripped of the drama it once contained, to be later recaptured as absurdly funny. "See that hole in the wall?" Cormac asked pointing this time to a facade corner, "A Brit was standing just there, and a bullet was fired from across the street [scarcely ten meters] and . . . [he paused and laughed] it didn't hit him. He was lucky," he said, putting his finger on the hole the bullet left on the wall. His laughter was a kind of self-mockery, a commentary on how poorly prepared militarily they were, a metacommentary on their status as ordinary men using arms in an extraordinary situation, rather than shrewd terrorists.

For Cormac the past was brought into the present through spatial connections, which in turn led to categorical connections. Henry Glassie has beautifully described, in his study of Ballymenone, the primacy of space in Irish rural culture as a site through which history and myth are conflated: "Space joins past events to each other, and it unifies past and present in two ways: progressively and mythically" (1982, 201). In the working-class districts of Belfast too "space functioned as a mnemonic artifact that stored repertoires of historical narrative and collective action" (Feldman 1991, 27). Not only does space sediment collective history, but it also crafts personal experience by investing the urban landscape with intense subjective meanings that endow the past with a visible immediacy, blending time and personal experience into a collective history through the mechanism of localized memory. In so doing this collective history does not function as a nostalgic narrative of times gone by; rather it projects itself into the future by acting as a mythical chart to explain and legitimize action in the present. The future is read in the marks of the past through the memory of what people were fighting for.

Women are also subjects of this history; their positions differ slightly from those taken by men. They are not the shooters, but the carriers. Anne takes the thread of the story from Cormac:

> I was once moving gear [ammunition] with Cormac's mother. I had a lot of plastic bags wrapped around my body so it made noise when I walked, and she was carrying guns beneath her cardigan. I was scared to death. We were walking and came across a patrol, and I began to wince, "Oh Jesus this is it." I saw myself in Armagh jail, tortured . . . and she says "Stop it and keep cool!" The next thing she stops by the British who were in the corner and says, "Ack, son, you must be freezing here, all day outside without a cup of tea." And he says, "Yes ma'am. Where are you going?" And she says, "We are only going across the street, son, to do some messages [errands]." And the Brit says, "Alright, ma'am, go on"—without searching us or anything! And this was a woman of sixty!

In this story the older woman acquires the properties of the mythical trickster by outsmarting a far more powerful enemy through her intimate knowledge of locality and manipulation of the soldier's filial respect for elderly women. There is a connection in this story between the invisibility of women's bodies, bodies that can conceal weapons, and the exposed deployment of armed soldiers. The topography that armed soldiers attempt to master through the mounting vigilance of their presence hides behind the materiality of facades a social geography of resistance. Absence rather than presence appears here as the condition of political agency. Precisely because of this condition resistance becomes symbolically condensed in the bodies of women. For as subjects of history women have also been erased from the public arenas of politics and war. In Anne's narrative, resistance is predicated on this political invisibility, on the assumption that inasmuch as women do not belong to the public arena, when they walk the streets they are not really there. In the story the women encounter the soldiers at midpoint between the home and the laundry room, and by virtue of their presence, the streets cease to be a battleground that must be controlled and become an interstitial space linking domestic arenas, thus lowering the soldier's guard. The concealment of resistance that the bodies of the women, with their occult weaponry, materialize is made possible ironically by the open disclosure of their presence. Thus the act of control that visibility entails becomes for the soldiers a form of deception; what the soldiers see is precisely what they miss. There is a correspondence between community space and the bodies of women. This familiar local space, like the women's bodies passing through it, is opaque to the soldiers; and like the women's bodies, the space conceals resistance. As I discuss in chapter 2, the penetration of this landscape of resistance is predicated on the transgression of women's bodies and women's homes.[4]

In Bombay Street, new houses stand now in place of the ones burned during the riots of 1969. These houses, now facing the peace line, are protected by wire fences and screens enclosing the tiny backyards and windows. Paint and stones are intermittently thrown from one side of the peace line to the other, especially during the summer celebration of the victory of William of Orange over James II. Such territorial encroachments follow highly patterned ritual forms that are repeated from year to year (Kenney 1991; Buckley and Kenney 1995). Traces of damage remain on the screens, reminders of an omnipresent menace. In marked contrast, Clonard monastery stands further up Bombay Street still gathering faithful for the June novenas after many decades.

Ghosts and other folk beliefs that are usually identified with rural culture comprise an integral part of Catholic working-class culture in Belfast. Mingling with people, ghosts also hover in the corners of the narrow streets of the Falls Road area. Near Clonard monastery, the ghost of a monk saved Cormac from an British army ambush:

> I was out with my friend Danny one night. It was the early days of the troubles. We were waiting for a soldiers' foot patrol to come by. As we were waiting we saw a monk pass silently. It was a very tall monk. "Have you seen that?" I ask to Danny and he says, "Yes." We looked around the

39

corner, and there was nothing. He could not have had time to go into a house or the monastery. There was nothing he could have hidden behind either, but he had disappeared. It was a ghost. We were so scared that Danny said "Let's get the hell out of here," and we came to my house.

His wife intervenes: "When they arrived I knew they had seen a ghost; they were white pale." Cormac continues: "The question is that there was a patrol very close to where we were standing and they would have ambushed us if we had not left. So the ghost saved our lives." Cormac was sorry that he was now the only witness to the presence of the ghost. Danny had been killed by the British army in a scandalous "shoot to kill" operation.

But ghosts do not always have such a benefic effect. During June 1989 a female ghost dressed in turn-of-the-century costume appeared in one mirror of a young family's house in Beechmount. She pushed the man who lived in the house angrily against the walls causing several injuries to his head. She demanded the family vacate the house, which she claimed was hers. Accounts of this appearance were the talk of the neighborhood for quite awhile. People gathered around the house in the evenings with a mixture of fear and excitement, intrigued by the story and ardently debating its truth. Holy water, popularly used to dispel bad spirits (including the police), was sprinkled inside and outside the house, and even the Archbishop was called to perform an exorcism. All to no avail. The ghost persisted in her abuse and her demands. After a few days the family abandoned their home. Given the shortage of housing this was not a decision lightly made. During this time the rumor spread that people had been killed in that spot by the "Black and Tans" (the British mercenary soldiers vilified for their brutality during the war of independence) and that the ghost was probably one of those who had been killed. Was this ghost a return of a repressed history, the objectification of actual violence, or both? "Ghost tales map the history of death in local space disrupting the linearity of time" (Feldman 1991, 67). Life changes, but the past in its multiplicity of mythical forms has a persistent way of coming back into the present, nagging and pressing, organizing experience into forms of actions. This is what Northern Ireland singer Christy Moore may mean when he sings that "the cries of the dead are always in our ears."

Belonging

People in West Belfast have a strong sense of belonging to that place. This belonging has different levels of reference, the most immediate of which is to neighborhood. Until the mid-1970s it was not infrequent for

40

people to marry, raise their children, and grow old in the same neighborhood in which they themselves were born (Boal and Douglas 1982; McAteer 1983). With the redevelopment that followed 1969, many people moved out of their "home" districts to new ones. Yet their feelings of identity were still connected to the area in which they were raised, where many visit and return regularly to attend social events. "Belfast," Carol, a nationalist from North Belfast, told me, "is a group of wee villages," in the sense "that everybody knows each other, and there is a great identification with your area." In her work in loyalist areas of Belfast, ethnographer Mary Kenney also encountered these strong feelings associated with one's neighborhood. She termed these deeply rooted loyalties "pride of place" (1991, 41).

The old sense of community has, to a certain extent, disappeared with the increasing individualization of private life, a process intensified with the displacement accompanying housing development over the last twenty years. Anne recalled with nostalgia the days when neighbors knew each other and could count on each other in moments of need: "I don't have any relation with any of the neighbors now, everybody is in their own house and I barely know them." Rose, a young woman from a small Catholic enclave in North Belfast who had moved with her husband to a new housing state in West Belfast, felt very homesick: "I miss the community. I cannot visit my mom's and my sister's house as I used to everyday, and I don't know anybody here."

Despite the loss of much of the local closeness recreated in the novels of Michael McLaverty and romanticized in my informants' memories, people's sense of community remains strong. Aware of the political importance of this sense of community, in 1986 republicans in West Belfast began to organize an annual week-long festival in which political demonstrations and parades combined with cultural and social activities would be held each August to celebrate the local history of nationalist West Belfast. Coexisting with neighborhood loyalties, the more inclusive concept of West Belfast has gained strength, boosted as much by militarization and the victimization that people of the area have shared since the 1970s, as by the pride that people of the area take in their achievements as a community.

The concept of a West Belfast community entails not only social but also political and class identity. In spite of existing differences in political allegiance and economic position among the people of West Belfast, there is an association in local parlance between the area of West Belfast and the identity of working-class nationalists. This identity is important in relation to others (e.g., loyalist or middle class) who are also territorially located in Belfast political culture (Boal and Douglas 1982) and crucial to the delineation of social interactions.

During my first visit to Belfast I was living in Queen's University dorms on Malone Road, the residential area to which Belfast's upper class moved at the turn of the century and where an ethnically mixed population of middle-class intellectuals resides today. In my initial interviews with West Belfast activists and residents I was invariably asked where I was staying. When I answered "Malone Road" often the attitude of my interlocutor would shift—after several seconds of silence—from a friendly demeanor to a more distant and sometimes hostile one. Knowing nothing of territorial differences at that time, I was puzzled by this; soon I started saying I was living at the university hoping that this would prove a more acceptable setting. Later in my fieldwork I became aware of the extent of the antagonism that residents of West Belfast feel for the residential area of Malone Road, particularly for the intellectual and professional nationalists who lived there. People resented the insulation of these middle-class Catholics from the suffering and violence of everyday life in West Belfast. From their perspective, such insulation allowed middle-class nationalists to make the kind of righteous political judgments about ghetto violence that people immersed in it could not afford to make. A saying from the early years of the conflict encapsulated these feelings of bitter resentment: "Malone fiddles while the Falls burns."

Names of Empire, Metaphors of Suffering and Redemption

Bombay Street, Kashmir Street, Cawnpore, Lucknow, Benares . . . It is ironic that these narrow rows of tiny red brick houses, springing up in the shadow of the Lower Falls linen factories, celebrate memorable campaigns of the British Empire. These streets of unskilled laborers and linen mill workers were laid out during the heyday of the British Empire when the production and export of linen in Belfast depended on the markets opened by the Empire. They trace a connection between the proletarianization of this area of former meadows and the colonization of exotic lands, between the colonized at home and the colonized far away. There are few streets in the Lower Falls whose names recall the Crimean war and the Balkans: Sevastopol Street, Inkerman Street, Odessa Street, Balkan, Cyprus, Bosnia, Servia, Belgrade, and Roumania streets. They were built by the Ross family, owners of a local linen factory. Many of these streets were ransacked by the British army during three days of curfew in 1970. Most were demolished at the beginning of the 1980s, after surviving more than a century and housing far more bodies than space had reasonably allowed. These streets arose with the British Empire, and their history is inextricably linked to colonial expansion. Long after the echoes of Empire were quelled in other parts of the world, the coming of the British troops to Northern Ireland in August 1969 was a reminder that the northeastern corner of Ireland was still under British dominion. This realization was not, however, immediate. Indeed, for almost a year British troops were welcomed as rescuers of the besieged Catholic ghettos.

The relationship of the Irish people to the British army has been historically more ambiguous than republicans now like to admit. Irishmen served regularly in the British army up to the nationalist war of independence of 1918–1921. After partition, the British army was an outlet for young unemployed men in Northern Ireland, of whom there were always excessive numbers in Catholic communities (Jones 1956). Northern Catholic Irish were intimately familiar with the British army, but not with having it operate in their midst. A year after they entered the streets of the Falls, British soldiers imposed a curfew on the area, searching houses for guns and IRA men. This operation was perceived as an assault on the community and dispelled any vestigial ambiguity (Burton 1978). The British army became, unequivocally, an army of occupation.

The Lower Falls was eventually redeveloped, and new houses were built at the beginning of the 1980s. The new streets were restructured to suit military surveillance (Faligot 1983); they were built according to a design of concentric cul-de-sacs with only one entry street, rather than the crisscrossing streets that characterized the old neighborhoods of row houses. The new streets retained their old names with their reminiscences of past imperial glories in exotic places. The resilience of these names reasserts not only the local sense of place but also the status quo of Northern Ireland itself. Names define reality, create history, and shape memory. The change of political regimes is too frequently followed by battles over name changes, as recently witnessed in the former Soviet Union and Eastern Europe. Naming is a form of rewriting "history," erasing traces of past lives, burying dissenting versions, and refashioning memory. This is often the prerogative of those holding economic and political power; a prerogative, however, that seldom remains uncontested. The Lower Falls and Clonard, with their array of imperial miseries written on their streets, were also strongholds of the IRA who have created their own inscriptions on the walls.

On Kashmir Road, a placard reads: "Clonard Martyrs." Republicans call it the "roll of honor," the list of IRA members from the Clonard area who died "in active service against British imperialism." Similar mementos can be seen in other Catholic districts. One could argue that these images of martyrdom are in dialogue with images of empire contained in street names. In a sense they represent an answer to the assertion of empire. As juxtapositions in space they comment on each other; the IRA's roll of honor challenges British political hegemony. The names of colonial sites, reproduced after the old streets were destroyed, long after those parts of the world were lost to British rule, seem a pervasive affirmation of the Britishness of Northern Ireland. It would be wrong to see them, however, in active dialogue with each other. These images pertain to different historical periods and speak of different historical conjunctures. In the republican imagination, however, these distinct historical moments are not unconnected. They are unified through a central theme in nationalist culture: suffering, as a predicament of the Irish people under British rule and as a path to political redemption.

Metaphors of suffering and aggression characterize the majority of murals throughout nationalist West Belfast. Many of the murals appeared in the late 1970s, spontaneously painted by community youth as part of the campaign in support of IRA prisoners. After the hunger strike of 1981, murals of IRA activism have been more directly authored by Sinn Fein as part of their ideological campaign (Rolston 1987; Sluka 1992). Some murals, drawn from Christian imagery of suffering, depict IRA members as victims and saviors. Others identify the IRA martyr with the warrior Cuchulain, the mythological hero of Gaelic Ulster. Sometimes the metaphors of suffering are more abstract, such as one depicting Ireland bearing England's cross. Or another which depicts a naked man crucified on the cross of the English flag (see figures 2 and 3). A mural in Beechmount, the neighborhood in which I lived, recreates the historical victimization of Ireland by Britain through the metaphor of the prisoner's body. Setting the scene with Cromwell's conquest, historical time is depicted flowing mythically through images of interrogation, torture, and corrupt trials, culminating in the figure of a naked body of the protesting prisoner of the late 1970s, an allegory of unvanquished Ireland (see figure 4). These mural images form a counterargument to images of vicious terrorists that, as Curtis (1984) has shown, are permanently disseminated through the mass media.

Resistance is a central notion in the political culture of Catholic West Belfast. A mural in Sebastopol Street, painted in honor of the twentieth anniversary of the conflict, depicted a battle between the IRA and the

2. "In Loving Memory" of killed IRA members from the local area. The plaque on the wall lists their names. The mural represents mythological hero Cuchulain in a guise evocative of crucifixion yet bearing arms to suggest death in battle. (Reproduced as a postcard by Republican Publications.)

3. Irish men crucified by Britain next to Ireland carrying the cross of British colonialism.

4. The violence of state against nationalists allegorically represents the violence of Britain against Ireland.

5. Mural on the facade of Finn Fein offices in the Falls Road portraying 20 years of military occupation.

6. Mural on facade of Finn Fein offices in the Falls Road celebrating
IRA military prowess.

British army framed by a giant message: "August 69/89. 20 Years of Resistance: Victory to the Irish People" (see figures 5 and 6). This mural is
part of a different set of images that portray the IRA as an army of liberation, fully equipped and in the offensive against the British army.
Ideas of suffering and conquest form an "argument of images" (Fernandez 1986) that legitimize for republican nationalists the practice of
violent aggression against the oppressor. This is made explicit on another mural where Mairead Farrell, the IRA militant killed in Gibraltar,
is quoted: "I've always believed we had a legitimate right to take up arms
and defend our country and ourselves against British occupation."[5]

I focus on this mural, for it touches on a crucial theme in the cultural
elaboration of republican violence, that is: the gendered meanings of
suffering. The mural takes the form of a processual sequence, suggesting continuity of the fight through suffering (see figure 7). It portrays a
semi-naked man lying on the ground after he has been killed. Looking
at him is a woman with her head bent in the unmistakable posture of
grieving. She is holding a baby in her arms, extended as if showing the
dead man—presumably his father—to the infant. Next to her figure a

47

7. Women as mediators of male resistance against colonial violence. Mural is damaged by paint bombs.

young man in a determined, almost military, attitude moves forward. The model for the mural is a memorial for the republican dead erected in county Kerry in 1960. The time sequence the image conveys is at once chronological and circular. The young man is obviously the baby following his father's steps. The woman stands between the two, the witness and, as such, the mediator of historical continuity. Through her, historical memory is inscribed, and historical consciousness is maintained in the next generation. The image makes clear that this consciousness rests on suffering. The symbolic locus of suffering, however, is not the same for everybody.

Men encounter suffering in the violent death generated by an unjust

8. "Solidarity of Women in Armed Struggle." National
liberation binds together women from the IRA, PLO,
and SWAPO (Namibia). (The mural was reproduced
as a postcard by the collective "Just Books.")

social order. Here, death is not the outcome of a fair confrontation, but
of unilateral aggression. The dead man in the mural could not appear
more vulnerable. Not only disarmed, he is semi-naked, his protruding
ribs a sign of misery and poverty. This victimized body, which appears as
a passive receptacle of violence, constitutes, however, the production
and legitimation of the young man whose determination is now trans-
lated as violent resistance: "We have the right to take arms." In republican culture, men's suffering is encountered in the space of violent in-

9. Graffiti against strip searching of women republican prisoners.

tervention in the social universe. This kind of suffering, conceptualized predominantly in physical terms as torture or death, is elaborated in mythological terms as heroism or martyrdom.

The victimized man does not occupy, however, the symbolic center and emotional load of this image. Rather the inexpressible mute suffering of the woman, like the Mater Dolorosa, triggers emotional identification. This refractive image lies beneath martyrdom; people identify with the mother's suffering, rather than with that of the son. In republican culture men's suffering is inscribed in their own bodies through their fighting; women's is inscribed in the bodies of others: fathers, sons, brothers, husbands, or friends. Socially recognized suffering, culturally meaningful suffering, is articulated for women around the complex of motherhood. The implications of this economy of suffering that reduces women's historical agency to the passive bearing of testimony have not escaped republican women who view Christological images of this kind with ambivalence or outright dislike. It is an irony that the words encapsulating the meaning of active resistance embodied in a young male figure were uttered by a military woman killed in active service.

Motherhood is not the only symbolic locus of culturally constructed female experience. Nor is a mother's pain the only site of female suffering given voice in the urban landscape. The emergent feminism of the late 1970s altered female representations in republican imagery. An instance of this change (and of its international as well as precarious character) was a mural (now expunged) in the Upper Falls in which an IRA woman is portrayed alongside a South African and a Palestinian bearing arms. A feminist symbol encircles them. In this image the allegorical suffering of the motherland is not emphasized; instead, the transnational solidarity of oppressed women dominates (see figure 8). A giant graffiti along Beachmount Avenue reads: "STOP! STRIP SEARCHES" (see figure 9). It arose out of a campaign waged by women prisoners against body searches. Women prisoners equate the emotional pain of having their bodies forcibly exposed to meticulous and intimate exploration to sexual violation. Their sex is an inescapable dimension of their political experience, for it is primarily there that intimidation and punishment are inflicted.

THE POROSITY OF GENDERED SPACE

In the search for the cultural space of nationalist women, two images come to mind: one, the red-bricked linen factories still standing in the Lower Falls as a mute vestige of the past, absurdly lingering in the present. The other, a photograph, published in the local newspaper *Irish News*, of Janet Donnelly, a young woman with her child in her arms, alone in the middle of her house destroyed by the British army in a house search—an all too familiar image for people in West Belfast. The first image speaks of the space of capitalist exploitation; the second shows the invaded space of intimate relations. Both images are important traces of women's historical experience in Catholic West Belfast.

In the Falls, where male unemployment was chronic, women provided an essential portion of the family income. Falls women worked in the linen mills from the beginning of the nineteenth century until the 1950s, when the cheaper production of synthetic fabrics drastically reduced the demand for Irish linen (Bardon 1982; Budge and O'Leary 1973). Women spent more than a century moving between the intimate space of household reproduction and the capitalist space of industrial production. How did this experience shape the social consciousness of Falls's women? In the oral histories and folklore of the linen mills, women recalled the solidarity among female workers above all else (McAteer 1983; Messenger 1975). Geraldine McAteer, a sociologist and folk historian of the Falls whose mother worked in the local mills, traced a connection between this female space of material production and the female space of political confrontation opened with the Lower Falls curfew of 1970, which I discuss in chapter 2. The perception was echoed by other nationalist women who saw the hundreds of women that marched through the Falls, breaking the soldiers' barrier that had sealed off this area of former mill workers, to bring food to the women under curfew, as expressing the same kind of solidarity female workers had experienced in the factories.

The solidarity that brought women together in political activity through the 1970s stemmed from an existing network of female relationships closely knit around street houses and the workplace. The house was far from being a secluded female space. Visiting was so common in the Catholic areas that people used to keep their front doors open. During the high point of sectarian assassinations in 1972, many people were killed inside their homes and repeated warnings appeared in the local papers of Catholic West Belfast to keep doors closed as a security precaution. Yet a Falls community worker noted how difficult it was to convince people to close their doors. At the time of my fieldwork, and despite the continuing occurrence of Catholic assassinations, many houses in the Falls still kept their doors open all day long.

The social character of the household space seemed to have diminished at the time of my fieldwork. People still visited but not with the assiduity that appears to have been the norm twenty years earlier. The image of Janet Donnelly in the midst of her ruined house is, however, a persuasive sign of its politicization. During my fieldwork I saw mementos of republican "martyrs" or Celtic crosses and harps carved by republican prisoners displayed in many republican houses constituting an interior landscape of political allegiance and defiance. It is a landscape of defiance because the house, as the epitome of private space, has hardly been a bastion of security. House searches in Belfast have been a routine part of the security operations, and signs of republican sympathies too often lead to harassment or more serious punishment. There is an analogy between house searches and strip searches: nationalist women interpret both as violations of their bodies and personal integrity. In nationalist culture, state violence perpetrated in the space of the house is interpreted as the epitome of English violence to the Irish nation. Concomitantly, by a metonymical operation, women's suffering becomes the most powerful representation of the nation's suffering. In the raid the house most potently becomes a metaphor of the country and women an allegory of the nation.

If the house is the space of intimate relations, caring, and protection, then it has also been a place for hiding "terrorist" men. The importance of safe houses to the political operability of the IRA has been analyzed by other scholars (Feldman 1991, 42–44; Sluka 1989). The logistic structure of political violence is articulated, however, through a web of intimate relations sustained by women. Although this connection has apparently been overlooked by social scientists, it has been explored to some degree in plays and novels. In Michael McLaverty's *Bring My Brother Back*, generally considered the best work of fiction on the ethnic conflict in Northern Ireland, the emotional life of the main character Alec is rooted in the caring relationships of the family home. Alec's mother produces and reproduces such emotional space. When Alec becomes a member of the IRA and the police begin to look for him, it is another woman, a neighbor, who hides him. Both knitting the web of intimate relationships and sheltering wanted men are important parts of what constitutes the symbolic space of women as a cultural locus different from that of men. The stories of women that I offer in the following chapters about their experiences of "the troubles" reveal a profound connection between what Raymond Williams has called a "structure of feelings" (1977, 128) and the performance of political violence. The analysis of such connection provides a view of political violence as a thoroughly gendered structure of power that reaches into the domains of intimate feelings and familiar spaces. Conversely, emotion, so often disengaged from social analysis, emerges as a political force that must be examined rather than assumed. In chapter 3, I explore the particularities of this connection to the formation of a specific form of political subjectivity embedded in the opposition of nationalist women to state violence.

Gender Trouble and the Transformation
of Consciousness

T HE CIVIL RIGHTS Campaign of 1969 and subsequent events constituted a watershed in the historical consciousness of nationalists in the
North and a turning point in the personal biographies of many
women.[1] The early 1970s appeared to them as a time of self-discovery
and political education, which provided a necessary space for reflecting
on gender social positions. Their recollections are often framed by
statements like these:

> I was a typical Irish woman, wife and mother in 1969. I never thought
> about politics. Society didn't encourage you to think about it and I was
> very busy raising five small children and it was hard enough to make
> ends meet. I got involved in 1971 with the introduction of internment.
> My son was interned at the age of sixteen and held for eighteen
> months. When the hunger strike ended I felt that I just couldn't go
> back into the house again. It just wasn't enough for me. I was too aware
> of the social problems in the community.

> * * *

> In 1969 I was living in Bombay Street I became involved in the marches
> and tenants' associations by seeing what was happening. It made a
> change for me. I wasn't a housewife anymore. I became more aware of
> injustice, of the interdependence of people for help, and of interna-
> tional politics.

> * * *

> It was with the civil rights movement and seeing the state reacting the
> way it did, that you realized what you were up against. When the civil
> rights movement started I had two small children. I think it was at that
> time that I began to question everything.

The unfolding of political events and women's active participation in
them triggered the emergence of new forms of political consciousness
that led to widespread "gender trouble." I use this expression in a double sense. First, *trouble* is the word commonly used in Belfast to refer to

the recurrent outbreaks of ethnic confrontation. Thus people often speak of the "troubles of the 1920s," the "troubles of the 1930s," or simply "the troubles" when they refer to the current conflict. There is a degree of ironic intimacy in the use of such a mild word to characterize repeated periods of ethnic violence—as if this were a domestic conflict, recurrent and familiar, with well-known rules and expectations. However, the tensions produced in the home as an effect of the involvement of women in popular resistance were narrated by women in clearly political terms. In contrast to the familiar forms in which political conflict was cast in popular discourse, domestic conflict was *defamiliarized* in the narratives of women. By using "gender trouble" in the context of Belfast I wish to emphasize the overlap between what is generally conceived as two separate forms of conflict. In the following pages I attempt to show that the boundaries distinguishing the political and the domestic fields are indeed unfixed. In so doing I intend to show that the practices of resistance undertaken by women constitute a privileged scenario wherein to examine the mechanisms of social change. Second, my use of "gender trouble" echoes, of course, the title of Judith Butler's (1990) critique of gender as a stable category of identity. Precisely the instability of gender signification endowed the women's activism I describe in this chapter with parodic effects, unintended consequences, and multiple interpretations, both allowing for social change and setting its limits.

Women's practices of those early years of the conflict bring into relief the forms in which state practices are organized within a system of gender difference. Thus, for example, key political events, such as the curfew of 1970 and policy of internment in 1971, seemingly impervious to gender constructions, were structured from the beginning in a genderized form. I analyze women's practices of popular resistance within this gendered context to show the shifts of gender meanings that accompanied both state violence and women's resistance. This process of engagement was transformative both politically and personally. At one level, the female protagonists of this chapter thought of their political experience in the early 1970s as a radical change of political and gender consciousness. At another level, change in political consciousness is also how republicans conceptualize what happened to the entire nationalist community, a transformation that has been encapsulated in the repeated slogan "off our knees," the title chosen for a popular documentary about the Northern Ireland civil rights movement. This mirroring process makes women's political experience a privileged, if unexplored, site for understanding the changing political culture of Belfast's nationalist community.

The Curfew of 1970 and the Staging
of Female Solidarity

The repression of the civil rights marches and the subsequent intimidation that forced Catholic people out of their homes in some districts shocked Catholic people, but not until the curfew imposed by the British army on the Lower Falls in 1970 did women of all ages begin to be involved in street protests and committees. The confrontation leading to the curfew began in the Lower Falls with a series of house searches in pursuit of IRA men and arms. As the military filled the narrow streets of the area with vehicles people began to gather and stand watching the search operation unfold. The search escalated into a major riot after a military vehicle killed a man standing on the curb. In an effort to control the situation the army imposed a curfew.

According to the Belfast newspaper *Irish News* (July 4, 1970), at 10:20 p.m. on July 3, "a helicopter with a loud speaker circled low over the rooftops and announced that a curfew was being imposed on the area and anyone caught out of doors would be arrested. Saracen armored vehicles lined along the Falls Road." By midnight an armed force of fifteen hundred surrounded a population of barely ten thousand civilians. The military fired more than fifteen thousand rounds of ammunition, and the narrow streets were deluged with CS tear gas. Riots spread, and at least three hundred Catholic families were evacuated from their homes. In the following days residents made reports to the press and citizens' defense committees about soldiers wrecking houses, smashing windows and doors, and stealing property. Young men were forced to lie flat on their faces on the street or to kneel with their hands at the back of their heads while being interrogated (Sunday Times Insight Team [STIT] 1972). The whole episode lasted three days, during which five civilians were killed.

Less than a year before this episode the Lower Falls had been badly damaged by loyalist crowds aided by the B-specials—the voluntary, part-time police. They burned houses, and people's lives were threatened. The sight of a well-equipped army taking over the sky and streets was an experience that my informants remember as terrifying; it left a profound imprint on their memory. Twenty years later, Rose, a nationalist woman in her fifties, still expressed unextinguished anger and anxiety when recalling the curfew:

I was living in Conway Street [Lower Falls] when the curfew happened.
It was terrifying, unbelievable. When I see in television how Jews were

intimidated in Germany, or how blacks are treated in South Africa, I realize that there is not much difference in the way we were treated. I really know how a Jew or a black person feels. There were soldiers all around. The helicopter announced that nobody should come out of their house. In those days the soldiers were much worse than today. They were dragging men out of the houses, kicking and beating them with the butts of their rifles, throwing them to the ground. It is terrible to have to see that and not be able to do anything. That feeling is the worst: that you can do nothing. It was terrifying; you would not believe the way they wrecked houses. My house was searched, the television smashed to pieces on the floor—everything broken. And there was no food, some people had tins of beans, others had nothing, and no milk [for the babies]. Then the women came from the upper Falls with bread, milk, everything they could. Oh, they were welcome!

Some women I interviewed, too young at the time the curfew was imposed to understand what was happening, could recall the voice from the helicopter ordering everybody inside their houses, the oppressive smell of the tear gas, and the kerchiefs soaked in water and vinegar that people wrapped around their faces to counteract the effect of the gas. They also remembered the fear. Christine was fourteen at the time of the curfew. Her mother had recently given birth to a baby and was in bed. Her father was working in England. She recalled that the baby needed milk, and they did not have any in the house. Without thinking she ran into the streets to get the milk, and she heard a soldier yelling at her to stop or he would shoot. She was so worried about the baby that she did not care; she reached the shop and got the milk: "I didn't know what was happening then, you did it all for the family, you know, but soon I learned by experience what the British meant."

In these narratives the curtailed access to milk was unfailingly emphasized by a tone of resentment in the women's voices. In the working-class communities of Northern Ireland, buying and cooking food is done by women on a day-by-day basis. Milk is a basic element of the daily diet, particularly for young children. But milk also has a deeper significance; as in other cultures, it conveys the qualities of nurturance and care for which women are held responsible. Milk is thus both a metonymic representation of food and a symbol of emotional nurture. The inability of women to provide milk during the curfew encapsulated the enforced impossibility of providing for the physical and psychological well-being of family members who were exposed to the soldiers' mistreatment. Thus the impotence—characterized by Rose as "the worst feeling"—and the relief brought by the women from the Upper Falls—which made some women cry with emotion—were paramount in women's narratives about this time.

The Belfast newspapers, the *Irish News* and *The Belfast Telegraph*, gave ample coverage to the women's march. With a big headline—"3,000 Strong Army of Women Help to Feed the Lower Falls"—the *Irish News* of July 6, 1970, reported the women's march:

> Troops at barbed wire barricades were taken by surprise by the chanting, singing and yelling women. They marched down the Falls waving shopping bags, bottles of milk and loaves of bread. Some wore aprons, mothers clutched the hands of small children, some were at their Sunday best after coming from mass. An army spokesman said later that they had "looked the other way" during the march. Many of the women carried placards with the words "British army worse than the Black and Tans, women and child beaters."

As I alluded to earlier, Black and Tans, the British mercenary force used in Ireland during the War of Independence (1918–1921), were known for a level of brutality that gained for them an immortal place as the embodiment of death in Irish political folklore and popular history. By identifying the soldiers deployed in 1970 with the Black and Tans, women were tracing a parallel to a deeply resented historical situation. Furthermore, by accusing them of beating women and children, this defiant crowd of women was manipulating gender stereotypes of helpless femininity. The resultant image posed a powerful and odious force (Black and Tans) against a powerless people (women), thereby underscoring the shamefulness of the army's actions and delegitimizing its authority.

The women's march broke the ban on political demonstrations imposed by the minister of Home Affairs. According to *The Belfast Telegraph* "the army decided to turn a blind eye to the contravention" (July 6, 1970, 3), apparently not knowing what to do with such a group of uncontrolled women shouting abuse at them. Had this been a demonstration of men the soldiers would have responded with tear gas and bullets, but to shoot women with kids and prams stacked with cans of beans and bottles of milk who resembled all too much the women of their own working-class neighborhoods seemed too ridiculous; the soldiers were disconcerted and horrified at the sight of what they might have interpreted as female hysteria. The curfew was lifted shortly after the women walked through the Lower Falls cordoned area at 9:00 a.m. on July 5. Whether or not the decision to lift the curfew had been made previous to the appearance of the women, in the participants' consciousness the women had ended it.

The curfew has frequently been analyzed in the literature of the Northern Ireland conflict as a disastrous episode in political relations. No mention has been made, however, of the gender significance of the event. On a general level, local nationalists interpreted the curfew as an attack on the community, but wrecking houses and the denying access to food endowed the army's actions with additional gender meanings. Inasmuch as the curfew invaded the culturally dominant space for women and blocked fulfillment of their social role as mothers, it was a direct attack on the women themselves. For the thousands of women who marched down the Falls with their children and their prams full of food defying the soldiers' cordon, the gendered significance of the curfew was clear. Women—not men—organized themselves into a march; women were accompanied by their children, and women carried the food. Arriving at their destination, women—not men—came to encounter them. The slogans on their banners rendered public the meaning of their action: "British army worse than Black and Tans, women and child beaters"; they made it clear that the curfew was not a neutral action against the whole community but a highly gendered attack.

The lack of milk became, in women's consciousness, the epitome of British depravity. The nationalist women who took to the streets in solidarity with the women under curfew were prompted not so much by political ideology as by the shared understanding of maternal meanings and the feelings attached to them: the forced impediment of providing for small children or protecting others in the face of violence is understood as immoral and unjustified. Like in *Antigone*—a play of recurrent appeal in Ireland—the law of moral obligation to family is superior to that of political law that commands obedience to a superior power. And when the latter interferes with the former, instead of protecting it, then injustice is produced, the moral order upturned, and action demanded. Motherhood becomes then a major site of ethics (Scheper-Hughes 1992). Their march was spontaneously organized, yet it rested on established ties of kin and neighbor. For the women of the Falls breaking the curfew has achieved the quality of a myth of origin, the starting point of women's popular resistance.

Abuse, ill-treatment, and arbitrary arrests became daily occurrences after the curfew. Teenagers, who formed the bulk of the rioters, were easy targets for the army. Their mothers began to speak out. The march protesting the curfew had left women with a reinforced sense of solidarity as well as a taste of collective power. They soon began to organize new actions. At the end of February 1971, a group of women organized a demonstration outside the Law Court of Belfast in the city center to protest the continued indiscriminate arrests under the Special Powers Act. This was an unusual event because Catholics were banned from demonstrating in the city center. Rose recalled the story vividly while we were in her living room sipping tea one afternoon:

> We went to the court to protest for two lads who had been arrested for wearing combat jackets [forbidden under the Special Powers Act]. We went there—all women—dressed in combat jackets and carrying hurlic sticks, something Irish, we thought.[2] As we arrived at the court there was a crowd of Orangies [loyalists] waiting. We were beaten up by men and women alike. One [nationalist] woman got her little finger broken and hanging from her hand, and they [loyalists] would not leave her alone. The police was watching, and they didn't move a finger. Finally we were arrested and charged with disorderly behavior. We were taken to the police station, and they wanted to search us, you know, a strip search. I was so embarrassed; I would not have done it for the doctor. You know what I mean, we . . . Catholic women. . . . So I said: "No way, I'm not stripping, no way!" We made such a fuss they didn't search us, and we were finally brought to the judge and he dropped the charge of disorderly behavior. So I raised my hand and said: "Your honor, if we are not charged with disorderly behavior, can I have my hurlic stick back?" Everybody applauded, and the judge said, "Yes." Now, if somebody had told me before that I was going to go to court protesting I would not have believed it, you know, I would have said "No, not me . . . " But you learned—bad as it was—that you had to.

It is this sense of learning that lingers, filling the space with memory. It's a learning by shock, a loss of innocence that forces women like Rose into the uncertainty of political practice and the feelings of anger that come with it.

Both Catholic and Protestant newspapers reported the incidents in their front pages. While their reports coincide in the description of the confrontation between Catholics and Protestants, their headlines indicate a clear disjunction in relation to police behavior. The headlines of *The Belfast Telegraph* read "Factions clash in city center. Many arrests." The *Irish News* on the other hand opened its report with "Siding of RUC with anti-Catholic mob." Both newspapers reported that the police had arrested more than forty Catholics, most of them women, "after scuffling and fighting broke out between rival mobs in downtown Belfast. . . . There was a confrontation between the Catholic crowd and a rival Union-Jack waving crowd of Protestants who had gathered on the other side of the street. On several occasions groups of women, dressed in combat jackets, black berets and carrying hurlic sticks were chased and arrested by police" (*The Belfast Telegraph*, February 26, 1971). The *Irish News* in criticizing the partiality of the police, reported that "no attempt was made to arrest Protestants who struck at women being arrested, and who refused to move from the courthouse building" (February 27, 1971). The Northern Ireland Civil Rights Association protested "the vicious conduct of the RUC yesterday when the right of peaceful protest was interfered with while counterdemonstrators were given police protection as they screamed abuse and inflammatory remarks at women who were protesting the proceedings taking place in the court under the Special Powers Act" (*Irish News*, February 27, 1971). That night a group of five hundred women—according to the *Irish News*—or fifty women—according to *The Belfast Telegraph*—marched to the police station on Springfield Road in protest of the arrests that had taken place outside Belfast Court.

Like Rose, many women have the sense that the change in their lives was forced by the deep disruption of community and family life. Talking about women's motivations during that early political involvement, Brigid, who is now in her forties, said: "Many women had small children and had enough with raising their families. They would have preferred to go on with their lives as before, but they had no choice because their husbands were arrested and also their older sons. They had to do something."

This sense of choiceless decisions recurs in people's narratives, particularly when the subjects are women. This sense expresses an existential predicament, the confrontation of dilemmas that led to extraordinary forms of action. The concept of choiceless decisions embodies a moral discourse in which the social order is accountable for communal principles of justice that, when broken, make rebellion necessary. Such moral discourse is also expressed in the folk history and folk songs of the Catholic population of the North, in both the countryside and the urban ghettoes of Belfast (Glassie 1982; McCann 1985). Within the context of this moral universe, a choiceless decision is not an oxymoron. It encompasses a complex notion of freedom involving a subtle double critique. On the one hand, the idea of a choiceless decision questions the passive victimization of women in Northern Ireland; on the other, it challenges the liberal belief that human agents have free choice. For people like Brigid, human beings are never completely determined by social constraint; they can rebel. But neither are they absolutely free; their rebellion, if socially meaningful, is bound to moral imperatives.

As Northern Ireland feminists have noted, the strongest motivation for women's political action arose from motherhood, from the arrest of men and boys (Edgerton 1986, 61–79; Ward and McGivern 1980, 583). To Rose, "women became stronger and stronger as they [the British army] were trying to let us down. I don't know how women did it, how they carried on. Well, you see, you had to; you had no choice. As they were getting worse, a greater resolution grew among the women that they would not turn us down. See, women are the mothers, and any mother would do anything for their children."

In Irish Catholic culture the ideal-typical mother has been shaped, particularly since the mid-nineteenth century, by the cult of the Virgin Mary. The historical significance of the myth of Mary in Europe has been well documented by Marina Warner (1983). Although the cult of Mary began to develop in Ireland in the seventeenth century, it did not become a widespread symbolic representation until the second half of the nineteenth century, when the late marriage of men, according to historian Margaret MacCurtain, made the Mary of the Passion, the sorrowful mother, "an appropriate model for a generation of women the death of whose elderly husbands left them widows at a relatively young age" (1982, 539–43). For sociologist Liam O'Dowd, in Ireland "the Marian cult contributed to the Catholic idealization of motherhood while distinguishing the role of procreator and family provider from sex and sexuality" (1987, 13). In the aftermath of partition in 1921, the Church reinforced the control of the family and women's role in it, while simultaneously policing extrafamiliar sexual deviance. In this way the Catholic church promoted in Ireland a profoundly ambivalent view of women (O'Dowd 1987, 14). Ward and McGivern, speaking about the image of the Virgin Mary in the North of Ireland, observed that "the chaste, pure image of Mary with her passive, unquestioning role, has been a model for all young Catholic girls" (1980, 581). As cultural ideal the Catholic mother represents the emotional foundation of the family. She is the source of unconditional love, expected to protect and forgive her children and to mediate on their behalf when trouble befalls them. This model has frequently provoked feelings of guilt in those women who do not conform to it (Beale 1986). The Catholic establishment, along with the conservative government that emerged in the South after partition, gradually utilized this ideology to ground firmly gender discrimination. Article 41.2 of the Irish Constitution of 1937 confines women to the domestic sphere and defines motherhood as the social role for women:

"The state recognizes that by her life within the home, the woman gives to the state a support without which the common good cannot be achieved. The state shall therefore endeavor to ensure that mothers shall not be obliged by economic necessity to engage in labor to the neglect of their duties in the home." This provision was accompanied by legislation that banned divorce, prohibited contraception, and severely restricted salaried work for married women, thus leaving them in a position of stark structural inequality. Women fared little better in the North where the Protestant government was equally conservative and patriarchal in ideology and social legislation. The dominant Protestant ideology in Northern Ireland conceived of a woman as subordinate to the authority of her husband and idealized family, marriage, and motherhood (O'Dowd 1987).

The ideal was hardly a reality for working-class women in Northern Ireland, where female labor in the linen factories was a permanent social feature until the 1950s. The tension between cultural ideal and socioeconomic reality was more acute in the Catholic communities where male unemployment was chronically high. Married Catholic women were twice as likely as their Protestant counterparts to work outside the house (O'Dowd 1987, 28). This tension was to be heightened during internment.

THE IRONIES AND PARODIES OF INTERNMENT

Army stones women from the West Belfast area when objecting
to British destruction at a house search.
(*Andersonstown's News* [*AN*] December 6, 1972)

* * *

Women in Tullymore protest against the destruction
of footpaths.
(*AN* December 20, 1972)

* * *

Women protest outside Long Kesh against degrading
searches going to visits.
(*AN* January 10, 1973)

* * *

A meeting of 30 women in Turf Lodge form an action
committee. They are discussing techniques of community
policing in order to set a community control service.
(*AN* February 16, 1973)

* * *

Turf Lodge Women's Action Committee print a paper called
Action. The group will work for release of all political
prisoners, end of repressive laws and withdrawal of
British troops. They call for united community action.
(*AN* February 28, 1973)

* * *

Emma Grove awarded 35,000 pounds as compensation for the
loss of sight by a plastic bullet.
(*AN* February 28, 1973)

* * *

Tish Holland (17) was interned second after Liz Mckee. Tish's
brother Brendan is serving a prison sentence of 12 years.
(*AN* February 21, 1973)

The government of Northern Ireland introduced internment without
trial on August 9, 1971, at 4:30 a.m. Their objective was, through sweep-
ing arrests in nationalist areas, to dismantle the IRA that was allegedly
reorganizing itself after abandoning armed activity in 1962.[3] Internees
were held at three camps set to that effect: Long Kesh near Belfast (later
to become a high-security prison), Magilligan in County Derry, and the
ship *Maidstone* in Belfast harbor (Flackes and Elliot 1989, 402). The introduction of internment proved to be a highly controversial move that
escalated violence and further alienated the Catholic community (Burton 1978, 18). Although internment was supposed to target IRA sus-
pects, most internees were local men without IRA membership. Many
households were deprived of their main source of income, and hundreds of women were left to raise their families alone for the foreseeable
future (STIT 1972). Even more distressing for women was the internment of teenage boys. Several women I interviewed had had sons who
were arrested at the age of sixteen. Their collective outrage and distress
was conveyed in a letter signed by a "concerned mother of an internee"

and addressed to Cardinal Conway, which appeared on September 19, 1971, in the local weekly *Andersonstown News*:

> I am a Catholic mother of five children. My youngest son was arrested on his 17th birthday. He has been constantly harassed since the age of 15. . . . Where is your voice? Why are you not demanding the release of all the innocent men, women, boys and girls who are imprisoned without charge? Where are you when mothers and wives need comfort when their husbands and children are assassinated by the British army and other extremists? I, as a mother, am not asking, I demand that you do something immediately to start the release of all these innocent people.

The publication of this letter—in which a woman addressed a highly respected authority figure in a demanding and outraged tone—would have been simply inconceivable only two years earlier. Notice that the writer did not address the cardinal from the point of view of a woman, however, but from that of a mother. Motherhood, idealized by the Catholic church as the highest expression of womanhood in order to control individual women, offered a moral foundation from which women could confront the Catholic leadership. This letter expressed a growing frustration, not necessarily with local priests, but with the Catholic hierarchy that had been notably silent in the face of the unfolding political events.

Women, whose tightly knit communities allowed free flow of information, organized on their own streets to provide protection against military harassment and arrests. As internment continued women replaced men in the local branches of the Northern Ireland Civil Rights Association (Edgerton 1986), and young women began to involve themselves in the armed struggle.

To protest internment NICRA organized a massive civil disobedience campaign, which consisted of withholding payment of rent and utilities for council houses. Thirty thousand households joined the campaign. Because women were household administrators, they were the ones in the best position to enforce the campaign. To neutralize this action the government introduced the Payment for Debt Act of 1971 that permitted the government to withhold wages and welfare benefits from the paychecks of those people on rent and rates strike. This significantly reduced the budget of many families who were already finding it difficult to make ends meet and greatly impoverished women-headed households as sociologist Eileen Evason (1980) noted in her pioneering study of poverty in Belfast. The Payment for Debt Act also brought back the concomitant anxieties of debt, a familiar sword of Damocles in Belfast working-class communities. For example, Clare, a community worker in her thirties, described to me the anguish suffered by her mother, a former mill worker who had managed to avoid debt for most of her life and suddenly found herself indebted. Although internment led women into male arenas of political organization and street protest, their actions were interpreted according to the parameters of dominant gender ideology, as this comment from Clare reveals: "When it came to protests, it was always women. They took the initiative and they did it. There was a general belief that women were somehow by virtue of their womanhood more protected, that a woman was less suspicious than a man. I cannot ever remember a man organizing a protest; it was always women. Big groups of women and then young lads with stocks of stones behind to stone the soldiers when the women pulled back." The assumption that women were passive victims of war and therefore less likely to engage in subversive activities was manipulated by both men and women during the early 1970s. At the level of everyday practice, such an assumption led to gender reversals. In an inversion of tradition, women walked with men to ensure men's safety or women patrolled the streets at night while men stayed home. The IRA, by using women to transport ammunition, turned the hegemonic discourse of gender identity that rendered women invisible in the political world into a subversive technique.

In discussing the colonial assumptions that made veiled women suspect of subversion during the Algerian war of liberation, Frantz Fanon astutely observed that precisely the obsession to disclose the body of Algerian women enabled the veil to become both a symbol and a technique of resistance. Algerian women would wear the veil or shed it to attract or detract the attention of French security forces, thus playing the assumptions of colonial authority against itself. As Homi Bhabha has commented when the veil is displayed in the public sphere "it becomes the object of paranoid surveillance and interrogation . . . and when the veil is shed in order to penetrate deeper into the European quarter the colonial police see everything and nothing. An Algerian woman is only, after all, a woman" (Bhabha 1993, 63; Fanon 1967). Similarly, in Belfast, a woman wearing a coat eventually became suspected of hiding ammunition. The military attempted to counteract this possibility by literally uncovering the body of women, asking them to open their coats and their handbags at search points to expose them to the soldiers' gaze. As occurred in Algeria, the attempt to uncover subversive women in Belfast made the coat and a woman's body both a symbol of resistance and the very vehicle of political transgression. Women often refused to perform the humiliating operation of opening their coats to men's eyes, even if they risked arrest. But women could also open their coats to pass unsuspected, hiding weapons in their prams. In this case they became just women, complying to what they are told, and the army sees everything and sees nothing. In the words of Homi Bhabha, this negation both tactics entail "is a form of power that is exercised at the very limits of identity and authority" where the signs of identity can be redeployed as masks of insurgency (1994, 62). This subversive mockery is even more apparent in the performances of women who constituted the "hen patrols."

Of the Duck in Every Soldier and the Fighter in Each Hen: Gender Metaphors of Resistance

The action most celebrated in the narratives of nationalist women was the establishment of an alarm system against the British army. The army liked to conduct house raids and arrests during the night when people are less alert. This military tactic led local women to organize a warning system. Their aim was to warn the community and the IRA, which at the time amounted, in the words of one participant, to a bunch of local boys, of the imminent presence of the British army. From 10:00 p.m. to 6:00 a.m., the hours favored by the army for raids, women patrolled the streets on a rotating basis, taking turns following the soldiers everywhere they went. They called themselves the "hen patrols" in opposition to the "duck patrols," the popular nickname given to the night units of the British army. Each woman, carrying a whistle, would blow it to warn the community about the proximity of an army patrol, while simultaneously banging garbage bin lids against the pavement.

The use of humorous nicknames was a form of managing and, to certain extent, subverting what was otherwise a threatening reality. Such names are metaphoric assertions that, in James Fernandez's words, "make manageable objects of the self and of others and facilitate performance" (1986, 6). The duck metaphor symbolically disarmed the (powerful) British army by predicating on the soldiers an unthreatening animal identity. The hen metaphor, however, empowered the (disempowered) watching women by providing an imaginative scenario where confrontation between comparable parties—ducks and hens—could take place. Thus the initial power relation is imaginatively reversed, easing the move from fear to defiance. The gendered character of this metaphoric play must not be underestimated because it is the key to its subversive character. Hens are better known as chased creatures, rather than as pursuers. The humor evoked by the reverse image of hens chasing male fowl psychologically transformed a menacing situation into a laughable one and thus brought it under a certain degree of control. This transformation creates a space wherein action can occur and through which the paralysis produced by fear can be effectively counteracted. One can see this dynamic in Clare's recollections:

> We followed the soldiers everywhere they went. I remember one saying that he could handle the men, but not the women. We made a lot of noise. Noise can be frightening. There was a fellow being arrested in a house. We were outside making a lot of noise, and when the soldiers came we suddenly disappeared. You could hear a pin dropping. The soldiers who had all their rifles and had been kicking us in the demonstrations were shaking, panicking, while we were in our houses, giggling away behind the curtains. They were terrified. We waited five minutes and went back to the streets and started it all over again. I was in a house with this woman whose son had been interned and she said, "My God, Clare, I never saw a color like that in their face." They were yellow, terrified. All was over when the fellow was arrested. There was nothing you could do but bang the bin lids. But this time we went home afterwards and left them in the streets wondering what was going to happen to them. Who was going to open [fire] to them.

The effect of the metaphoric reversal I described is clear in Clare's narrative; the major emphasis in her account is women's power to frighten the military and the humor and delight derived from doing so. The humor was clearly there while narrating the story.

In October 23, 1971, two sisters from the Clonard Women's Action Committee, Maura Meehan and Dorothy Maguire, were shot dead by the military. Another, Florence O'Riordon, was badly wounded. In a short period of time, two more patrolling women, Rita O'Hara and Marie Moore, were shot, and Emma Groves, a mother of eleven, was blinded by a plastic bullet while standing by the window in her house. Women continued protesting military raids by marching and banging bin lids, but stopped their nightly patrols. The metaphoric game ceased to be effective when the military figured it out and took the unimaginable step of shooting unarmed women. In so doing, they were "really" shooting community resistance. Yet, if the bodies lying on the ground were symbols of resistance, they were also the flesh and blood of women with concrete identities and personal histories. The boundary between the symbolic body of community and the actual bodies of individual women had become indistinguishable. As embodied allegory, the female body emerged as a charged space wherein republicans of different persuasions and state forces would fight their battles. Similarly the porous line between house and street, domestic space and communal space, was blurred.

PUBLIC DOMESTICITY AND THE DEFILEMENT OF COMMUNITY

Internment and the widespread raids of people's homes blurred the boundaries between household and communal space and at certain moments practically erased them. Army raids transformed the secure intimacy of the household into a vulnerable space, susceptible to arbitrary violation by armed men. That the raids, accompanied by intimidation and destruction of property, were conducted in the predawn hours when people were asleep, unprepared, and disoriented on awakening, deepened the feelings of violation and vulnerability. The disproportionate and arbitrary nature of the searches, which sometimes included sealing off whole streets, asserted their character as collective punishments. The minimal results, obtained by the army and police in thousands of house searches conducted in the nationalist districts, make it difficult to avoid characterizing the raids and concomitant arrests as rituals of authority (Feldman 1991, Sluka 1989).

The military enactment of state power in a space culturally defined as feminine created a gendered colonial dichotomy. By forcefully entering the household the army was not only invading women's physical space but also violating their psychological and affective space. Many women described to me the experience in terms similar to these:

> I always knew when they were coming to our house. You just got the feeling. Somebody would blow the whistle, and the women would come out and support you. In my house we were in many ways very traditional Catholics. We never cursed, and suddenly these big foreign [not Irish] men would come into your house with their arms, and jackets, and boots and call your mom a bastard and a whore. There was nothing more humiliating, nothing that would make you more angry than

69

being in your own house and have the British army bullying you, wrecking your house, and making fun of your mom. I think that is what I would always remember until I go to the tomb—that my mother was constantly humiliated.

Stories like this were frequently accompanied by expressions of disgust, exemplified in the attitude of Moira, a young nationalist woman whose husband was imprisoned and who described the aftermath of the search of her house by saying, "You don't feel the house clean for days afterwards, no matter how much you clean it." There is an implicit but clear continuity between the body and the house in women's narratives of house searches. For Moira the humiliation, destruction, impotence, and anxiety accompanying such a house search was as defiling as a sexual assault. Certainly the verbal abuse of women and the arrest of their children blurred this line, if such a distinction can indeed be established between symbolic and physical violation.

Women's narratives recalled more often and more bitterly the arrest of their sons than those of their husbands. Political folklore memorialized the arrest of sons in the chorus of the most popular song against internment: "Armored cars and tanks and guns came to take away our sons." This is the first stanza:

> Through the little streets of Belfast
> In the dark of early morn
> British soldiers came marauding
> Wrecking little homes with scorn
> Heedless of crying children
> Dragging fathers from their beds
> Beating sons while helpless mothers
> Watched the blood pour from their heads.

Mothers, of course, were far from being helpless. In this song the image of the helpless mother constituted a collective representation that expressed the deep feelings of violation produced by both house searches and, by extension, the military intrusion in the whole community. Such female allegories of collective victimization have loomed large in Irish nationalist culture, proliferating during the first years of the 1970s and recurring periodically in the popular imagery of West Belfast. The image of the helpless mother provides an inherent moral argument that legitimizes (male) armed aggression against state domination. In this sense the song conveys the same message as the mural analyzed in chapter 2, and like the mural it does so through gender terms.

As the house became collectively vulnerable, the streets, enclosed by barricades and watched by women, were endowed with familial meanings and intimate knowledge. Reflecting on her involvement with the hen patrols, Mary said: "They were my political education. Although, at the time, I was not aware of it. All I knew was that I was defending my area, my family, my people." In her words area, family, and people were equivalent; they were interwoven, rather than different categories. Thus, they articulate the rhetoric of a nationalist community. Because the community was not politically homogeneous, there were profound and sometimes bitter political divisions among nationalists. But political factionalism was not incompatible with a sense of community and the solidarity derived from sharing the same predicament. Political division and communal solidarity should not be seen as opposed processes during the early 1970s, but as coexisting dimensions of the same process.

Tight communities became tighter; communal solidarity was reinforced at the same time that political differences widened. Open house doors, alleys, and backyards, provided free movement for IRA men. Women guarding the streets and demonstrating against arrests symbolized not only community solidarity but, more important, the rejection of a broader power relation between an army of occupation and an occupied people. The hen patrols constituted as much a parody of military power as a system of warning. They demystified the army as they counteracted practically its effects. Gender inequality provided a model through which the Catholic community, long familiar with gender metaphors in political and religious discourse, could express their frustration and defiance.

The manifest power differential between soldiers armed with machine guns and women armed only with whistles reflected the larger inequality perceived between English and Irish and perhaps that other, more immediate and more deeply felt, inequality between Catholics and the Protestant state.

THE POLITICAL HOSTAGE ACTION COMMITTEE

As the military policy of internment continued, female relatives of internees decided to start a broad campaign. A group of women called a meeting at one of West Belfast's republican social clubs, "The Felons," thus called in ironic reappropriation of the old British categorization of

10. Children playing in a street in Beechmount, near the house of the author.

Irish rebels.[4] The Political Hostage Action Committee, a predecessor of the Relatives Action Committees of the late 1970s, emerged from the meeting. Clare recalled the events:

> I remember that meeting well. We called together all the relatives of people interned. We decided we were going to fight collectively, together. At that time the IRA was fighting away, and Sinn Fein was seen as part of the IRA, and the British were making a strong international campaign against the IRA. Nobody mentioned the fact that the IRA existed because of internment; there was practically no IRA before. But internment got so bad that everybody joined the IRA. So we decided that if we wanted to make a point in the international scene we had to form a broad front. Women were all together in the buses to the prison and every time you went for a visit you heard of a new atrocity being done to the internees, and we would say "Jesus Christ you have to do something, we can't take all that." We wanted to do something. We were going to jail three fucking times a week! [Her voice was angry.] I remember one occasion when my mom and I went to visit our Mary [Clare's sister] who was interned in Armagh jail. She had very severe

11. Back alley near Clonard.

menstrual pains and when she came to the visit room she was pale and she felt sick during the visit—really bad. And she says, "I'm gonna have to cut this visit, I'm gonna have to go, I'm gonna be sick." And we carried her into the prison yard, and my mom stood there with our Mary in her arms, and our Mary was vomiting, she couldn't make it to the toilets, and all the screws [warders] came and surrounded her. I never seen my mum more helpless because that woman was her daughter. And you're standing there, and your daughter is sick in your arms, and they took her away. . . . Things like this happened all the time, you know, and they make you more and more bitter, and bitterness in itself is not good. You have to act, and everybody realized that. So at that meeting, we formed the Political Hostage Action Committee, and we decided we were going to picket Downing Street [the British prime minister's residence]. We decided the campaign was going to be a broad platform with major marches etc., so all got started up. These committees were formed in all the areas. We had our wee committee in our district. We organized functions to raise money, organized local pickets, updated information on the internees, and edited our local newsheet. We did an awful lot of things. It was not only an international campaign; it was also a local campaign. It was as much to keep local morale because people were very repressed, and we were very frightened, depressed. I mean it took quite a bit of nerve to actually start it up, you know.

Narratives of violence mediated and constructed the experience of actual violence, as I will discuss at greater length in chapter 4. Buses coming and going to the prison were a privileged space for the diffusion of such narratives. The women in these buses connected house and prison with an invisible but indelible tie that inscribed both spaces in a continuum of political contestation.

Women exchanged information about protest verbally: ways to claim benefits, tips about prison visits, and how to deal with men "on the run." Because of their close acquaintance with each other, women knew who among their number was articulate and would make a good speaker. Those natural leaders were in turn asked to talk at meetings or at police barracks.

Confrontations between women and security forces remained the most culturally charged ventures, largely because they became an allegory of nationalist resistance. Yet, women's encounters with the British army problematized nationalist representations of Ireland as helpless mother or passive maiden. The Ireland allegorized in women's resistance to the state forces more closely resembled the revolutionary Marian of Delacroix, marching decidedly through working-class streets, than the passive Cathleen ni Houlihan, waiting for her men to liberate her. Indeed, women's involvement in political resistance during the early 1970s constituted a process of reflection through which dominant gender discourse was challenged.

This challenge emerged more clearly with the end of internment in 1975; upon their release, many male internees found their wives unwilling to assume a secondary position in the household and return to their former tasks of housework and childrearing. The resultant domestic discord led to the breakup of many marriages. Some women attributed this widespread conflict to the different social experiences that men and women had undergone. Internment led to the imprisonment of many men and their submersion in the political culture of the prison. The prison became a school of militant nationalism where men learned republican history, ideology, and military organization; however, women were led to test their abilities in various social contexts. The hardship of coping alone with family needs amid great poverty and increasing militarization created new ties of solidarity among women and contributed to the development of a new sense of independence and self-identity. Men and women had followed relatively separate processes. Brigid put it this way: "Men were used to the women being in the house all the time. But with internment there was no dinner-at-five and children-to-bed-at-eight. Everything was disorganized then. Men did not realize that, because they were locked up. Then when they came out they expected to find things as they left them. But women were not willing to go back into the house again. It was a big shock!"

For some women, however, things were not so clear. For Anne marriage crises provoked deep anxiety. She had discovered a new sense of independence when her husband was jailed, but she felt she needed the security of her marriage. When her husband was freed, she worried that her continued pursuit for self-development would jeopardize her marriage. The dilemma between her needs for both personal growth and emotional security led to a difficult psychological crisis. Anne's husband was killed by loyalist paramilitaries in the mid-1980s. In a tremendously painful way his death resolved Anne's dilemma by forcing open the door to change. If married women involved in community activism were wrestling with competing—and frequently contradictory—needs, then a younger generation of women fighters had altogether different concerns.

A GENDER LAPSUS

Women were not interned until December 1972. The first woman internee, Liz McKee, was nineteen years old, and the second, Theresa Holland, was barely eighteen. The strong reactions in the local papers suggest that the internment of "girls" was shocking to the Catholic population, independent of political affiliation. Political and community organizations made public statements denouncing what they considered "callous disregard for human rights" and a step "before children land up in Long Kesh as well" (*AN*, January 3, 1973). The main West Belfast publications, the *Andersonstown News* and *Republican News,* both dedicated space to individual women internees, including photographs and details of their biographies—treatment not received by their male counterparts. Yet for the women interned there was nothing exceptional about their arrest; they were part of a generation that had come of age during the civil rights movement, and all had seen male relatives interned. Arrests were an everyday occurrence in the community, and they did not think of themselves as being any different from men. Gender difference was for them politically nonexistent. As Theresa, one of the internees, said, "There was no thought about women or feminism then; the idea then was the unity of Ireland. I never thought of myself then as being unequal with men." Not until they were jailed did interned women realize what difference gender difference made. Within six months 236 women were imprisoned, all of them republicans. Like interned men they were soon granted political status and organized according to the IRA military structure with an officer commander at their head. In 1975 the IRA called a truce, but the female prisoners were not consulted in the decision-making process. In Theresa's words:

> It was then that we realized we were women. We were in Armagh [jail], internees, remanded, and sentenced prisoners. We had been fighting, and we were told to shut up. Why could we not have a say in what it was going on? We had a meeting within Armagh and made a list of demands—the most basic of which was having a say in where the struggle was going. We got that. Then on our release we realized that once you get married you contend with two struggles because—no matter what—the woman is left responsible for the raising of children and the keeping of the house.[5]

If jail for the interned men was a school of militant nationalism, then for women internees it entailed a reflection on the politics of gender. They were militants and as such had—like men—risked their lives, been arrested, and were organized in the same military structure; but, when it came to decision making, their organization slipped into a hierarchical system of gender difference within which they were not peers, but, simply, women. Identity does not spring here from any pre-existing condition of being, an essence or material reality, rather identity is formed by imputation and sliding of meaning. The imputation of a feminine identity is performed by the exclusion of women from the realm of political decision that constitutes the community of militants. It is exclusion, absence, void, rather than presence, that constitutes the space of identity.

Such operation is made possible by the sliding of meaning in the concept of militant that is gender neuter, denoting a relationship with political activism, not a gender position. As militants, men and women are purported to be the same, yet they are not. In the arena of cultural representation and practice, *militant* is already marked by sexual difference. The gap created by the sliding of meaning is a gap between different orders of reality playing in political practice and materializing identity not as presence but as absence. Such a gap between the identity of militants and the difference of gender opened a space of signification that led women internees to take a new subject position in the arena of popular resistance. This change in the positionality of militant women generated a discursive transformation on the politics of gender that came to full strength in the late 1970s.

MISRECOGNITIONS

Feminists in Northern Ireland have often argued that the activism of the Catholic women of West Belfast did not substantially modify the balance of gender power relations. Sociologist and feminist Linda Edgerton (1986), for example, has suggested that women's activism against the repressive policies of the state was motivated by the same gender ideology that maintained motherhood as the primary responsibility of women in Northern Ireland. While this ideology furnished the motivation for political action, she argued, such involvement did not challenge the hierarchical system of gender that constrains the space and social possibilities of women. Thus, for Edgerton, women's political resistance during these years was—from a feminist perspective—fundamentally untransformative because women were locked in a dynamic of de facto transgression of gender roles while ideologically reproducing them. Although this argument brings into relief the structural contradictions that women often face in movements of resistance, it also forecloses important questions about how social and particularly feminist transformation occurs. What is left unexamined, for example, is the idea of ideological reproduction. Thus the political deployment of motherhood by nationalist women in Northern Ireland is understood by Edgerton as a form of gender false consciousness that maintains a system of gender inequality. Yet, as I have shown, the dominant gender discourse that propelled women to action was in fact modified in and through practice—that is, the military practices of the state and the resistance of women.

The interstitial character of women's political practices, the fact that they were situated in the margins of social and political space, placed dominant gender discourse *out of place* by introducing slippages of meaning and creating new social fields.

As in other parts of the world (Beall et al. 1989; Peteet 1991), the tension in Northern Ireland between transgression and reproduction of gender ideology did not constitute a mechanical operation but, rather, a dynamic process. By confronting new dimensions of social experience, many women challenged former understandings of the roles of mother and wife, infusing dominant gender discourse with new dimensions. This process did not occur outside the consciousness of women or in spite of false consciousness. Women in Northern Ireland were not unaware of gender hierarchy; it was simply taken for granted. Their involvement in popular resistance led women, however, to an increased appreciation of the political character of gender inequality. That is, gender relations came to appear as susceptible to transformation as were other social relations. The disruptions and new accommodations of gender relations, which intensified in the mid-1970s, represent the recognition of that possibility of change.

The discussion of the possibilities and limits of feminist transformation must complicate gender identity by exploring how gender functions as signifying form in a particular cultural universe. First, gender has been a recurrent metaphor in the construction of colonial and postcolonial identities in Ireland. In this chapter I have attempted to show how these constructions infused the political practices in which women were engaged with unintended meanings. The resonances that gender signifiers produce in the political culture of Northern Ireland make it quite impossible to understand gender power relations in isolation from colonial and nationalist power relations. Second, in West Belfast gender inequality is complicated by its inextricability from class and ethnic inequality. The discrimination against Catholics in employment and political representation confronted Catholic women with different social realities than those faced by Protestant women. Catholic women were also affected by the military occupation of Northern Ireland differently than were their Protestant counterparts (Moore 1993). Gender hierarchy is never a transparent system; it is always engendered as already marked by particular positions in a social universe. The facts of being Catholic and working class in Northern Ireland are not elements that can be added to an essential *woman*; rather they fundamentally constitute what woman is, making the task of defining gender power relations immensely complex.

Without taking the mutual construction of different systems of oppression into account, it is impossible to understand the transformative effect of the political involvement of nationalist women.

The hardship of the early years of the conflict has frequently obscured a great amount of joy women found in what they called a process of learning. This process involved a transformation of consciousness. Carolyn Steedman (1987) has written about class consciousness as an uneven and complex position in the world, learned rather than acquired, often through the exigencies of difficult lives. This view can also apply to gender consciousness. Women became collectively aware of the power of the state as it manifested itself in concrete forms that directly affected their lives, such as arresting their sons or their husbands, invading their houses, or withholding their social security benefits. In confronting the state, their position in the world as Catholic, working-class women in a Protestant-dominated British colony acquired new political meanings. The acute inequality of the political system of Northern Ireland became both progressively intolerable and progressively susceptible to change. This in turn affected other structures of inequality—from religion to gender—that women had formerly taken for granted. The emergence of a new consciousness was a rough and complicated process that had an impact on not only the personal identity of individuals but also the construction of concepts of nationality and ethnicity as I discuss at some length in chapter 7.

The argument about gender roles lurking beneath the political scene is a story forgotten by the crafters of nationalist-republican history. There is, of course, an intimate relation between power and memory. Although the republican movement has occasionally celebrated "women's role in the struggle," the challenge to gender definitions with its concomitant conflicts has been frequently forgotten.[6] By the end of the 1970s, the challenge posed by women became more compelling. This time the process would be very painful.

CHAPTER 4

The Ritual Politics
of Historical Legitimacy

T HE HUNGER STRIKE of 1981 can be viewed as a ritual event through which historical myth is transformed and re-created anew. Mythicized history, rather than hard facts and dates, Obeyesekere has suggested, is the material out of which national consciousness is formed; "myths are always in the minds of people, and sum up for them the 'meaning' of their country's history" (1975, 23). Republican historical myth contains powerful gender models of historical action—models that erase the historical agency of women in favor of individual male heroes.

In his analysis of the 1981 hunger strike, O'Malley (1990) has emphasized the continuity between this dramatic action and the republican tradition of hunger striking, concluding that the hunger strike of 1981 was a reenactment of republican historical myth. Feldman (1991) has, however, minimized cultural continuity and underlined instead the political discontinuities that distinguish the hunger strike of 1981 from former ones. For Feldman the central question is the instrumental effect of the strike on the republican movement rather than its construction within republican culture (1991, 219). I argue that, while the political effects of the strike are obviously of paramount importance, these effects cannot be separated from the cultural continuities that gave the hunger strike of 1981 its political form. Sole emphasis on the performative codes of the hunger strike leaves unexplained the emotional and moral force of this form of resistance. Nor does the code explain how the hunger strike was constructed as a gendered model of historical action in which men figured as the hero-martyrs and women as the supporters. This analytical gap between the cultural continuities and performative discontinuities can be bridged by understanding the hunger strike of 1981 as a historical ritual (Kelly and Kaplan 1990) of which both expressive content and performative power are inseparable dimensions (Tambiah 1985).

When Bobby Sands, leader of the hunger strike and artificer of the prison political culture, began fasting to death in protest against Britain he followed an international political legacy that had gained moral legitimacy since Gandhi. Yet, for prisoners, the political meaning of the strike did not stem from a pacifist conviction or strategy, "it was a prelude to [insurrectionary] violence" (Feldman 1991, 220). Sands was simultaneously reinterpreting while enacting a myth model deeply rooted in Irish culture (i.e., redemptive Christian sacrifice) by fusing it with mythological images of Gaelic warriors and socialist ideals of national liberation.[1] Simultaneously Sands was fighting with rational instrumentality a concrete political battle that influenced, at least temporarily, the balance of power between Britain and the republican movement in Northern Ireland, a fight that led the latter to a political reconfiguration.

The Irish writer Colm Toibin (1987) has compared narratives of Irish history to poetry; in the sense that both enable similar emotional moves. For the hunger strikers, fellow prisoners, and many of their supporters, history constituted as much a moral narrative as an existential predicament. As narrative, the past gave meaning to the present; it legitimized politics and charged actions with emotional power. As existential predicament, the prisoners perceived themselves as embodying the history of their country, and, as such, their actions effected as much the existence of the nation as individual lives. Consequently the hunger strike as a ritual of redemption was intended to bring an end to the suffering of the prisoners and, insofar as the prisoners were the embodiment of the nation, to terminate the suffering of Ireland under British rule.

FASTING AGAINST BRITAIN: THE INVENTION OF TRADITION

The 1981 Irish hunger strike became an international event, so much so that representatives of different foreign countries attended the funeral of the first hunger striker to die, Bobby Sands, or sent their official respects to his family. The U.S. government expressed deep regret. The president of the Italian senate sent his condolences to Sands's family. Thousands marched in Paris. The town of Le Mans named a street after him. In India the opposition in the Upper House observed a minute of silence in Sands's honor. Iran sent their ambassador to the funeral. The then-Soviet Union publicly condemned Britain for her policies in Northern Ireland. Poland paid tribute to Sands. Bombs exploded on British premises in Paris, Milan, and Lisbon; and there were demonstrations against British policies in several countries (Beresford 1987, 132).

Despite the embarrassment caused by this international political recognition, the British administration maintained a hard line toward republican prisoners by refusing to acknowledge them as anything more than criminals and dismissing the hunger strike as a "suicide." Although eager to negotiate a resolution to the conflict, the Catholic church had also condemned the hunger strike as suicide and warned the prisoners against committing mortal sin. The prisoners and their supporters—that diverse community of relatives, friends, neighbors, acquaintances, and fellow republicans of the Catholic ghettos—believed that the prisoners, far from suicidal, were fighting for their dignity with the last weapons left to them: their bodies, their lives.

Hunger striking has become part of modern political culture and has indeed been widely used by political movements in different parts of the world. It is therefore surprising that republicans do not generally allude to this internationally shared political weapon; instead, they draw on a past native tradition to illuminate the meaning of the fast. The hunger strike, I was often told, had a deep cultural resonance because it was rooted in an ancient Gaelic practice. *Destrain* (fasting) existed as a juridical mechanism for arbitration of certain disputes in Gaelic Brehon Law (Blinchy 1973; Kelly 1988). It allowed those who were unjustly wronged to fast at the door of the wrongdoer until justice was done. Death at the fast brought shame and moral responsibility on the wrongdoer.[2] Although Fergus Kelly (1988), a recognized scholar of Brehon Law, has noted the distinctions between hunger striking and legal fasting, the link of continuity between ancient Gaelic tradition and contemporary political practices is powerful in republican imagination (see also Vincent n.d.). For republicans the old Gaelic practice conferred meaning and moral legitimacy on a controversial political action and fashioned it in terms of, not an international political culture, but an essentialized Irish history. In so doing republicans constructed a political identity as direct descendants of their preconquest ancestors.

The interpretation of Irish mythology and folklore for nationalist purposes was not novel. Ironically it built on philological studies about Celtic cultures flourishing among nineteenth-century English intelligentsia (Curtis 1968). This body of knowledge, which literary critics Cairns and Richards (1988) have called "Celticism" echoing Said's "Orientalism" (1978), cast the Irish in the subservient position of a "feminine race" (as quoted in Cairns and Richards 1988). Such characterization gave rise in Ireland at the turn of the century to a nationalist cultural counterdiscourse in which the Irish figured as descendants of a noble and masculine Gaelic race. Integrated within nationalist ideology, such discourse provided images of the future nation and powerful models for political action. One of the most salient artificers of nationalist culture, William Butler Yeats, elaborated on the theme of the hunger strike in his play *The King's Threshold* (1904), in which a poet fasts against the king who abolished the customary right of the poets to sit on the king's council. In the first version of the play Yeats keeps the poet alive. In 1924, after the death in hunger strike of republican Terence McSwiney, Yeats rewrote the play; in his second version the poet dies, as do his followers.

By the late 1970s hunger striking in Ireland was, if not a survival of ancient custom, at least a well-known practice in political culture. For all its poetics of male heroism, hunger striking owed its political popularity not to republican men, but to suffragist women who first used it to exercise political pressure during 1911–1913.[3] As the tactic proved quite successful it was soon adopted by the republican movement that could after all count on a number of suffragists in its ranks (Ward 1983). In 1917 Tomas Ashe, president of the Irish Republican Brotherhood (a forerunner of the IRA), died on hunger strike for refusing to wear the prison uniform and perform prison work. Terence McSwiney, lord mayor of Cork and officer commanding the local IRA, died similarly in 1920.[4] There were hunger strikes in 1923, 1940, and 1946. In 1974 and 1976 respectively two IRA men, Michael Gauhgam and Frank Stagg, died on hunger strike in British jails while fighting for transfer to Ireland. Despite this obvious continuity, there is no reason to assume, as Feldman (1991) has also noted, that the hunger strike of 1981, led by young republicans many of whom grew up in the working-class urban ghettos of the north during the relative calm of 1950s, had the same meaning as those carried on earlier in the century. What then was the meaning of the fasting that resulted in the deaths of ten men in 1981?

Republicans talked to me about the hunger strike with deferential respect, almost awe. Their voices were lowered, their gazes often lost in distant space. Many houses had portraits of the hunger strikers or memorials of Bobby Sands hanging on the walls under the rubric "Our Martyrs," beside pictures of the Sacred Heart or the Virgin Mary. In the streets the disappearing Victorian landscape of Catholic West Belfast still showed in 1988 the vestiges of that time in the images of murals and old graffiti. Like Easter 1916, May 1981 seemed for republicans "the beginning of the end."[5] I turn now to the formation of that final beginning.

SYMBOLS OF IDENTITY, METAPHORS OF HISTORY

In June 1972, after rising tensions in the prisons and the unfolding of a hunger strike, Secretary of State for Northern Ireland William Whitelaw granted "special category"—de facto political status—to prisoners detained under the current policy of internment. In November 1975 the new Secretary of State for Northern Ireland Merlyn Rees announced a change of policy in the House of Commons. The new policy included an end to internment and the withdrawal of "special category" status for republican and loyalist prisoners. The last internees were freed on December 5, 1975. Interment had ended. A new phase of ghettoizing violence and creating a fiction of normality was launched by the British government. Under the codes of "Criminalization, Ulsterization, and Normalization" the new policy was part of a counterinsurgency plan to divest the IRA of political legitimacy by criminalizing political offense. Part of the program to depoliticize the conflict was to contain it within the confines of ghettoized areas while attempting to restore local institutions to a semblance of political normality.[6]

After March 1976, republican prisoners were to be considered and treated as ordinary criminals. Prisoners were ordered to wear prison uniform, although women were exempt from this obligation. Both were required to perform prison work. Republican prisoners had in the past rejected the uniform as a sign of criminalization of Irish republican history. Ciaran Nuget, the first political prisoner to experience the new policy, was forced to wear only a blanket when he refused to wear prison uniform; he thus inaugurated what became known as "the blanket protest," which lasted four and a half years.[7] The prison administration confined protesting inmates to isolation without reading materials or other sorts of stimulation. Prisoners, enclosed in their cells twenty-four hours a day and naked except for a blanket, were routinely sentenced to punishment cells. Prisoners—three-quarters of whom were between the ages of seventeen and twenty-one—left their cells only to go to the toilet, weekly shower, Sunday mass, and a monthly visit with relatives.

In March 1977 the prison authorities forbade the wearing of blankets outside prison cells. Thereafter prisoners had to leave their cells naked, exposed to warders' jeering at their bodies, especially their genitals, as well as frequent beatings. After eighteen months of this defiling treatment, republican prisoners responded with a "dirty protest." They refused to leave their cells to either wash or use the toilets. At first chamber pots were emptied through the pip holes in doors and through the windows. When these were boarded up by prison authorities, republicans began to smear their excreta on the walls of their cells. The indefinite continuation of this stalemate led in 1980 to the first hunger strike and, in March 1981, to the second hunger strike led by Bobby Sands.[8]

The British government argued that prisoners' suffering was self-inflicted because it could end at once if they conformed with the law and put on their prison uniforms. Republican prisoners deemed the uniform a source of pollution. One of the blanket men, Sean, told me that he would not even touch it or go near it: "It was folded up in the cell the day I got it, and I never touched it. I wouldn't even go near it." The uniform was odious to republicans because it represented a negation of identity, an erasure as political subjects. Republican prisoners thought of themselves as soldiers of an army of liberation fighting a war against Britain. This military identity transcended the individual self to constitute the terms defining a power struggle.

The philosopher Albert Memmi has reflected on the special significance attributed to military identity by anticolonial movements. Writing about the use of khaki uniforms by Tunisian rebels he wrote that "obviously they hoped to be considered soldiers and treated in accordance with the rules of war. There is profound meaning in this emphatic desire as it was by this tactic that they laid claim to and wore the dress of history" (1965, 128). Nation-states are not only symbolized but also legitimized by the conventions of military display and conduct within an agreed international order. Thus, to recognize an army is to recognize a legitimate player in that international arena, to acknowledge it as subject of rights regulated by the conventions of war, and therefore to legitimize its existence. It is not surprising then that armed organizations of national liberation emphasize their military identity because such identity is a claim to presence in an international order of things. The British refusal to characterize the conflict in Northern Ireland as a war, despite the continuous presence of an inordinate number of military troops, aims at erasing the IRA as a political subject who counteracts by always referring to the conflict as a war and their struggle as that of an army against another, more powerful army. Thus the refusal of the British government to recognize republican prisoners as prisoners of war and the emphasis on their criminal character entails a divestment of moral and political legitimacy, hence the assertion of military identity. The stubborn demand to be treated as prisoners of war is a demand for existential-political recognition, a desperate claim to presence. There is a literal sacramental character in this position that forbears the kind of figurative political play that would be involved for example in making the most out of the uniform, using it for one's political purposes against the prison regime (Zulaika 1988).

For republican prisoners, to wear a prison uniform meant to assume Britain's definition of reality and accept the judgment that Ireland's history was no more than a concatenation of criminal acts. That attitude negated both their national and personal identities. Moreover the prison uniform meant downgrading to the level of criminals not only themselves but also the community to which they belonged. Ultimately by wearing the uniform prisoners would admit that moral and ethical distinctions lay only in the weight of the dominant force because only an arbitrary date marked the distinction between a political prisoner and a criminal. Those republicans sentenced before March 1976 were considered prisoners of war and received the treatment accorded this status; those sentenced after that date were regarded and treated as criminals. Members of the same organization, who shared principles, goals, and gaol, were differentiated only by a decree. This decree, cast as "The Law," freed the British establishment from responsibility for the prison crisis.[9] For republicans to reject the moral value of the law that classified them *into* opposed categories was to defy the arbitrariness of a superior power, to reassert their dignity and political legitimacy.

The criminal/political dichotomy, which converted the prison uniform into such a highly charged symbol, was in the final analysis about ethical distinctions and historical legitimation. For republicans the new policy represented a criminalization of Irish history. A popular song at the time expressed this clearly:

> But I wear no convict's uniform
> Nor meekly serve my time
> That Britain's might call Ireland's fight
> Eight hundred years of crime.

As a negation of identity wearing the uniform constituted a loss of dignity. The importance of the word "dignity" became evident during my fieldwork. It epitomized the accumulated feelings in the experience of being working-class Catholic in Northern Ireland. As Una, a community worker, told me during the course of an afternoon discussion, "Some outsiders think they understand what is going on here, but they don't. They don't know what it means to be observed, humiliated, made to feel inferior, day-by-day in your own country." The same feeling was articulated by Bobby Sands: "That's a word: Dignity. They can't take that from me either. Naked as I am, treated worse than an animal, I am what I am. They can't and won't change that. . . . Of course I can be murdered, but while I remain alive, I remain what I am, a political prisoner of war, and no one can change that" (1982, 93).

Although the hunger strike was a pragmatic action to counter British policy of criminalization, the moral force that sustained it was articulated through feelings of alienation and dispossession such as those expressed by Bobby Sands. And the anger that can be read in the words of Una entail a politics of emotion that must be understood historically. They form what Raymond Williams (1983) has tentatively called a "structure of feelings." Williams defines structures of feelings as "social experiences in solution," related to specific social formations, particular generations, and social classes. Structures of feelings differ from formally held ideologies or systems of beliefs, but they are articulated with those in complex and varied ways: "we are talking about characteristic elements of impulse, restraint and tone; specifically affective elements of consciousness and relationships: not feeling against thought, but thought as felt and feeling as thought: practical consciousness of a present kind in a living and interrelating continuity" (1983, 132). Williams uses the concept of structure to emphasize a social experience that is not totally in flux but is articulated in "a set with specific internal relations at once interlocking and in tension" (1983, 132). This is not a fixed, closed structure but an embodiment of social experience in process. Williams's notion seems particularly appropriate to understand the political formation of the republican prisoners of the late 1970s. Belonging for the most part to a generation coming of age in the upturn of social relations that followed the riots of 1969, they shared similar social experiences and modes of feeling.

MEMORIES OF VIOLENCE, NARRATIVES OF DISPOSSESSION

Taussig has rightly insisted that people use, not conscious ideology, but dialectics of images and storylike creations to delineate their world, including their politics (1987, 367). The question I wish to discuss is how those "cultural formations of meaning" (rumor, images, song, story, etc.) are articulated through personal experience. For at the intersection where cultural constructions meet unique personal (or collective) experience modes of feeling are shaped, and new meanings created. The images and stories that crafted the politics of the young prisoners of the late 1970s and allowed them to survive naked amid excrement and violence are of a varied character. Asked how they became involved in politics women former prisoners recounted childhood experiences of political violence with remarkable consistency. The accounts of male prisoners of the same generation, which have been better documented, do not differ substantially.[10]

The protesting prisoners of the IRA in the late 1970s were the children caught in the riots of the previous decade. Mairead, twenty-nine years old when I met her, was sentenced in March 1981 to twenty years imprisonment for possession of a firearm. She had already served three years in Armagh jail while awaiting trial and had been there during the hunger strikes. Mariead was nine years old when the troubles started and twelve when she and her family moved, as a consequence of intimidation, from their predominantly Protestant district to Twinbrook, a new Catholic housing estate on the outskirts of West Belfast. Mairead's grandparents lived in the Falls Road, the heart of Catholic West Belfast, at the center of the intimidation, burnings, and killings of the early stage of the present conflict. When the troubles began she and her sister, staying with their grandparents on the weekends, witnessed some of the action:

> At eleven years of age we had to be actually escorted to and from the school buses by our teachers because the local Protestant youths living near our school would gather and throw bottles and stones at us. One day I can remember witnessing them trailing three young Catholic boys from the bus—a crowd of about twenty of them did it—and they gave them really bad beatings with sticks, and the rest of us were terrified and turned to get help from the other people standing by. But— whether because of fear of whatever—none of them would interfere. The young boys in question had to be taken to hospital; they were that badly beaten.

Mairead's family went back to the ghetto they had left in 1966 and, like many other refugees fleeing from other parts of Belfast, began to live in unfinished houses without doors, windows, electricity, water, or anything else: "I'm not kidding you; in fact the BBC made a Panorama film about the slum conditions the people in Twinbrook had to live in, and in the film they interviewed my mother and filmed us sitting eating on the floor by candlelight. I can remember hearing of a young boy of seventeen from the Twinbrook state being shot dead by loyalist gunmen at the garage where he was apprenticed at the Lisburn Road—that happened the night we moved to the [housing] estate." Mairead would later come to know the sisters of this boy, and they would tell her about the details of his killing. Mairead's world was changing dramatically and this change was becoming meaningful through whispers, memories, and stories narrated by others: "My granny would take us around the Falls and explain who had been killed. They'd recalled the Belfast riots of the twenties and thirties, the execution of Tom Williams and other such things."

Mairead's stories of early childhood not only morally legitimize present politics but also provide the very stuff that made her an IRA volunteer. When she explains her involvement in the armed struggle, conventional ideology, a set of systematized ideas about socialism or national liberation, does not come forward. Such political ideology came later during the formative years of imprisonment, which most republicans dedicate to readings, discussions, and political education. Instead, when she recalled the motivations that led her into armed struggle, she stressed her experience. Experience, as Joan Scott has argued (1991, 25), does not exist, however, outside the flow of discourse. In Belfast it was shaped, encapsulated, and conveyed through collective images and stories, through silences and the ongoing reshaping of ethnic difference taken place through the practice of violence. Thus Mairead said, "witnessing RUC/British army brutality had a profound impact on most of the young teenagers then." In fact, witnessing violence came again and again in the reminiscences of the people with whom I talked. "I learned my politics in the street, by witnessing what was going on," said Anne, another protesting prisoner. Witnessing had for these prisoners the force of self-evidence, the power of knowledge that cannot be contested and needs no further elaboration; a kind of knowledge that defies linguistic containment to infuse instead a form of political transcendence. The untranslatable character of such knowledge was encapsulated in a graffiti from the time of the hunger strike "for those who believe no explanation is necessary, for those who do not believe no explanation is possible." And yet what Mairead and Anne were trying to convey to me was not experiential knowledge, but the way in which such experience had constituted them as republican political subjects.

In another conversation, Pauline, a republican activist in her thirties when I first met her, evoked the smell of the houses burning in the Lower Falls where she had been living in 1969. She recalled the uncertainty and terror of abandoning the house with only a trash bag full of clothes, not knowing where to go or what was happening. The world, shaped by those early impressions, created a structure of feeling that led those young teenagers to become involved in a war they came to interpret as their own. That world was also rendered meaningful by earlier memories of older people—parents and grandparents—who were marked by the riots of the 1920s that gave birth to Northern Ireland and those riots of the depression in the 1930s. Individual experience was thus embedded in the discursive flow of collective memory that emerged as a frame of interpretation.

Bobby Sands was no exception to the formation of those early modes of feeling. He was fifteen when the troubles began. Like Mairead, of whom he was a friend, Sands was living in Rathcoole, a predominantly Protestant area. There were only six Catholic families on his street. One day the Ulster Defense Association (UDA), a paramilitary group that became notorious for assassinating Catholics, staged a march down his street. The Sands family kept the lights out while Bobby waited—sitting on the stairs clutching a carving knife. On another occasion he was coming home when two men stopped him. One produced a knife and cut him. Groups of youths began then to gather outside the house shouting "Taigs out!"[11] The intimidation increased until the Sands fled Rathcoole for a new place in Twinbrook in 1972. Shortly afterward Bobby joined the IRA (Beresford 1987, 58–59).

If the politics of emotion of republican prisoners were shaped through practices of terror and the discourses of ethnic difference that accompanied them, the prisoners would redeploy those discourses as political weapon by becoming in turn the latest embodiment of an old colonial trope: the savage Irish.

REHEARSING THE WILD IRISH

The Irish literary critic Seamus Deane has said that, "The language of politics in Ireland and England, especially when the subject is Northern Ireland, is still dominated by the putative division between barbarism and civilization. Civilization still defines itself as a system of law; and it defines barbarism (which by the nature of the distinction cannot be capable of defining itself) as a chaos of arbitrary wills, an Hobbesian state of nature" (1983:11). The use of the barbarism/civilization dichotomy to represent political relations between Ireland and Britain has a long history. Edmund Spenser advocated in 1596 a harsh military policy as the only path to civilizing the Irish. In 1649 Cromwell plundered the country, and 85 percent of the land in Ireland was expropriated and given to Protestant planters and Cromwellian soldiers. In some parts of the southwest hundreds of Irish were sold as indentured servants to plantations in the West Indies (Curtis 1985). Massacre and dispossession ingrained as a recurrent motif in folklore and nationalist rhetoric left a deep print in Irish historical consciousness. The images of terror associated with the name of Cromwell were recreated in the new songs that flourished in Catholic districts during the years of internment: "Round the world the truth will echo / Cromwell's men are here again / England's name again is sullied / In the eyes of honest men." Allusions such as these gave state and communal violence a mythical-historical dimension charged with moral content. The association with Cromwell positioned the soldiers on the side of the wrongdoers and gave the IRA and community activists moral legitimacy. This perception was reinforced by the incongruities of the British government's practice and discourse; they vilified the IRA as a murderous and hated group of terrorists while using generalized violence to intimidate the Catholic minority.

The enduring image of the savage Irish in British representations of Northern Ireland is expressed in many instances; two will suffice as examples of the wider pattern. The BBC broadcast a series of interviews on the *Tonight* program in the spring of 1977 during which Bernard O'Connor, a schoolteacher, and Michael Lavelle, a production controller at a factory, made allegations about the use of torture at Catlereagh interrogation center. After the program the Conservatives in England and Unionists in Northern Ireland protested strongly, accused the BBC of aiding terrorism, and demanded tougher security measures. The *Sunday Times* added to the controversy by stating that "the notorious problem is how a civilized country can overpower uncivilized people without becoming less civilized in the process" (as cited in Curtis 1984, 55). The preoccupation with degeneration has been lasting in British colonial history and indeed in bourgeois culture, as Stallybrass and White (1986) have pointedly shown. The problem is not the legitimacy of overpowering the "other"—that is granted by the other's inferiority—but how to avoid contagion while in contact with them.

A more recent instance of the resilience of British anti-Irish prejudice is the reply of former Lord Chancellor Lord Hailsham to the suggestion made by the Irish government in September 1989 that the Diplock courts in Northern Ireland—trials without jury and presided over by one judge—should be replaced by a more suitable alternative, such as three-judge courts. Lord Hailsham dismissed the suggestion as silly and ignorant. To the argument that the Diplock courts were a deep grievance for the nationalist community Lord Hailsham answered, "That is because they don't think. It's as simple as that, they just don't think and on certain subjects they are incapable of thought" (*Irish News*, September 19, 1989).

Perhaps nothing embodies the image of the wild Irish more clearly than the image of the terrorist. He is the "other" par excellence, a criminal depicted as bloody-minded psychopath with apelike features maintaining an armed tyranny over the nationalist community.[12] This image, popularized through cartoons, forms also part of a propaganda war that attempted to delegitimize the IRA and legitimize the permanent deployment of the British army (Darby 1983; Faligot 1983, 61–63). British soldiers in Northern Ireland have openly expressed their anxiety at moving through a terrain perceived as impenetrable, unknown, and full of danger. In this sense British soldiers perceived the geography of Belfast ghettos as exotic and untamed as, according to historians, Elizabethan soldiers had perceived the Irish landscape (Foster 1988, 5–11). Yet little in West Belfast distinguishes it from the working-class neighborhoods of Liverpool, Newcastle, or Glasgow, the hometowns of the British soldiers. Not much differentiates their styles of life, customs, or language, except, of course, the multiple army posts and police barracks dotting the area as landmarks competing for historical hegemony with the chimneys of the now-abandoned linen mills, and the murals and political graffiti endlessly obliterated with paint by the army and repainted by the "natives." The impoverished landscape of West Belfast is familiar, and yet, like the remote Irish woods so disliked by colonial soldiers and so disordered in the descriptions of Elizabethan officers, the landscape of West Belfast still conceals resistance. For the British soldiers it remains impenetrable, even if every street and household is under the gaze of the most sophisticated surveillance. And by virtue of this perceived impenetrability, the landscape becomes defamiliarized and the people who inhabit it strangers.

The soldiers' perception is, however, far from a spontaneous sense of estrangement. They are trained in special sessions to see the population and the environment as something of which to be wary and to tame (Faligot 1983). Their patrols, arbitrary searches, and continual harassment anger the population that regards the military with obvious distaste, which in turn reinforces the soldiers' perceptions of the Irish as hostile strangers. The contradiction is clear: while the problem of Northern Ireland is defined by the British government as one provoked by an organized bunch of criminals, their policy criminalizes—de facto—the whole Catholic population.

In 1976, the British government defined IRA members as criminals, yet the treatment of these criminals differed from standard procedure. Torture was used to extract confessions, and special courts without juries were created to try them. The prisoners' refusal to accept this incongruity was represented as a new instance of their barbarism. The horrific imagery of degradation that the "no-wash" protest provided was, for British mainstream commentators, proof of the bizarre nature of the Irish (see for example *The Guardian*, March 16, 1979, and *The English Times*, October 24, 1980).

After Bobby Sands began to fast in March 1981, all attempts at mediation by Irish politicians, human rights organizations, and the Catholic Church failed. In the middle of his fast Bobby Sands was elected member of Westminster parliament by 30,492 votes. People in the nationalist ghettos thought that the British government would now be obliged to recognize the political character of the prisoners. The British prime minister made her response famous: "A crime is a crime is a crime. It is not political, it is a crime" (Beresford 1987, 115). This intransigence alienated the nationalist community even further and convinced many people, who were previously uninterested in republicanism, that the only language Britain would understand was the language of force.[13] British intransigence aimed at breaking the republican movement and undermining their popular support fueled IRA popularity. After the success of Sands's electoral campaign Sinn Fein initiated a process of reorganization to lead a more comprehensive political strategy known as "the armalite and the ballot box" (a combination of political organization, electoral campaigning, and armed struggle), which secured them representatives in the local and Westminster elections. As important as this shift in Sinn Fein's strategy is the deep scar left in the consciousness of many nationalists by the British policy during the hunger strike. A well-known female community activist framed the legacy of the hunger strike in terms of a moral obligation to continue their struggle: "Nobody who went through that experience can say that it didn't profoundly affect their lives. No matter what happens we cannot give up the struggle now." The hunger strike as historical event acquired a personal meaning, as much for the prisoners within the prison as for their supporters outside.

BOBBY SANDS: SELF-SACRIFICE AS REDEMPTIVE HISTORY

Some commentators of Irish republicanism have emphasized the mythology of sacrifice within this movement to claim that such mythology is the leading force of the IRA (Dalton 1974) and/or the foundation of their support in the Catholic ghettos (Kearney 1988). The appeal of this view is epitomized by Northern Irish poet Seamus Heaney who has interpreted Ulster violence in the atemporal frame of a Gaelic myth of sacrifice to the goddess Earth. In the view of these commentators republican violence appears as a continuation of ritual sacrifices in which the goddess of the land is substituted by "Mother Ireland."[14] This kind of explanation is clearly problematic: it assumes that myths have a force of their own, capable of determining people's behavior; moreover, it runs dangerously close to the old anthropological distinction that endowed the primitive with a prelogical mode of thought while reserving rational thinking for modern civilized man. In the contemporary version of this distinction the terrorist often replaces the savage as the embodiment of irrational thinking and/or an example of subjection to myth. Myths, however, require social contexts in order to become something more than interesting stories. It is through the mediation of consciousness and social relations that myths come to constitute meaningful frames of interpretation for one's existential or political predicament and became powerful "models of/for reality," in Geertz's sense (Geertz 1973).

Explanations that root IRA violence in the power of ancestral myth fail to explain why people respond to such mythology at certain moments but not at others. By failing also to account for the responsibility of the state in creating, maintaining, and/or fueling violence, such explanations lead to the presupposition that while state violence follows rational motivations, republican violence follows mythological ones. As Walter Benjamin (1978[1920]) noted long ago, all socially relevant violence is linked to, not separated from, the workings of the legal apparatus. To think otherwise might be certainly comforting, but is to fall prey to the fallacy of attributing to the state a rationality and autonomy from social relations that it does not posses, as Herzfeld has insightfully argued in his analysis of Western bureaucracy (1992).

The mythology of sacrifice, ancestral or Christological, as the alleged cause of the current political violence in Northern Ireland seems to me a new origin myth that conveniently permits commentators to ignore the field of sociological and political power relations at play. Furthermore it reinforces the extended stereotype of the Irish as irrational myth followers and hopelessly prone to violent character (Foster 1993). To say this is not to deny the existence of a mythology of sacrifice in the nationalist community, especially in its republican sector; rather, it is to deny that such sacrificial narrative explains IRA violence. Such violence is entangled in the history of British colonization in Ireland and in the practices of domination and inequality to which colonization gave rise in the North. IRA violence might be interpreted and legitimized through mythical narratives as well as other kinds of political discourses, but neither of them stands in a simplistic causal relation to violence. Having said that, I can now analyze how the symbolism of sacrifice embedded in Catholic mythology became at the political conjuncture of 1981 a meaningful framework for political action.

The heroic symbolism of republican culture has its origin in the turn-of-the-century Irish cultural revival. W. B. Yeats perhaps did most to create the image of the sacrificial hero that became so important to the imagination of the 1916 uprising.[15] If Yeats reinvented a glorious mythological past populated with Gaelic warriors, Padraic Pearse infused it with Christian imagery and revolutionary action. A leader of the 1916 uprising, Pearse conceived heroic sacrifice in the romantic tradition, as an act of renewal, and firmly believed that the sacrifice of a selected few would stir the dormant spirit of the nation and lead it into its own statehood. Not coincidentally, the day chosen for the revolt was Easter Monday.[16] The rebellion, without popular support and badly organized, was crushed rapidly; the participants were arrested, and their leaders executed. Yet Pearse proved in a sense right, for the intended exemplary executions provoked generalized social disturbances in Ireland that ultimately led to the war of independence and the Anglo-Irish Treaty of 1921. Easter 1916 became mythologized as a crucial event, in not only republican historical consciousness but also the official nationalist history of the new Irish nation.

By the 1950s the political significance of sacrificial heroism for nationalists in Northern Ireland had faded. Not until the violence of 1969 did this symbolism endow political action with new meanings. The metaphors of sacrificial martyrdom and Gaelic heroism then took on a new "force"; that is, they comprised not only a cognitive structure but also an emotional experience defined by "the subjects' position within the field of social relations" (Rosaldo 1989, 54). For, as Fernandez has indicated, "metaphors can only become meaningful if the domain into which they operate are important arenas of activity for people" (1986, 24). The early 1970s were characterized by great instability, uncertainty, and political debate. This was accompanied by a revival and creation of ballads and rebel songs, *ceili* sessions, and reinterpretations of Gaelic mythology incorporated as precolonial history into republican history. The symbolic power of this historical narrative was evident during the blanket protest. It provided models of identification and political legitimation. Intertwined with Gaelic imagery, the blanket protest was anchored in a profusion of Christological metaphors emphasizing the sacrifice of republican prisoners.

Although such imagery was clearer in the republican communities, the prisoners, socialized in the strongly rooted culture of Irish Catholicism, also resorted to its metaphors and symbols to create and sustain the affective moods that allowed them to endure the unimaginable duress of prison life. Allen Feldman's differentiation between the meanings of the hunger strike in and outside the prison is, I think, too sharply drawn (Feldman 1991): he argues that prisoners did not share the Christological model so pervasive among their relatives and supporters but that they planned the hunger strike as a strategic military action to be waged with their bodies. I suggest, however, that both discourses were simultaneously at play: the rational discourse of military strategy and the expressive idioms of religion and myth. The prisoners planned the hunger strike according to rational political assessments. At the same time they went to mass, prayed the rosary, read the Bible, learned Gaelic, recounted myths, and discussed socialism. Bobby Sands, the ideologue of the hunger strike, produced cold and evaluative political communiqués as well as a poetic narrative filled with religious images and feelings. It is possible that many prisoners might have rationalized and dismissed religious forms of symbolic expression at a later time. After the hunger strike the prisoners grew self-conscious of Christological elements in their ideology, in part because such elements were used to accuse them of sectarianism and in part because the hunger strike led to an ideological radicalization along Marxist lines. Self-conscious republicans worked to distance themselves from the image of Catholic paramilitaries in their effort to promote a more internationalist image of an army of liberation. Yet such self-consciousness was not shared by everyone. I encountered prisoners who had no problem speaking about the sustaining role religion played during the trying times of the dirty protest and hunger strike. This notwithstanding, I agree with Feldman that the relatives and supporters resorted more to this framework of interpretation than did the prisoners themselves.

Pauline, a prominent republican activist and not particularly sympathetic to religion, told me that the hunger strike was "a dramatic time for all of us but especially for the families. They say about Jesus, well Bobby Sands died for us all." Mairead serving sentence during the hunger strike reiterated the religious parallel in her discussion of endurance: "You gather strength when you think of [the suffering of] the people on the outside and when you think of your comrades, from their deaths, because you know they have died for you."

There is virtually no house in Catholic West Belfast that does not have an image of the Sacred Heart and an image of the Virgin Mary, just as there is no house that has not experienced military searches, police harassment, or the loss of a close relative or friend to political violence. Religion is as deeply anchored in Catholics' experience of the world in Northern Ireland as is dispossession. The Penal Laws introduced by Britain in 1695 associated Catholicism with Irishness.[17] After the partition of 1921 Catholic-Irish identity intensified in the North as it became—more clearly than ever before—a parameter of one's position in the new political structure. Just as being Catholic in the new statelet signified being disadvantaged and discriminated against, religion continued to provide a discourse of ethnic identity. Eamon McCann, a well-known socialist activist, begins his classic story of growing up in a Catholic ghetto with the words: "One learned quite literally at one's mother's knee that Christ died for the human race and Padraic Pearse for the Irish section of it" (1980, 9). In the sociological conditions of the North, Catholic religiosity was, in spite of the fiery opposition of the Catholic hierarchy, susceptible to radical interpretations. Relations between republicans and the Catholic church, which had always been problematic, grew increasingly tense as conditions deteriorated in the prisons.

The Church's condemnation of the prisoners' protest alienated many supporters who found too great a disjuncture between religious convictions, priests' political opinions, and their own loyalties. A middle-aged woman from the West Belfast district of St. James explained her disenchantment with the church:

> My cutting point was when so and so was killed, and the priest would not allow his coffin into the church for his funeral. I thought that was terrible because let's put things straight: If somebody steals you something, that's stealing isn't it? Well that's what England has done: steal a part of this country. And I thought, this priest has been in the war, and what is the difference? People go to war and kill hundreds of other peo-

ple for no other reason than to steal somebody else's land, and they get a proper funeral. And what is the IRA doing? Fighting a war against Britain who stole this land! And they are Catholic men, and they cannot get a proper Catholic funeral? I told this to the priest, and he had no answers. So I said "This is it!" And I didn't go back to church.

Not everyone was able to resolve the tension between religious obligations and political convictions so easily. Another republican, the wife of a blanket man, distanced herself from the church because the priest used the sermons to question the morality of the prisoners. Yet she confessed a sense of guilt for not attending church despite firmly believing in the integrity of her moral reasons for doing so. Criticism of the Church was part of a complex struggle to give new meaning to an existential situation characterized by uncertainty, distortion, and upturning of social relations. Out of the institutional frame of Catholicism, some people discovered new meanings and new expressions for their religiosity in the available political field. A republican former prisoner described her feelings: "I am not an atheist. I don't think I could ever be. But I don't believe in the Church. It is difficult to be critical of the Church because it is so much a part of your upbringing, and we had never heard before of a feminist Christian or a socialist Christian. But people are looking now for other models, like the theology of liberation, for instance."

During the years of the blanket protest and during the hunger strike there was a proliferation of images in leaflets and murals portraying the prisoners as Christ-like figures. The physical appearance of prisoners (with long hair and beards, their bodies covered only with blankets) strengthened this identification. As conditions worsened in the jail and solutions to the stalemate seemed far from sight, the parallel with the religious model of Christ became stronger. For the relatives and—to a lesser extent—for prisoners this model contained the moral legitimation for their struggle in the face of widespread condemnation from the Church, media, and political establishment. In the anxious uncertainty of waiting for a resolution, praying became a rehearsal of wishes, to use the aphorism of the Bulgarian philosopher Elias Canetti (1978). During the blanket protest the prisoners went to mass and prayed the rosary daily. When the hunger strike began they started praying the rosary twice a day. "Praying was a form of drawing strength," explained Eileen, a young republican, when I inquired about the meaning of prayer during the prison protest. She continued, "Even I—who am not very much of a believer—prayed when I was arrested."

Many prisoners were believers, as were their supporters on the outside. Bobby Sands certainly was. His writings are filled with religious imagery, metaphors of sacrifice and hell that capture an experience bordering on the surreal. *The Crime of Castlereagh*, written while "on the blanket," is a poem of 145 stanzas in which he talks about interrogation and jail.[18] Sands imagines the space of Castlereagh interrogation center with its cells and its corridors as a hell filled with devils torturing him, trying to eat his mind and tear his soul apart; they trick him into evil deals, offering comforts in exchange for his secrets. His poetry expresses a double consciousness triggered by the disjunction between a discourse of social morality defined by the LAW as the embodiment of justice and the use of such discourse for the social reproduction of discrimination and injustice.

> This Citadel, this house of hell
> Is worshipped by the law.
>
> Some bear the stain of cruel Cain,
> These are the men of doom.
> The torture-men who go no end
> To fix you in that room.
> To brutalize they utilize
> Contrivances of hell,
> For great duress can mean success
> When tortured start to tell. (982, 44)

Castlereagh, like Long Kesh, is imagined as a liminal space that represents neither life nor death, where detainees appear as Christological phantoms: "Each looked like a loss, each bore a cross / Upon his bended back" (1982, 55).[19]

In Sands's evocation of the interrogation center, which could very well be superposed to the reality of prison space, the parameters of reality appeared blurred. Space is distorted, unmastered, changing, pregnant with fear, threats, and promised comfort. There is no control of time; permanent lights make day and night indistinguishable. To elicit uncertainty and confusion in the detainee is a big part of the interrogation game. One is left to one's innermost solitude to confront the ultimate dilemma of confession, that crucial operation of power producing truth through "the body of the condemned" (Foucault 1979).

In extracting confessions the point is not the congruity of fact and evidence but the fabrication of social truths.[20] An important component of the truth-punishment relation is, of course, the humiliation of the confessant. Obliged sometimes to confess nonexistent realities incriminating him or her and others, she or he is deprived of individuality and of the last ground from which to resist the arbitrariness of power. Yet confession also represents a tempting relief from the agony of interrogation. Hence the dilemma, the distorted reality and displacement of meanings that, as accounts of interrogation relate, frequently confer a hallucinatory quality to the reality of interrogation (Taussig 1987).

In his poetry Sands represents himself on a journey between life and death. Despite its nightmarish quality there is a literalness in this space of death, for Sands did not know if he would come out of jail dead or alive. This literalness became chillingly real during the hunger strike. Several scholars have argued that the experience of extreme forms of violence such as it is experienced in torture often eludes rational discourse (Kleinman and Kleinman 1994; Das and Nandi 1985; Scarry 1985; Taussig 1987). Reality may lose its contours and appear as a bad dream, leaving an indelible mark on those who have walked through it. Sean, a blanket prisoner, expressed this idea one night when talking about the time he spent "on the blanket." In the course of our conversation he suddenly said: "For some people prison time is like a nightmare from where they never come out again—even if the sentence is served and they can go home." His words brought to mind the question raised by the mother of a republican prisoner in a conversation about prison violence: "How do you explain a nightmare?"

For Sands powerful metaphors and poetic language provided the semantic and emotional space to elaborate his experience. He represents his jailers through the bestial imagery that dominates the inferno in Catholic eschatology:

> A demon came his eyes aflame
> And round him was the law.
> They danced like in Hades and rats in plagues
> And Christ I froze in awe.
> They spun a cord this gruesome horde
> On loom of doom and sin,
> To make a noose that would induce
> A tortured soul within. (1982, 56)

By casting interrogators and prison officers in the guise of demons Sands represented in cosmic terms a political conflict as an epic struggle between good and evil with Christian overtones, thus creating for himself the identity of martyr and redeemer:

The time had come to be,
To walk the lonely road
Like that of Calvary.
And take up the cross of Irishmen
Who've carried liberty. (1982, 64)

Lila Abu-Lughod (1986) has suggested that poetry provides a cultural narrative for articulating deep feelings that would be inappropriate to express in other forms of everyday discourse. By resorting to culturally stylized images and metaphors, she argues, poetry can persuade people toward action, especially in situations of intense personal suffering. Thus the religious imagery and emotional vulnerability contained in Bobby Sands's poetry stands in vivid contrast to the hardened, uncompromising attitude of Sands the military leader and officer commanding the IRA in Long Kesh prison. Both the poetic and politico-military discourses are inextricably linked cultural devices through which Sands, and his comrades, constructed different collective and personal meanings during the prison protest.

In the last stanza quoted above Sands creates a clear identification in his allusion to Calvary between the individual journey to death and the collective journey to freedom. The prisoners endowed the transcendence of religious metaphors with historical meaning and legitimacy. The Ulster mythological warrior Cuchulain and a long list of republican martyrs were condensed in the ritual complex of Christological sacrifice. As Feldman has noted, this sacrifice, not of pacifist but of military character was deliberately aimed at increasing insurrectionary violence (1991, 237). The prisoners in Long Kesh thought that their actions were turning the course of history. With this profound belief in historical redemption and the emotional strength derived from religious identification Bobby Sands immersed himself in a hunger strike to death. Such identification was so strong that Sands was already convinced of his death when he began the strike. The first line of his fast journal reads: "I am standing on the threshold of another trembling world. May God have mercy of my soul" (1982). He ritually marked this threshold between life and death, oppression and freedom: he took a bath, cut his hair, and shaved (Feldman 1991, 245).

The prisoners had politically weighed the decision to go on a hunger strike for more than a year. The decision was made, contrary to the media interpretations of the time, against the wishes of the IRA leadership.[21] The prisoners saw it as a political last resort. Once the crisis esca-

101

lated and the decision to fast to death had been made, the hunger strikers seized and deployed the politics of redemptive sacrifice, pervasive in their different forms in republican and Catholic cultures.

The "force" of the redemptive sacrifice metaphor can be seen not only in the graffiti and murals of the urban landscape but also in how it moved people in the political arena. Metaphoric assertions people make about themselves or about others "provide images in relation to which the organization of behavior can take place" (Fernandez 1986, 6). In the Catholic ghettos demonstrations and riots escalated. If the nationalist community moved in the direction of revolt, then the loyalist community was drawn in the opposite direction. If Catholic walls cried, "Don't let Sands die," Protestant wards demanded, "The time is now for Sands to die" (Rolston 1987). Tension rose as the countdown went on. Paramilitary assassinations increased, and so increased the number of people killed by British troops in nonriot situations.[22]

Sean MacBride, recipient of the Nobel Peace Prize in 1974 and founding member of Amnesty International, commented that "the hunger strike must be understood in terms of the historical memory of British colonial misrule" (1983, 5).[23] This historical memory is of course a contested subject in Ireland. But whatever the different constructions, historical memory plays a deep role in political legitimacy. Historic actors do not play in either an atemporal space or a symbolic vacuum. The prisoners protesting in Long Kesh, especially the hunger strikers, saw themselves as the perpetuators of eight centuries of tradition of resistance. The force and immediacy of this history are easily grasped in Bobby Sands's writings in which he condenses men from different generations and sociopolitical contexts into a single historical situation: "I remember and I shall never forget, how this monster took the lives of Tom Ashe, Terence McSwiney, Michael Gaughan, Frank Stagg, and Hugh Coney" (1982, 91).

History for republicans is not merely an intellectual legacy. As narrative, history makes meaningful the present as it unfolds in existential experience. Without the encompassing narrative of history, political action would have no direction. Thus Pauline, the republican encountered earlier in this chapter who could still smell the burning houses of the Lower Falls she left behind as a child, could comment: "Some people say we have to forget history, but we have to remember it because history repeats itself, and we have to be prepared." And Mary, another republican, would corroborate: "The troubles in 1969 caught us completely unprepared, but that shouldn't have happened. We should have known better with the history we got." History as a succession of events is not conceptualized by republicans as a linear progression. Such conception is after all linked to the enlightened optimism of imperialism. Set *against* the colonial power of Britain, history appears to republicans as a succession of stages each representing the same drama in different times. Chronology provides the scenario for a recurrent transcendent theme—colonial oppression and national freedom—that in turn endows with meaning the inchoate feelings of dispossession. Thus for the republican prisoners history was not a detached knowledge learned at school, but the articulation of a structure of feeling. "History was forced on me," said Anne, a committed republican serving sentence in Armagh jail during the hunger strike. Such an assertion conveys the kind of inevitability contained in tragedy because tragedy is ultimately about inevitable paradoxical dilemmas. For the hunger strikers their dilemma was either to accept the definition of criminality—in which case they were psychologically if not politically defeated—or to die—in which case they were also damned. The resolution of an existential paradox requires the resort to an altogether different domain of experience. Thus the hunger strikers saw their death as an historically transcendent action, one that would simultaneously unlock them from their prison and free Ireland from her colonial nightmare. Inasmuch as this single liberating action was performed by men in congruence with republican constructions of history, *History* was also imagined as a grand heroic male narrative.

In the women's prison of Armagh and outside the jails, however, women had started challenging that male heroic narrative, as I shall discuss in the following chapters. Three women, Mairead Farrell, Mary Doyle, and Mairead Nugget, had embarked in the hunger strike of 1980 that preceded the strike in 1981 and had finished with no fatalities. The women prisoners had defied the expressed opposition of the leadership of the republican movement in joining the men in the dirty protest. Their participation in the first hunger strike came as a logical step in participating on equal footing with the men in the prison struggle, and in so doing they challenged the male heroics of historical narrative. When the prisoners in Long Kesh decided to undertake a second hunger strike, Sile Darragh, then officer commanding the women prisoners in Armagh, made an impassioned plea to the leadership of the IRA to allow her to embark on a hunger strike—a plea that was denied (Beresford 1987, 74, 77). Sile told me that women did not join the second hunger strike because the small number of women prisoners could not have sustained the sequential form of the second strike.[24] Other women prisoners gave an additional explanation: the reason for the categorical opposition to women hunger striking at this time lay in the IRA fear of the devastating ideological effect that the death of a young woman prisoner could have had on the republican movement. The IRA had already being accused by the media of playing with the lives of their male militants for propagandistic purposes; to be seen as callous manipulators of the lives of women was a risk they were not willing to take. After some wrestling the women agreed to stand out of the path taken by their male comrades.

As existential predicament and as nodal event in a historical narrative, the hunger strikes were nowhere more tragic than in the experience of the women who held in their hands the fate of the hunger strike.[25] Women—the closest relatives of strikers, often their mothers—had to decide in the last crucial moment when the strikers lost consciousness whether to save the lives of their sons and in one instance husband by politically betraying them or to remain loyal to them by letting them die. Siobhan, a prominent republican, reflected about the inexpressible anguish of these women's dilemma in which the meaning of motherhood appeared deeply anchored in class position: "It was traumatic for the mothers because it's a reversal of all what it means to be a mother, a reversal of all what you have done for your son. You've struggled all your life to put food in their bellies, sometimes at the expense of yourself, and to watch them die of starvation."

The Gendered Politics of Suffering:
Women of the RAC

In 1976, AFTER FIVE years of violence and the failure of various attempts at a peaceful resolution, the dominant mood in the nationalist community was exhaustion and weariness. With the end of internment the plight of new prisoners did not attract much interest. Only the prisoners' relatives, whose numbers were growing, were deeply anxious. They soon felt compelled to take action and formed an organization to publicize the situation of their sons and husbands: the Relatives Action Committees (RAC). Its members were primarily women, mostly mothers. In 1976, while the Women's Peace movement was the center of media attention,[1] the RAC women—clad in blankets to bring the prisoners' reality to the streets—passed virtually unnoticed. The RAC experience opens a discussion about the play of subjectivity in political practice and therefore about the relation between subjectivity and social transformation.

Taking a cue from Foucault and Lacan, much feminist scholarship has linked women's subjectivity to operations of exclusion within cultural representations (Butler and Scott 1992; Cornell 1993; Scott 1988; Steedly 1993; Visweswaran 1994). I have been arguing that this focus on representation is critical to an analysis of the politics of nationalist women. Yet, as Jane Flax has pointed out, "political action and change require and call upon many human capacities including empathy, anger and disgust"—and I may add, pain—"that are not always expressed in language" (1992, 458). How do those emotions enter the arena of cultural representations? What effects do they produce in political practice? How are they organized within a system of gender difference? In addressing these questions, I am concerned here not so much with language as with the embodiment of emotion in social action. In chapter 3 I discussed how the politics of emotion worked to produce a historical discourse of male heroism. In chapter 4 I analyze the women relatives of political prisoners to show the different ways in which emotion worked to embody specific kinds of female political subjectivity.

Bringing the Suffering Close to Home

The Relatives Action Committee was formed in 1976 by women who had close relatives in jail. It originated in Turf Lodge, a particularly poor district of Catholic West Belfast, on an Easter Monday. One of the founders remembers:

> There was trouble in the prisons, and this woman came to my house and started talking about the taking of political status away and about what were we going to do. It was a beautiful day and I told her "I could do without this today. But, anyway, you go get some women and I'll go and get some women and see if we can have a meeting." We arranged to have the Whiterock Hall for the meeting, and there was quite a large group of women there, and a couple of men, but mostly women. We were a bit abstract about what we wanted. So we decided to have a number of meetings locally to discuss the situation in the prisons, and then we decided to have another meeting and invite everybody to come along to it. So we had our first meeting, and we discussed various names, and we decided to call the organization the Relatives Action Committee, and we made a press release, and from then on we gathered information on the prisoners, and we organized ourselves in the local areas and elected representatives so that people would not have to come to meetings all the time. The situation in the jails deteriorated terribly. No clothes, no radio, no reading material except for the Bible, no medical care, nothing. How the prisoners survived, I don't know! The meetings were open to everyone, and there were representatives of the political parties. It was quite difficult because you had to listen to them talk about their party etc.; and what in theory I suppose was a good idea, in practice it was not great. I remember at the time being quite upset, and a lot of other women were too. Because we were very single minded; we wanted something to be done in very practical ways. A lot of people were burnt out because you were traveling all the time to meetings and campaigning, and it was very difficult. But we were very determined. We were mostly women, mainly mothers, and a few men, mainly fathers, but very few. I think this is because this was something that affected women, their lives, very strongly. If your child is in prison you want to do everything possible for them. And they were in such horrible conditions. . . . It really affected women very deeply.

The majority of women of the RAC were housewives at the time. They were drawn into organizing, public speaking, lobbying, and publishing by concern for their sons. The British government had unfolded a propaganda campaign against the prisoners, and very little information about conditions inside the jail reached the public eye. The women of the RAC did everything possible to break the silence around the republican prisoners and to publicize their plight. At the center of women's preoccupation was the prisoners' suffering. In an effort to bring that suffering close to home, the RAC deliberately utilized expressive methods. They believed that if people only knew what was happening in the jails they would support the prisoners. To convey the reality of their sons' situation the women wrapped themselves only in blankets and took to the streets of Catholic districts with banners and posters to make the invisible visible. The women chained themselves to emphasize the harsh conditions of captivity of the prisoners and kept fast vigils at different times. They blocked roads, occupied government premises, picketed courts, distributed leaflets, hung posters, and contacted ecclesiastical authorities who could mediate in favor of the prisoners. Women from the RAC went on to campaign, in their blankets, outside the northern ghettos. Some of them chained themselves in front of the house of the British prime minister at 10 Downing Street , London. Others went to the Republic of Ireland and toured Europe and America, always in their blankets. They were arrested and harassed.

The RAC did not induce immediate support. It took four long and painful years to build the mass support that characterized the political conjuncture of 1980–1981. From the perspective of Clare, a republican community worker, this conjuncture constituted a second wave of activity, a historical landmark wholly embedded in the chronological marking of personal biographies:

> In 1980 you had another rebellion, like another wave of revolution, as in 1971. You would have, for instance, people interned in 1971, out by 1973, by 1975 they got a job and a family and were carrying normal lives, and by 1980 they realized "Jesus the British are still with us, and they are going to crucify us." They got used to a kind of normal life, and 1980 just brought all the 1970s back again and much worse. Suddenly everybody wanted to do something. But it took four years to mobilize all the people, and during all those years there were mainly women in local action committees who did all the work.

Along with the political work of information and lobbying, the public image of these women clad in blankets constituted a powerful symbol of maternal suffering that brought to the surface the depth of pain defining the Catholic experience in Northern Ireland. Maternal suffering refracted a broader collective pain, stirring a mixture of personal and social guilt. This sense of guilt was utilized in republican rhetoric to gain support for the prisoners. Beside the photographs of demonstrating silent mothers, the weekly *Republican News*, repeated again and again the same question: "Are you going to let them die?"

The crucifixion metaphor used by Clare—"the British are still with us and they are going to crucify us"—provides an image that condenses experiential reality and organizes a whole array of feelings. As we saw in chapters 1 through 4, republican murals which began to be painted at this time often evoked crucifixion themes to portray both the prisoners' struggle and the suffering of Ireland. Such metaphorics of suffering articulated a discourse of political redemption and historical legitimacy among male prisoners. But how was suffering both as discourse and feeling articulated for women? How does pain work within sexual difference? What kind of effects does it trigger in political practice? What dissonance of feeling is produced by occupying different subject positions?

THE NATIONALIST PASSION OR THE MOTHER AS SYMBOL OF COLLECTIVE SUFFERING

In Marian Catholicism the image of the crucifixion forms part of a configuration in which Mary, mother of Christ, figures prominently. The Virgin of the crucifixion is a sorrowful mother. As we saw in chapter 2, her suffering is refractive. Through her, the Son's pain and agony is enlivened, she is the medium through which identification with Christ's suffering is attained. As Marina Warner has noted: "The momentum of Mary's myth, which always seeks out a parallel to Christ's life in hers, made her Calvary the nodal point of his passion" (1983, 211).

The theme of the sorrowful mother of God, which developed in Europe around the twelfth century, acquired special intensity in Ireland after the devastating famine of the 1840s (MacCurtain 1982). It was further elaborated in the nationalist collective representation of a grieving Mother-Ireland, which begins to appear in ballads and songs of the late nineteenth century (Zimmerman 1966). One of the best known examples of this kind of production that became popular in Northern Ireland after 1971 (McCann 1985) is the song "Four Green Fields" in which an old woman (Ireland) grieves the ravaging of her four fields (Ireland's four provinces) and the bondage in which one of them (Ulster) remains:

> "What did I have?" this proud old woman did say
> "I had four green fields, each one was a jewel,
> But strangers came and tried to take it from me
> I had fine strong sons, they fought to save my jewels
> They fought and died, and that was my grief" said she.

> "Long time ago" said the fine old woman
> "Long time ago" this proud old woman did say
> "There was war and death, plundering and pillage
> My children starved, by mountains, valley and sea
> And their wailing cries, they shook the very heavens
> My four green fields ran red with their blood."

> "What have I now?" said the fine old woman
> "What have I now?" this proud old woman said
> "I have four green fields, but one of them's in bondage
> In stranger's hands that tried to take it from me
> But my sons have sons as brave as were their fathers;
> My fourth green field shall bloom once again" said she.

The rhetoric of Mother-Ireland appears recurrently in republican publications, particularly during the first half of the 1970s. The image of a grieving Ireland is constantly interwoven with the image—more immediate to people's experience—of maternal loss. Thus an article published in 1971 in the republican weekly elaborates on the theme of a mother who has witnessed the killing of a boy in a riot: "She was helpless as she saw the fathers and sons beaten and kicked to the ground. With a mother's pain she realized he was dead. She had wanted to scream out against that sight, scream for the boy, for his family, for his unknowing mother. That boy was her own son, every mother's son. Quickly she turned to make sure her own 14-year old was still with them. He wouldn't always be fourteen, but already he was a man too aware of his duty to protect" (*Republican News*, March 10, 1971). During Bobby Sands's funeral Owen Carron also alluded to his mother's suffering: "It is hard to be a hero's mother, and nobody knows that better than Mrs. Sands who watched her son being daily crucified and tortured for sixty-six long days and eventually killed. Mrs. Sands epitomizes the Irish mothers who in every generation watch their children go out to fight and die for freedom" (*Republican News*, September 5, 1981).

Sands's mother's sorrow—more than his sister's, son's, or wife's (completely effaced from the story)[2]—allegorically represents the suffering of the country inasmuch as the country is represented as a mother in republican imagery. In this imagery women are represented as passive figures, waiting witnesses. Even when women engage in manifest acts of resistance they tend to be represented as symbols rather than political subjects. In 1976, for instance, a short column in the republican weekly, reporting a vigil held by women in protest for the conditions of prisoners, read: "the hunger for justice is symbolized by the sacrifices of the women who are prepared to endure the rigors born by their relatives in the now notorious H-Blocks" (*Republican News*, December 4, 1996). The commentary was framed beside a photograph of a group of women wrapped only in blankets under a banner that read "Mothers Hunger For Justice." In spite of the rotund affirmation of this banner that places the women holding the vigil as subjects on their own right, their action is represented by the reporter as a symbol of the actions of others, namely their imprisoned sons. In nationalist representations, the source of women's power does not stem from their engagement in action but from the endorsement of their sons, whose sacrifice causes them so much grief. At another symbolic level, this economy of pain that genderizes social practice is encapsulated in the ubiquitous tandem images of the Virgin Mary and the Sacred Heart of Jesus that decorate every Catholic house in Belfast.

The mother-son cultural relationship is also reinforced sociologically in Belfast. Kin and affinal families live in the vicinity of each other in Catholic working-class districts, and close ties among members of the extended family are often kept through life. Men and women usually live in the parental home until marriage, but men tend to return to it in the event of separation while women rarely do. The common pattern for a separated or divorced woman is to settle in a house of her own with her children. "Mom's home," as the parental house is commonly called, seems a more available recourse for men than for women. One of my close neighbors told me humorously how her brother-in-law had abandoned the marital house at 3:00 a.m. after a fight with his wife to go to "mum's home," despite the serious risks of encountering an army patrol or a loyalist death squad on his way. As he was walking the street, he was indeed spotted by the military, beaten, and taken to their local headquarters where he spent the night.

12. A wall on the patio of Clonard Monastery shows an image of the Virgin of Fatima. In the back the chimney of a linen factory now closed.

13. Hunger striker dying with madonna irradiating grace over him. In the back the silhouette of the H-Blocks of the Long Kesh prison.

111

The death and arrest of large numbers of young men during the last twenty years of violent conflict have endowed collective representations of motherhood with powerful political meanings (see figures 12 and 13). The politicization of the Catholic Passion is best represented in the images evoked by women and "blanket men" simultaneously praying the rosary during the hunger strike: the former on a street corner, the latter in their prison cells. The women pray under the statues of the crucified Christ and His virgin mother, which stand on a corner of Falls Road; the prisoners pray under the vigilant eye of the prison warders. As the former quote from Clare reveals, by 1980 these images had become an allegory of the suffering of a whole people—indeed of a country—represented in the mural in which Ireland carries the heavy cross of Britain.

Prison Visits

The politicization of the bond between mothers and sons is nowhere better enacted than in the setting of the prison visit. Mothers are not, of course, the only women who regularly visit the prisoners. Yet their presence is particularly salient and constant, being accentuated by the youth and unmarried status of most prisoners. Women travel at least weekly to the prisons to provide the awaited parcels of food, clothes, books, news, and emotional and psychological support. They check on the health and morale of their sons and husbands and safely smuggle out messages and letters for friends and acquaintances. This interdependence reached a paradigmatic level of political communion during the late 1970s and the hunger strike. Visits were then restricted to thirty minutes a month, and parcels were prohibited. Like their sons and husbands, the women used their bodies to smuggle precious forbidden goods. Tobacco, pen refills, a headache tablet, and perhaps a letter, all wrapped tightly in small packages the size of a cigarette, were hidden in the vagina or mouth to fool the warders who body-searched visitors. After the search, women removed these parcels in the toilet and passed them on to the men amid close surveillance and high anxiety. The men then put them in their rectum or mouth or inside their foreskin.[3] The exchanges were reciprocal. The prisoners had to manage to pass on to the women letters and communicados ("comms") written in minuscule handwriting on cigarette paper and addressed to people outside the prison. Communication between the prisoners and the outside IRA leadership relied heavily on women relatives. The emotional link between mothers and sons, so elab-

112

orate in the political culture of Irish nationalism, assumed a corporeal dimension during the prison protest that gave it a chilling literalness.

Emotionally, visits were times of great anxiety. For the prisoners it meant going through mirror searches, one of the most hated of surveillance practices. This consisted in forcibly squatting the naked prisoners over a mirror to search their anus, a practice that was deeply humiliating for the prisoners. They also risked beatings and punishment cells if caught exchanging parcels or "comms." For the women visits represented the permanent shock of confronting their sons or husbands deteriorated physical state, the visualization of their pain, and the impotence and frustration of meeting half an hour a month, sometimes less, surrounded by other visiting prisoners and prison warders. Roisin's husband spent three and a half years "on the blanket":

> I hated going to the jail. That wrecked me. I had to take a nerve tablet every time because it upset me so much I was shaking. For three or four days before the visit I had these nerves; that is probably why I have a bad stomach. While you were there you would hear all different stories about what was happening inside the jail. That they were dragged from the cells by the hair, beatings and all. It was terrifying for us [relatives] because we saw them once a month, and we could only wonder what will be next. I brought the kids for the visits because I felt they needed to see him too. Once there, the kids would start: "Daddy come home!"—crying and hugging him. One time we went to visit, and the guards had forcibly shaven his head. He had no hair, and at first I was looking around in the visiting room and couldn't recognize him. When I finally did, the kids saw him, and they were so terrified they screamed! You had to go through three hours of waiting for half an hour visit. You could talk nothing on that time. The visits were in small cubicles, you could see everybody and the screws could see in every box and you knew you were watched and you were uncomfortable and very tense. Most of the times I went back home without saying the things I wanted to say and had to go home and write him a letter. We were smuggling letters to them and that was the only way I could say things I wanted to say. I carried the comms in the mouth and we had our wee tactic, we kissed and that is how it was passed. I used to go in with one letter and come out with six, if somebody had spoken to me I would have choked. I got letters for other people who hadn't got a visit. Other people did it for me when I didn't have a visit. It was terrible. But the searches were the worst.

113

One of the most distressing aspects of the visit situation was the body search to which women and their children were subjected before seeing their relatives. These searches deeply humiliated many women for whom modesty was an important value. For Roisin it was the worst part of the visit: "I hated it. I hated getting searched, a stranger palming all over you. You didn't have to strip, but you may as well strip. They went over every part of your body. And sometimes you had a sanitary towel on, and they told you to take it off and throw it out to them, which was very degrading. There is no way I would have done that. I would have refused my visit before taking it off in front of them." The emotional toll of prison visits on women was enormous: "I always left the prison devastated; it was worse than not seeing him," said Roisin. Rose, the mother of a prisoner, emphasized the anxiety and impotence of worry: "Worry never goes away. They are in jail, and you think about them all the time and worry. And you still have to keep up morale for the men. But when you were back home, alone again, that was another matter, you know. You went down then."

UNLOCKING THE PAIN

The principal motivations for women to organize themselves in the Relatives Action Committee were the unbearable conditions that their relatives were enduring in the prisons and the pain that their suffering brought to themselves. Passive waiting was for the mothers and wives at home psychologically unbearable. Waiting looms large in the narratives of Belfast nationalist women: waiting for their children and husbands to come home alive, waiting to see them in prison, waiting for them to be released. Waiting becomes in their narratives an immense space of uncertainty filled with worry, a worry that, as Rose said, never went away. It was worry that gave you the nerves, that wrecked the stomach and put you on the tablets; a worry that takes the place of life or makes life not quite there but somewhere else. "During the blanket protest all I did was worry sick about all that he was going through," said Roisin, "everyday something will come up that maybe all would be over but it never did. You're still living on the edge because he can be singled out by a screw for having been in jail. He can be lifted [arrested] any moment, he can be killed. Every time he is not home early I worry, I wonder if he is OK, I watch every car that comes around my door. You have your door locked constantly for fear of assassination. . . . I live like this every day. He doesn't understand what it means to be waiting and worrying. He gets harassed all the time, stopped by the cops, I have to live with that. He doesn't understand that I worry that he might be shot, and when he comes late because he has been drinking in the pub that angers me, wrecks me. Men are so selfish, they can just put on the coats and walk out of the door." It has been estimated that during the 1970s, thirty-five million tranquilizers were consumed annually in Northern Ireland (population, one and a half million); significantly twice as many women as men were dependent on them (Ward and McGivern 1980).

In Roisin's words, like those of other women, waiting emerges as the anguishing feeling of having one's life on hold through the projection of somebody else's life being on hold, a gnawing feeling. There is a gendered economy of feeling that connects agency and space so that men wait for their lives in prison, women wait for the lives of others outside prison. Women's waiting becomes an allegory of an imprisoned existence, in the sense that in Northern Ireland the lives of everybody are on hold, that the country is just a big prison. Waiting, Crapanzano (1985) has noted, is being locked in a present that is always subordinated to a contingent future: a present (de)formed by floating stories of terror and abuse, like those heard by Roisin in the waiting room of Long Kesh; a present that denies itself because it is always anticipating, hoping—sometimes against hope—as during the hunger strikes. For the mothers and wives of prisoners, waiting was filled with dread, anguish, and guilt. These women said that they felt constantly guilty for their sons' and husbands' pain, that the suffering of their relatives was always on their minds. Suarez-Orozco (1992, 242) has noted that similar emotions of guilt and interrupted grief were motivationally important for the Argentinean women who formed the *Mothers of Plaza de Mayo* to demand the return of their disappeared children. Like the *Mothers of Plaza de Mayo*, the grief and rage of the mothers of republican prisoners became an engine of their political radicalization, channeled and elaborated into a project of political resistance that transcended their individual predicaments.

Action was for the prisoners' relatives both a political need and a psychological necessity. Mary, who had a teenage son "on the blanket," put it in these terms: "I just couldn't sit in the house. I had to go out and tell the world what was happening and what they could do. The whole stress and anguish took a big toll and had a direct effect on the health of women. If I hadn't been involved I would have had a nervous breakdown by now." Maura McCrory, a prominent member of the RAC, also corroborated the liberating effect of political action: "There was immense relief in just letting emotions hang out, women meeting women, talking about the strains on their families. You could see confidence build up as they let their tongues loose for the first time, talking with each other, listening to each other. Women who were nervous wrecks, who'd never attended a committee meeting in their lives, came back to life in wee draughty community halls." (McCafferty 1981, 84–85).

This involvement in the RAC, aimed at the eradication of the prisoners' suffering, simultaneously helped prisoners' relatives to cope with their own suffering. Women drew on the religious imagery of the Christian Passion to procure community support through empathetic understanding of the prisoners' predicament. The women themselves found some solace in the model of the Virgin Mary; yet, they could not identify with her passive endurance. So while collective representations of the time associated the mothers of the prisoners with the Virgin Mother of the Calvary, the mothers of the RAC had subverted the model by actively turning their private suffering into a collective project of resistance. The need to fight for their individual sons became a struggle for all the prisoners and ultimately for a whole new project of social justice. Thus Mary, who became a prominent republican activist after the hunger strikes, felt that: "I had to do something not only for my son but for all the men and women who were in prison. . . . At the end I had become too aware of the social injustice. I realized the struggle went beyond the prisons, that there was poverty, unemployment, discrimination."

Some scholars have affirmed that during the hunger strike "mothers were filling mythological roles" (O'Malley 1990, 118). This assertion, however, ignores that (1) myths, like other cultural models, are necessarily transformed in social practice; and (2) transformation is often accompanied by political and personal changes. To interpret the actions of the prisoners' mothers as mythological enactments is also to ignore the personal and political motivations, the social and psychological processes that involved women in four years—or in some cases a lifetime—of political activity. One must remember that, as in the case of internment, the government's policy of criminalization, not religious or nationalist mythology, set the ground for the women's resistance. The position of women during the dirty protest and the hunger strike was not a passive mythological enactment but the result of a complex political subjectivity thoroughly embedded in and shaped by social practice. It is important to differentiate here between the politics of emotion deployed by the republican movement in their political rhetoric and the politics of emotion underpinning the activity of the RAC women. In re-

116

publican rhetoric the suffering of mothers was strategically represented as a symbol of nationalist dispossession. The suffering of the nation was condensed in the suffering of the mother. This discourse of maternal suffering was aimed at securing ideological support through the empathetic identification with the grieving mother. In this rhetorical discourse the figure of the mother often occupied mythological positions. For the actual mothers who constituted the backbone of the RAC the situation was different. Their suffering was not so much a rhetorical trope as the motivating force of a form of political action that departed considerably from the mythical paradigm of nationalist motherhood. The mothers of the RAC did deploy suffering as a weapon, but this suffering was not the embodiment of the nation of republican rhetoric; it was the concrete suffering of their incarcerated sons that lay hidden from public opinion, a suffering that they sought to publicize and in so doing terminate. As political argument and political force, the suffering deployed by the RAC also differed from that of the prisoners: inasmuch as it was not their own suffering that they used as a weapon of resistance but the suffering of others that they launched as a discourse of injustice. Thus at neither the motivational level nor the ideological level was the suffering of the mothers of the RAC allegorical or redemptive. Rather it constituted a political discourse that ran against the grain of dominant British and republican narratives and opened a space to unmapped forms of personal and social transformation.

Some women involved in the RAC had acquired political experience during the intense disturbances of the early 1970s. That experience was, however, confined to the local dynamics of Northern Ireland. The majority had never abandoned Ireland, if indeed they ever left their local community. Ghettoization, militarization, and poverty made it difficult to transcend local boundaries. Their involvement in actions as daring as traveling to Europe and the United States to campaign and lobby for their relatives, demonstrating wrapped only in blankets in the midst of London, and participating in the UN conference on women of 1978 opened new domains of personal experience. Maura McCrory, a leader of the RAC, conceptualized this experience as "a power of defiance and a sense of not being afraid any more." The empowering sense of political engagement generated a profound personal transformation for some of these women. In their own words they became more political, more aware of the social reality in which they were immersed, and more cognizant of their human potential beyond the roles of wife and mother. They also became aware of the obstacles to developing that potential. Maura McCrory noted publicly that their involvement had for many

117

women caused tensions in their home life and made women aware of the social pressure to conform to dominant gender roles.[4] As I discuss in chapter 6, interwoven with the RAC struggle for the prisoners was also a feminist battle to redefine gender relations in the republican movement. This process brought to the surface existing tensions in the gender structure of republican politics, which can be perceived in the silenced figure of the prisoner's wife.

GENDER TENSIONS IN REPUBLICAN (INFRA)STRUCTURE

Roisin's husband, Anton, was on the run for almost a year before he was arrested and joined the blanket men for three and a half years. The Brits came one day looking for him, and they wrecked the house so badly that Roisin and her two kids had to move out. Anton, who was out at the time, went on the run, and Roisin began moving from house to house, living for short periods of time with different relatives, often feeling like an intruder and a burden. Finally Anton was lifted, and Roisin settled in a squatted house.

> I had nothing, no furniture, nothing. I stood in the middle of this house and I cried and cried. I got bits and pieces of furniture from people. Financially it was terrible. A carpet was a luxury, a fridge or a TV was a luxury. There were weeks I and my kids didn't have a bite to eat. I felt very lonely. I sat for nearly two years and never went outside the door. People said to me "go out," but I couldn't afford to go out and socialize. I couldn't get a baby sitter. Thinking was constantly on my mind. Anton sort of understands, but he doesn't know what it is like. People don't understand that when your husband is in jail you are lacking on something, you are losing something. Your finances go down, you go down, everything stops. It's like being dead. Nobody understood, people must have thought I was used to it because I put a hard front most of the times. I got indebted just to buy food, it was all chips and chips, I couldn't afford meat. I was also angry. I felt sorry for Anton but I also resented him for leaving me on my own with the kids. It was the worst time I have ever gone through in my life. Anton said that I would never have to go through it again. I said "I hope not." But he got out and went into the movement again and was arrested a year and a half later. I was so annoyed I was not going to go again to see him in jail. Just the thought of it made me sick. I was prepared to wait for him but I didn't want to go near the jail again. But I felt sorry for him and went up to

118

jail and that was me starting all over from scratch again just when I thought we were settled, and I had a new wee baby then. Eventually I got a cleaning job. I brought the kids with me because I couldn't get them minded. That job made me want to go out. Anton didn't want me to go out of the house. He was jealous, he thought that if I went to a dance I would probably meet somebody else. The way things were at the jail was that if the relative of a prisoner was at the dance and saw me she would mention it and word would have gotten to Anton, so I preferred to tell him directly if I was going out because otherwise he would have thought that I had something to hide. He drove me crazy with his jealousy. Then when he came out all he did was talk about the fellows he had left behind. Maybe I was hard but I said "I'm not sorry for them after what I have gone through."

The cultural elaboration of maternal suffering has obscured the more problematic political meaning of wives' suffering. The prisoners' wives' support for their husbands was not devoid of ambivalence. Their imprisonment in the late 1970s was not the result of a general policy, as during internment, but a consequence of their membership in the IRA, a choice in which the women had had no part. Although they supported their husbands politically, they also resented them for worsening their situation and that of their children. "For many prisoners' wives" said Maureen one afternoon, "there is a degree of bitterness at being left without a choice. Yet after a while they find a job, get on with their kids and their new life. They change. And their husbands come out of jail and expect them to be the same. A fair number of marriages have broken because of that." Prisoners' wives were confronted with financial and emotional problems that mothers ordinarily did not face, especially loneliness and isolation. "It is harder for young women with small children to raise on their own," said Margaret while we sat in a crowded republican club waiting for the beginning of a homage to Bobby Sands. Margaret's partner is serving seventeen years. "My children are all reared; but at the same time, my daughter is married and the sons hurry in and out just for meals, so I am alone when I get home and I miss him for company." She introduces me to a young woman, "She has three small children and her husband got three life sentences," says Margaret later on. There's a silence hanging between us. "It's hard," Margaret says, as if that was all that could be said.

Prisoners' wives are required to be superwomen with the fit rarely being acknowledged. Despite the serious emotional and material hardship faced by women whose husbands become imprisoned, the ideology of unconditional love was, and still is, projected onto the wives, who were required to provide their husbands with unfailing emotional protection.

Sexuality radically separates, at least at the level of consciousness, the figures of the mother and the wife. Unlike the mother, the wife was frequently suspected of sexual deception and by extension of deception to the nationalist cause. Unlike the mother, the wife was perceived socially as a potential sexual betrayer. Surveillance of prisoners' wives by prisoners' friends was not uncommon in nationalist communities during the 1970s. "Life is hell when your husband is in jail," said Anne one night, remembering how it was for her. Anne's husband was killed in 1984 by Michael Stone, the infamous loyalist who threw a grenade during the course of a republican funeral in 1986 and killed three people. "It is hell because you haven't cut your tie with your husband yet you don't have him either," says Anne. "Women with their husbands in jail cannot go out with other men. It is not only the pressure of social reprobation, but also friends of the husband would tell the man who approaches his wife to leave. Nobody would do the same if the case was the opposite and the wife was in prison." For Maureen "the issue of relationships and affairs is not as badly perceived now as it was before, in the seventies. Then if a woman went out with another man she was just a whore, but the republican movement has learned that things are more complicated for women than just wait loyally for their husbands. So today if a prisoner's wife goes out with another man there is more tolerance about it." Even when a wife remained faithful to her husband—as was true in most cases—the new self-management of her life frequently led her to consider unacceptable former definitions of gender roles and to demand on her husband's release a more equal share of family and social responsibilities. This adjustment in gender relations was then, as now, usually not accomplished without conflict.

The commitment of republican nationalism to armed struggle has been a source of permanent gender conflict, in tension with its ideological and structural underpinnings. That is, IRA violence relies upon a network of integrated domestic units—safe houses—to provide for logistic infrastructure; at the same time it profoundly disrupts domestic arrangements. One way of minimizing this inherent tension was to promote a gender ideology that emphasized the heroic sacrifice of IRA men and the unfailing loyalty of women-mothers. Many women, however, are only too aware of the contradictions involved in that ideology, and have actively challanged it. Maureen thinks that to be in prison is not a state that women should pay for. She thinks that there is always an element of selfishness in the person who chose to be an active militant and go to jail, in the sense, she says "that he gets the inner satisfaction of his decision, the comradeship, the education in jail, and the social recognition, they still are the heroes. Women have to carry on with the less heroic task of looking after the children, make ends meet and sustain emotionally their men. And they don't get the recognition." For Roisin the ideology of male heroism was not devoid of bitter irony:

"It was a nightmare for me in every way when he was in jail. I coped alright on my own. I hardened a lot. I had to be strong. Some of his so-called friends didn't want to know about me and the kids, but when he got out of jail they all rallied around. He was the hero. I resented that. I know that it was me who kept his strength up all the way [through the blanket protest]. I did my duty; I waited. I could have gone off, me and the kids, find somebody else. Sometimes I think I should have."

The tensions surrounding republican gender politics were publicly articulated with the emergence in 1978 of a republican-feminist organization in West Belfast, Women Against Imperialism, but the rising tensions were fueled by the dirty protest of IRA women prisoners in Armagh jail.

CHAPTER 6

The Power of Sexual Difference:
Armagh Women

Aᴼᵀᴱᴿ ᴛʜᴇ ᴡɪᴛʜᴅʀᴀᴡᴀʟ of political status from prisoners, the republican women in Armagh went on a work strike, refusing to sew prison uniforms or do laundry, the mandatory jobs for regular inmates. The protest carried with it the loss of usual privileges: remission of sentences, visits, parcels, hours for free association, and education. As opposed to their male comrades, the women in Armagh were not required to use a uniform; as was true for all women prisoners in Britain, they could wear their own clothes. In Long Kesh, the blanket protest converted the prison uniform into a complex metonymy of a timeless republican struggle. In an inverted correspondence yet similar metonymic move "the Armagh women" used their own garments—berets, black skirts—to improvise IRA uniforms that would symbolize and reassert their denied political identity. In search of those small pieces of apparel, trivial in themselves yet deeply significant in the encoded world of prison regime, in full riot gear military men, kicking and punching, entered the cells of IRA prisoners in Armagh on Thursday, February 7, 1980. For the women prisoners the events of that day sparked their "protest of dirt." For more than one year thirty-two women, the majority of whom were under twenty-four years of age, lived in tiny cells without washing themselves, amid their own menstrual blood and bodily waste. Infections were rampant, and skin, sight, digestive, and hearing problems were common. Like their male comrades in Long Kesh, the women in Armagh were protesting against the British attempt to criminalize them.

The Armagh dirty protest sparked a process of cultural change. Unlike the transformation provoked by the women (mothers and wives) discussed in chapter 5, a change revolving around culturally hegemonic images of femininity, the political effects of the Armagh dirty protest were triggered by the symbolism of menstrual blood that tapped on an experience of femininity excluded from public discourse. Such transgression made manifest the shifting constructions of gender and sexual difference while simultaneously showing the dynamic work of symbols in political practice. I begin my analysis by discussing the events that embarked women prisoners in the dirty protest.[1]

THE ASSAULT

On that Thursday the noon dinner arrived to "B" wing, which housed republican prisoners on the "no-work" protest. As the women lined up at the counter to get their dinner, the governor came into the wing followed by approximately thirty male officers who formed a semicircle around the women. Another thirty female officers joined them. Mairead Farrell, leader of republican prisoners, was informed that there was to be a general search. Cell searches were usually carried out when the prisoners were in the exercise yard or at Mass on Sundays. This one, therefore, seemed odd. When Mairead Farrell asked about the presence of male officers she was told that the search would be faster that way.[2]

When the prisoners began to object to this unexpected search, male warders immediately attacked them. Some women were thrown to the ground; others beaten and kicked. Prisoners were pushed into two association rooms where they remained for three hours without food or drink while their cells were being searched. "At about 3:00 p.m.," according to a letter Eilis O'Connor wrote her parents, "we were told we were going back to our cells, one at a time, but that we had to go to the Guard room to get searched. We all did this and went back to our cells which were wrecked, clothes all over the place" (McCafferty 1981). Mairead Farrell wrote, "The officers came to take Ann Bateson down to the prison authorities [the governor]. I was outside Ann's door. The officers jumped me, punched and dragged me into a cell. Then male officers dressed in full riot gear charged upstairs for Ann with shields and batons. They pulled her out beating her and dragging her to the prison authorities. The same happened to Eileen Morgan, Eilis O'Connor, and Rosie Callaghan."[3]

This was Ann Bateson's narrative:

> I was sitting in my cell when three male screws [officers] burst in with riot gear. The three of them held me on the bed, then grabbed me by the arms and legs, and dragged me out of the cell. At the same time they kept punching me. When they got me out of the wing, eight female screws took me from them. Helped by a male screw, they carried

me spread-eagled downstairs. The male screw had his hand around my neck the whole time. I thought that I was going to choke. I was carried into the guard room, still spread-eagled, and I was held in this position during my adjudication [reading of charges and punishment]. My trousers and jumper were nearly off me at this stage, but the governor told the screws to hold me in that position and not to let me down. When my adjudication was over I was trailed out. The male screws took me at this stage and threw me into an empty cell. One of them kicked me while I was lying on the floor. They then stood outside the cell and banged the door and turned the light on and off.

Rosemary Callaghan also described her experience:

At around 3:45 p.m. on Thursday Feb. 7th, numerous male and female screws invaded my cell in order to get me down to the governor. They charged in full riot gear equipped with shields. I sat unprotected but aware of what was going to happen as I had heard my comrades screaming in pain. I was suddenly pinned to the bed by a shield and the weight of a male screw on top of me. Then my shoes were dragged off my feet. I was bodily assaulted, thumped, trailed and kicked. I was then trailed out of my cell, and during the course of my being dragged and hauled from the wing both my breasts were exposed to the jeering and mocking eyes of all the screws, there must have been about twenty of them. While being carried, I was also abused with punches to the back of my head and my stomach. I was eventually carried into the governor; my breasts were still exposed. While I was held by the screws the governor carried out the adjudication, and I was then trailed back and thrown into a cell.[4]

The notes and reports sent out by the other women echo those quoted here and were confirmed in subsequent interviews with the former prisoners. The women were locked in their cells without access to toilet and washing facilities. According to the prisoners, male officers ran the wing on the following days. Mairead Farrell described the situation in another letter smuggled out: "We got something to eat. Still not allowed use of toilet facilities. We have been forced into a position of "dirt strike" as our pots are overflowing with urine and excrement. We emptied them out of the spy holes into the wing. The male officers nailed them closed, but we broke them using our chairs."

The prisoners maintain that the beatings that prompted the women into the no-wash strike were strategically planned. As McCafferty (1981) notes on that day the women had been offered an unusually good meal of chicken and apple pie, which made them come out of their cells at once when they were opened. Before dinner common prisoners had been locked inside their cells, and education and religious administrators sent out of the prison quarters. "We were so excited about that chicken! We should have known something was up," said Bernie, recalling the scene one afternoon. Most male officers who conducted the search had been drafted from Long Kesh prison. The search itself does not seem a convincing justification for the presence of male officers or the institutional violence deployed. Women officers had carried out searches on past occasions during exercise time or during Mass—when the women were not in their cells—to avoid confrontations. Even if a confrontation had been intended, the searches could have been conducted by female officers. Why were male officers brought in if it was not for a gendered form of punishment?—one that would subjugate not only militant prisoners but also women?

The questionable character of the violent search was voiced if only timidly in the British press. The British National Union of Students with a membership of 1.2 million positioned itself against giving political status to prisoners. Yet they voted to organize a national campaign "against the inhuman treatment of women prisoners in Armagh jail" (Lucy Hodges, *The English Times,* March 19, 1980, 3). However, the close vote— 296 against 214—hinted at the polemical and ambivalent quality that the dirty protest of Armagh women would provoke among different social sectors. The Labour party also expressed concern about reports "that women in Armagh jail were being attended by male warders, were locked up for 23 hours a day and were being denied proper sanitary and medical facilities" going on to say "while the national executive should oppose terrorism, it should also oppose repression and torture in Northern Ireland" (*The English Times,* June 10, 1980, 2).

The prisoners were moved to a different wing of the prison on February 13 with only their prayers and rosary beads for personal belongings. They were housed in "A" wing; two to an eight-by-twelve-foot cell with two beds, two chamber pots, two plastic mugs and plastic knives and forks. The dirty protest was on. Mairead Farrell described the prisoners' situation in a new letter smuggled out of jail to her family:

The stench of urine and excrement clings to the cells and our bodies. No longer can we empty the pots of urine and excrement out the window, as the male screws have boarded them up. Little light or air penetrates the thick boarding. The electric light has to be kept constantly on in the cells; the other option is to sit in the dark. Regardless of day or night, the cells are dark. Now we can't even see out the window; our only view is the wall of excreta. The spy holes are locked so they can only be open by the screws to look in. Sanitary towels are thrown into us without wrapping. We are not permitted paper bags or such like so they lie in the dirt until used. For twenty three hours a day we lie in these cells.

The women's dirty protest has been treated by commentators as an appendix to the struggle of male prisoners, receiving a brief remark, sometimes in parenthesis, in accounts of the prison-protest (Beresford 1987, 73–74; Feldman 1991, 174) or, at best, a short chapter (Coogan 1980b). The predicament of Armagh women before 1979 elicited little political interest or energy. The greater number of male prisoners (more than four hundred), the longer duration of their protest, and the brutality of their conditions garnered all the attention of both the media and the republican movement. The core of the feminist movement in Ireland was opposed to republican violence and considered the Armagh protest just a mimicry of Long Kesh's. They thus found no reason to devote attention to the conditions of Armagh women. Republican supporters, however, also minimized any gender specificity to Armagh protest by representing it as the result of the same worsening conditions that men had experienced in Long Kesh prison. When I asked women prisoners what they thought about the imputation of mimicry, they emphatically denied it. Yet their responses were not uniform. All coincided that the political meaning of Armagh protest did not differ from that of the men's protest. Some insisted in the similarity of conditions leading to the protest in both Armagh and Long Kesh prisons. Other Armagh women, however, while unequivocally asserting that their protest had the same political meaning as that of the men's, also affirmed that it was the product of different circumstances. These nuances of interpretation over the status of Armagh struggle may seem just little quibbles. Yet the fact that this quibbling should be about issues of identity and difference points to more fundamental questions about gender and sexual difference, questions that the Armagh protest unintentionally brought to the surface of the political arena.

There is, of course, a clear similarity between the men's and women's protests. After all, they shared the same nationalist culture of the North, were socialized in the same sociological milieu, had similar experiences growing up, and belonged to the same organization. They had similar political understanding, aims, and beliefs. Nevertheless, I argue that the significance of the dirty protest of Armagh women cannot be separated from its inextricable connection with the play of gender and sexual difference in the production and deployment of power. I also suggest that at the cultural and personal levels the meaning of the women's dirty protest differed from that of the men's. Such difference was encapsulated in the menstrual blood as both a symbol of the protest and a signifier of a reality jettisoned from public discourse.

In his book about the prison protest, Tim P. Coogan begins his chapter on the Armagh dirty protest with these words: "The dirty protest is bad enough to contemplate when men are on it. But it becomes even worse when it is embarked on by women, who apart from the psychological and hygienic pressures which this type of protest generates, also have the effects of the menstrual cycle to contend with" (1980b, 114). The words of Coogan, a seasoned political journalist, echoed a generalized reaction of disgust to the appearance of menstruation in the political field. Indeed, the image of a group of young women—many in their late teens—living without washing themselves and surrounded by their own excreta, urine, and menstrual blood in bare tiny prison cells to protest a government decision was horrifying and incomprehensible for most people. It proved embarrassing for republican men who tried hard to dissuade the women from their protest. The prisoners acknowledged that there was significant opposition from the republican movement. Brenda, one of the protesting prisoners, told me her brother was appalled: "He would say 'Come off. It's not right for women to do this!' Sinn Fein would say 'Don't do that. It's easier on men.' They didn't want us on dirty protest because of our periods. They didn't say that; they said that we were women, that we were different. But we knew it was because of our periods. These were men who had killed, had been imprisoned and they couldn't say the word 'period!'"

In Brenda's narrative the word "period" emerges as the unspeakable sign of sexual difference that must remain outside representation. Its mere utterance is threatening; men cannot bring themselves to say the word. Its eruption into public representation through the dirty protest transgresses the established boundaries of gender difference in ways that cannot be controlled: "It is not right for women to do it." Women, proper women, do not show the marks of sexual difference. To do it is, for Kristeva (1982), to question the construction of gender identity, that is, to challenge the cultural representations of femininity that separate sex from motherhood and place a prohibition on the representation of the substance that links them. The transgressive power of menstrual blood comes from an excess of signification that threatens the boundaries that constitute the social order. This transgressive char-

127

acter of menstrual blood triggered reactions of incomprehensibility and horror.

When approaching the subject, women prisoners insisted on the enforced character of the protest, their lack of choice. While this is literally true of the first days following the search of cells by male officers, afterward it was not. In actuality women could have come "out of the protest" and returned to use washing and toilet facilities. Literalness, however, is not the substance from which human culture is made. The enforced character of their protest refers to deeper levels of significance than the factual possibility of using the bathroom. It is at once literal and metaphoric.

Their insistence on external coercion reveals a degree of anxiety about the comprehensibility of their behavior, an awareness that most people find the idea of unwashed women repugnant. Women prisoners themselves found it difficult to speak in detail about the protest, a difficulty that their male comrades did not seem to share. Armagh women recognized that they were more reluctant to talk about the dirty protest than men were, but they often found themselves at a loss to say why. Brenda, an exceptionally outspoken former prisoner, said that talking about the protest produced strong feelings of vulnerability and embarrassment: "In the no-wash situation the men were looking the way we were but with the exception that they didn't have periods. Every month that was an embarrassment because you were bleeding and you were trying your best to stay clean but you couldn't because you were not getting a change of clothes. So it really was quite disgusting. It is very difficult in many ways to talk about that." The feeling of embarrassment is produced by the presence of a reality that cannot be articulated in existing discourse without disrupting it. The embarrassment and vulnerability at the sight of menstrual blood echoes the embarrassment produced by sexualized violence, another reality that Belfast women find difficult to put into words.

One crucial element in the descriptions of the events leading to the dirty protest can hardly be overlooked: male officers searching women's cells and (mis)handling women's bodies. The symbolic violation that the house searches represent is also embodied in the assault of the young women prisoners. Thus, the use of penal practices with sexual resonances was aimed at subduing not only individual prisoners but also, by extension, the community to which they belonged. If the women defending the streets of the ghettoized community in the early 1970s became an allegory of people's resistance, the officers' assault on incarcerated "girls" was a humiliating affirmation of institutional power, one in which notions of sexual abuse and male dominance were deeply implicated and had important political consequences. To understand the meaning of the officer's attack and the subsequent dirty protest, it is necessary to consider different areas of cultural significance.

SEXUALITY AND THE POLYVALENCE OF DOMINATION

The Catholic discourse in Ireland, North and South, has converted sexuality into a taboo subject. There is no sex education in schools, and it is difficult for women to talk explicitly about their sexuality (Beale 1986; Fairweather 1984). Sexual matters, rarely discussed in the context of the family, are the object of much embarrassment when they are not safely disguised in joking. Many women commented, some times with resentment, about the painful process of learning from scratch about sex or childbearing. Modesty is deeply rooted among young girls and women in Ireland, and its transgression produces deep feelings of humiliation and shame. Remember the categoric refusal of an arrested woman to undergo a strip search in chapter 1: "I wouldn't have done for the doctor, you know?"

The Armagh prisoners were very young women, many of them still teenagers. They were socialized in a strict Catholic morality that strongly emphasized modesty. The handling of women prisoners' bodies by male officers was deeply distressing. At least in one case, that of Rosemary Callaghan, the handling and beating was accompanied by exposure of the body as well as by moves highly evocative of sexual assault: "I was suddenly pinned to the bed by a shield and the weight of a male screw on top of me," and later "during the course of my being dragged and hauled from the wing, both my breast were exposed to the jeering and mocking eyes of all the screws." She was forcefully held in front of the prison governor with her breast still exposed; the episode being "totally embarrassing and degrading."[5]

The importance of disciplinary techniques of the body in the production and deployment of power, particularly visible in total institutions like the prison, has been extensively elaborated by Foucault (1979, 1980). Among the discourses and practices constituting the political economy of the body, sexuality, he argues, "appears as an especially dense transfer point for relations of power, one endowed with the greatest instrumentality" (1980, 103). Relying heavily on Foucault, Feldman (1991) has analyzed the use of bodily techniques by male republican prisoners during the dirty protest. Although Feldman does not comment on sexuality as a relevant dimension to the men's protest, it is crucial to the women's. Sexuality emerged in the eighteenth century as a (scientific) social construction playing a crucial role in inscribing power relations of various kinds: not only between men and women but also between social classes, "races," and colonial others.[6]

Political practices articulated through an explicit or veiled sexual discourse, such as the military assault on the Armagh prisoners, are undoubtedly power mechanisms. To interpret them *only* as disciplinary techniques that inscribe power relations in the body, however, is to miss the cultural and psychological dimensions that make their use possible in the first place. Practices such as sexual harassment during interrogation, strip searches, or male military assaults involve complex emotions around which the formation and transformation of subjectivity takes place. For Foucault it is precisely the formation of subjectivity (the construction of docile and unthreatening subjects) that constitutes the whole rationale of disciplinary and punishment techniques. It is the "soul" not the body that is the target of disciplinary power. Yet if the transformation of subjectivity is what is at stake in the bodily disciplines of the prison, the directions that such transformation may take escape the panoptic control of the prison to hinge on a multiplicity of contingent cultural, historical, and personal circumstances. As Garland (1990, 158–85) has argued, punishment cannot be understood solely in terms of power and rationality; the subjectivity of the actors must be seen not only as the product of rational techniques of control but also a crucial element in molding any resistance to them. For the women prisoners, unlike the men, the subjectivity of the dirty protest was inscribed within the permutations of gender and sexual difference.

Emotions and affects generated by manipulations of the body are always powerful components of the social order. The narrative of Rosemary Callaghan, aimed at denouncing physical punishment as disciplinary mechanism, ends with the feelings "it was most embarrassing and degrading." Without attention to the feelings permeating the protest and their historical configuration it is difficult to grasp the meaning of thirty-two women living for more than a year without washing, surrounded by their own excreta and menstrual blood.

The male officers' assault can be interpreted as both an institutionalized attempt to discipline through punishment and an assertion of male dominance on the bodies of women. This latter is of course one of the most common forms of subduing women. The fact that after the initial blows the beatings and handling of women were done in a generally individualized fashion in the enclosed space of the cell by armed men perceived to be profoundly anti-Catholic was doubly humiliating and distressing. The women, Mairead Farrell reported to her family, "were in a state of panic," and it took a while to calm them down.[7] These women, who had taken pains to assert "their difference" from the ordinary inmates and had taken pride in their political identity, needed some kind of action to relieve personal humiliation and regain political leverage. Thus, I suggest that at the level of consciousness the dirty protest was politically motivated, but it also involved a deeper level of personal motivation. Indeed, all former prisoners were quick in remarking to me that the morale among the women skyrocketed after they embarked on the dirty protest. And several observed that "the anger kept us going." To understand the meaning and operativity of these emotions, I explore another dimension of the politicization of the female body, what one could call the colonization of the female body by the state forces.

COLONIZATION OF THE FEMALE BODY

Women have systematically complained since the early years of the conflict about sexual harassment by British soldiers and Royal Ulster Constabulary (RUC) officers. Recent research has shown that sexual harassment of women by security forces is indeed widespread and particularly systematic in areas considered to be hostile to the security forces (McVeigh 1994, 124–34). While men may be stopped and questioned when walking on the streets, women are also likely to be the object of sexual remarks. They have become very skillful at ignoring both the words and their source, to the point that a view of the streets of Catholic West Belfast in 1988 could have left an outsider with the impression of having seen wandering ghosts rather than actual uniformed bodies. The conspicuous military presence is erased in a deliberate act of public non-recognition. This "erasure" and the sense of surreality that sometimes provokes was expressed in a poem by a local woman, Ann Zell:

> When you walk our streets
> you are not there
> or we are not there
> or the streets are not there.[8]

The extent of this visible invisibility was dramatically conveyed to me by the encounter of a girl no more than nine years old with a soldier. The girl having just turned a street corner bumped into the machine gun of a patrolling soldier looking to the other side of the street. The barrel of the machine gun hit her in the stomach. The girl continued walking—impassive, not a gesture in her face, no hesitation in her pace—as if what had just hit her was nothing more than a draft. The soldier, noticeably startled, muttered an apology after a few seconds, but the girl had already left him behind.

In private the soldiers' presence is acknowledged as women express their resentment of the sexual slurs they have so carefully ignored in the street. During the early 1970s, women were required to open their coats at military checkpoints as part of the security measures against terrorism. Male visual inspections of the female body were sometimes accompanied by sexual comments. To Catholic women the act of opening their coat to the intent gaze of a strange man amounted to an act of undressing with concomitant feelings of embarrassment, degradation, and guilt. Frequently women refused to open their coats to male soldiers, sometimes risking arrest.

The practice most feared by women is the strip search and the most dreaded context that of interrogation. The Association for Legal Justice, an independent legal and human rights group formed in Ireland in 1971, has collected statements from women concerning police and military intimidation of a sexual nature. A much publicized case concerned a thirteen-year-old girl, arrested during the night in 1978, who was obliged to stand with her menstrual blood running down her legs because she was denied a sanitary napkin. A case filed in 1979 details the ordeal of a pregnant woman who was submitted, while under arrest, to three internal medical examinations without her consent and without substantiated reason. She was verbally abused about her sexuality and that of her family. In 1977 an eighteen-year-old woman was forcefully strip-searched while under arrest, tied to a table, and internally searched twice by a male soldier. These three women were released after a few days without charges.

The possibility of a successful legal suit against the RUC or the British army for sexual harassment is virtually precluded by the judiciary in Northern Ireland, which has acted at the service of the police rather than as independent administrator of justice. A case which received public attention during the time of my fieldwork was that of Geraldine Skillen, mother of three young children, from one of the poorest areas of Catholic West Belfast. While coming from a local shop Geraldine was stopped by the RUC. After being insulted ("swore at"), she was forced into the back of an RUC armored vehicle where she was sexually abused by two male officers. She was then charged for disorderly behavior and assault and fined by a magistrate who dismissed her charges of sexual harassment and assault.[9]

The Armagh women also experienced sexual harassment during interrogation. Many of them were embarrassed to talk about it. Brenda described it in some detail:

> They start asking you whatever is that you were arrested for, and then they would mention the name of a man and say, "Did you fuck him?" and continue, "You Catholic girls just fuck anybody, you sluts. You know we can rape you right here, and nobody is going to believe you, because you are all fucking taigs." The abuse is filthy, continuous sexual abuse. I had big breasts when I was young that always embarrassed me. And they said "Who gropes them? Everybody in the IRA has gotten their hands on them at some point. . . . We know all about you: you all have your legs permanently opened for the cause and for Ireland." You just want to disappear. This is a man the age of your father, and he is talking like this to you. You just want the floor to open and swallow you. Then they go back to the initial question and then back again to the sexual abuse. You are sitting there pretending it is not upsetting you— but it's really upsetting you. You are seventeen and these men are older and they come in relays. It is very disturbing. And how do you complain about verbal abuse? They just deny it! This routine can go on for seven days. I know girls who have signed statements just to finish with it. When I was arrested they brought another girl that they were accusing of blowing up a boutique. It was her first time, and the interrogators started all this sexual abuse. She couldn't take it and signed a statement saying that she had blown the boutique, and she had not done it. She got fifteen years for something she had never done! It took four years for her case to come up again when another woman who had been arrested for something else confessed she had blown the boutique.

Another protester was arrested when she was seventeen and beaten by several policemen during interrogation. At one time she was left alone with a policeman who pushed her against the wall and pushed his body against hers saying, "I am going to fuck you. Yes, you would do me." She was terrified at the time, and more than ten years later she became noticeably tense when attempting to speak about it.

The "event" leading to the dirty protest, the warders' assault of February 7, 1980, must be considered within the broader context of militarization of nationalist districts, with its legacy of political practices in which institutional and sexual forms of domination are fused. In this sense it was neither an isolated nor a unique event. But it must also be located within the particular dynamic of the prison. Tension in Armagh jail had been rising since the withdrawal of political status in 1976. In 1978 a squad of male prison officers had assaulted remanded prisoners (those waiting trial) and locked them in their cells twenty-four hours a day for several weeks. This punishment was made more severe by very hot weather, leaving "a legacy of bitterness" among the women (Coogan 1980b, 114). The "no-work" protest, with the concomitant lack of exercise and low quality diet, had also produced a deterioration in the health of the women prisoners. Their situation was aggravated by petty restrictions in the use of the toilets and provision of sanitary napkins, which prisoners confirmed was causing growing irritation (see also Coogan 1980b; McCafferty 1981).

Death was adding its toll of emotional hardship. Many of the protesting prisoners were suffering the loss of significant others. Mary Doyle, who would later go on hunger strike, lost her mother in a loyalist bomb explosion. The mother of Maire Og Drumm was killed by loyalist paramilitaries while recovering from a cataract operation in the hospital. Other prisoners lost brothers, sisters, and fathers. Rosemary Simpson lost her husband and her mother. Of thirty-two protesting prisoners, ten lost close relatives; most were killed by loyalists or the British army. Emotions were suppressed, "bottled up inside." Brenda recalled:

> Moira Drumm's daughter was in the cell next to mine. She heard on the radio that her mother had been assassinated. She was screaming, and the screws came and opened the door and said, "Your mother is dead" and closed the door. That was it. The radio said all the details: how she was hiding behind the bed to protect herself . . . and this was an elderly woman. And to know that your mother died this way and that the prison officers had waited until she heard it on the radio to tell her. The killing happened at 9:30, and the screws didn't come until 10:30 to make sure that Moira heard it on the news. That is cruel. I don't know how she coped with that. It was hard to realize that her mother had died because she could not really see her. A lot of women lost family members. It was very hard—particularly if they don't allow you to bury them. It caused problems for Pauline when her father died. She couldn't really believe it. You suppressed so much; you keep it inside most of the time. When Bernie lost her father they came to tell her that she was not going to get parole. And she just started screaming, and the whole cell got wrecked, and she was put on a restrainer. She lost it! The

governor charged her with destroying prison property for wrecking the cell, and they punished her to solitary confinement. She was in no condition to be put in solitary confinement. That is inhuman.

Bernie remembered the death of her father as a very trying time. The prison authorities attempted to blackmail her by allowing parole to see her father for the last time only if she abandoned the protest. She did not come out of the protest, but the psychological pressure of this dilemma was for her horrific. For her the mourning process stopped. "Grieving," she said, "did not come until I was released." Yet to suppress the work of mourning does not imply that the emotions disappear; they remain there, more or less inchoate.

There was indeed a lot of pain, grief, and anger in the prisoner's tight community, and these emotions were amplified when the normal process of mourning was deterred. Prison regulations impeded the affected women from seeing the body of the lost one for the last time and sharing the pain of loss with family and friends. Mourning was not a possibility in prison. On the one hand, the hard conditions of the protest required the repression of devastating emotions in order to maintain collective morale. On the other, display of emotional weakness rendered a prisoner vulnerable to warders' harassment.

The dirty protest crystallized potentially destructive emotions by endowing them with materiality and political direction. The hostility of the guards increased, but so too did the total solidarity among the prisoners increase. The anger of the prisoners had a clear focus and could be utilized as a source of strength. Prisoners repeatedly affirmed that the anger kept them going. Living surrounded by piss, menstrual blood, and excrement was extremely difficult to endure, but at the same time the feces and the blood were a permanently deployed weapon against the prison officers. One of the Armagh women clearly articulated this double dimension of the protest: "The dirty protest was very difficult, but it was a way of dealing with the situation. It was focused; it gave us something to fight against. I found being in prison much more difficult after we finished it." The dirtiness of the prisoners was indeed a dreaded source of pollution for the warders. Notions of dirt and purity are crucial, as Mary Douglass (1966) pointed out, in organizing ideas of savagery and civilization, establishing social boundaries, and formulating cultural classifications. Dirt and cleanliness were, of course, crucial in inscribing class distinctions within a social and moral landscape. Within bourgeois culture, the bodies of the working class and urban industrial spaces they inhabit became the epitomy of dangerous and dirty animality (Stallybrass and White 1986). Dirt is polluting because it is "matter out of place" (Douglass 1966, 35); by appearing where it is not supposed to transgresses cultural classifications and boundaries. As "matter out of place" the dirty Armagh women challenged the categorical distinction between savagery and civilization threatening to blur the line altogether. Armagh officers wore masks, insulating suits, and rubber boots that shielded them from the polluting condition of the prisoners. Prisoners noted that the guards did not like to touch anything belonging to prisoners even though they used gloves. They felt defiled coming in contact with prisoners. "They didn't like to touch you during the dirty protest," said Brenda, "so that became your little weapon. You threw piss at them or tried to dirty them, you know?" As the protesting women looked increasingly dirty, the female guards tried to counteract defilement by making themselves up and doing their hair.

The Armagh prisoners' dirty protest represented, like that of Long Kesh prisoners, a new form of political violence, one that entailed the use of the body as a political weapon. I have argued elsewhere that as an instrument of power, the dirty protest constituted also the symbolic articulation of powerful feelings (hate, rage, and pain) that prisoners could not express in other forms without risking psychological and physical injury. As a weapon, the dirty protest was configured as a compromise formation in the Freudian sense of the term, that is, as the crystallization of a conflict between prisoners' desire of mimetic violence against the guards and the need for restraint to preserve some physical and psychological integrity (Aretxaga 1995, 131–32). At this level the men's and women's dirty protests were not very different from each other. After two years, the men's dirty protest reached a political impasse as a form of resistance by having exhausted itself in a circular violence between prisoners and guards. Such impasse was ultimately broken by the hunger strikes (Feldman 1991, 227). The Armagh protest, however, originated a set of meanings that challenged well-rooted gender models in the nationalist culture and sparked a movement of personal and social transformation. The image of the menstrual blood lying on the excreta-covered cells became a complex symbol of sexual difference that forced a public discussion about the politics of gender in Northern Ireland. For the women prisoners themselves, the menstrual blood provided the *matter* for reflecting on gender identity as nationalists, and as working-class women.

MENSTRUAL BLOOD

Inside the walls of Armagh prison filthiness was tainted with menstrual blood. Journalist Tim Coogan, visiting the jail at the time, wrote: "I was taken to inspect 'A' wing where the dirty protest is in full swing. This was sickening and appalling. Tissues, slops consisting of tea and urine, some faeces, and clots of blood—obviously the detritus of menstruation—lay in the corridor between the two rows of cells. . . . I found the smell in the girls' cells far worse than at Long Kesh, and several times found myself having to control feelings of nausea" (1980b, 215–16). What can make thirty dirty women more revolting than four hundred dirty men if not the exposure of menstrual blood? An element that cannot contribute much to the fetid odors of urine and feces, but can turn the stomach. What Coogan expresses with his body—it literally makes him sick—is the horror and repulsion triggered by the sight of *that* which constitutes a linguistic and visual taboo. A horror that he cannot articulate linguistically. Through his own body, Coogan also inscribes a crucial difference between men and women prisoners.

Such difference was also manifest for republican supporters. Eileen, a founder of the RAC, told me that her father was very ill during the dirty protest. One day when she and her sister went to visit him in the hospital, he asked about the women protesting in Armagh: "How are the girls?" They were surprised that, ill and suffering as he was, his first thought was for the female prisoners. Eileen related this incident to underscore how shocking the idea of young women, "girls," locked in a cell without washing even through their periods was for people. Marie, the mother of an Armagh woman, said without hesitation that the no-wash protest was more degrading for the women than for the men, simply because of the menstrual cycles. Ironically, it was this difference that Armagh women were trying to eradicate by joining the dirty protest.

Women did not belong to prison in popular consciousness, even though they had participated in armed operations and had been imprisoned in rising numbers since 1972. Most nationalists perceived women's presence in jail as a product of an idealistic youth and the freedom from family commitments. As one Armagh woman, Fiona, put it "people thought that women's involvement was just a passing thing; they didn't take it very seriously." Through the course of my fieldwork, some women former prisoners acknowledged that republican men still assumed that

137

after marriage a woman would abandon political activities that entailed risk of death or imprisonment. Although this frequently happens, it is by no means always the case. The image of male prisoners, however, did not have an age reference. Although the majority of male prisoners were young, it was not rare for them to be married and have children. In contrast to male prisoners, female prisoners were permanently thought of as girls, as many of the Armagh prisoners acknowledged. Their cultural space was in this sense liminal. Neither men, nor completely women, they were perceived at a general social level as gender neutral.

Women prisoners did not consider gender a significant element of differentiation either. Female members of the IRA had fought in the early 1970s to join this organization rather than its feminine counterpart Cumman na mBan. Thus, they had consciously rejected gender as a differential factor in political militancy. To prove that gender was irrelevant to military performance in a male organization de facto entailed downplaying women's difference and interiorizing men's standards. At the level of consciousness gender difference was, when the dirty protest began, completely accidental to its meaning. From the point of view of Armagh women their dirty protest was no different from that of the men; it was the same struggle undertaken by equal comrades for political recognition, and on this ground the women fought the opposition of the republican movement to their protest. The emphatic reassertion of the sameness of prisoners' identity, regardless of gender, must be understood as an attempt to counteract the overshadowing of women prisoners under the focus of attention given to male prisoners. Such eclipse was partly a consequence of the fact that women were not required to wear prison uniforms and thus were not subjected to the dramatic conditions that men prisoners were. From the start the lack of uniform asserted a gender difference that obscured their political visibility. At this level, the dirty protest was for Armagh women an attempt to erase that gender difference introduced by the penal institution and to thus reassert their political visibility. Yet the menstrual blood negated this negation by underlying sexual difference. In other words, menstruation objectified a difference that women had carefully obliterated in other dimensions of their political life thus revealing the ambiguities of identity and shifting the meaning of the protest. That is, while their political identity as members of the IRA entailed a cultural desexualization and the dirty protest entailed a personal defeminization, at a deeper level the exposure of menstrual blood subverted this process by radically transforming the asexual bodies of girls into the sexualized bodies of women. In so doing the menstrual blood became a symbol through which gender identity was reflected, pushing to the surface what had been otherwise erased.

In Irish Catholic culture sexuality and the body are taboo subjects. This taboo is particularly strong regarding menstruation. As in most cultures around the world, in Ireland menstrual blood is considered impure and the bodies of menstruating women, dirty. Traces of menstrual blood, like pads or tampons, are hidden and quickly thrown out, especially if there are men in the household. There is a feeling of psychological dirtiness, embarrassment, and vulnerability at the exposure of menstrual blood and the inability to erase it or wash it away. Such taboo excludes women's experience from language and has rendered the meaning of Armagh dirty protest invisible.

The cultural and personal meanings of menstruation in the carceral context are explored in a very short story, "A Curse," written by a Northern Ireland writer, Brenda Murphy (1989). The story is about an arrested young woman who gets her period between interrogation shifts: "She sat up and looked about her. The yellow dimpled walls covered in graffiti stared back. She coughed and felt the ooze between her legs, the familiar ooze, the heat, the wetness. Her mother called it 'the curse.' A curse it was for her right then" (226). Menstruation as an elemental sign of womanhood also marks women's social vulnerability. It is at the level of representation a metonymy linking sex and motherhood and a sign of the dangerously uncontrolled nature of women's flesh in Catholic ideology from which only the mother of god escaped (Warner 1983). In the context of arrest it is a sabotage of the body. The arrested woman asks to talk to a policewoman. The male warder refuses. She is forced to speak to him: " 'I've taken my period,' she said simply. 'I need some sanitary towels and a wash.' He looked at her with disgust. 'Have you no shame? I've been married twenty years and my wife wouldn't mention things like that.' What is the color of shame? All she could see was red as it trickled down her leg" (Murphy 1989, 226–27). Two hours later she is taken to the washing room. The "shameful" feeling of uncleanness is mirrored in the sordid dirtiness of the bathrooms: "They walked down a corridor and a door was opened to reveal a toilet, wash basin and urinal. The stench was overwhelming. The girl went in. The toilet was blocked. She tried to flush it but it didn't work. She put on the sanitary towel and went to the basin. No soap, no towel, no hot water. She splashed her face with water, drying it on the bottom of her sweater" (227). In contrast to its dark sordidness stands the accusing artificial brightness of the interrogation room: "She stepped past the policewoman, who walked her upstairs to the interview room. It was exactly as she remembered it. Bright, electric, windowless" (227).

That Brenda Murphy, herself a republican former prisoner who participated in the dirty protest, chose the theme of menstruation to talk about the experience of arrest in her story is in itself significant. In doing so she breaks a taboo of silence that made women's personal and political experience invisible. The narrated arrest is her own, and for her the story can also be read as a commentary on the Armagh dirty protest. Brenda, who spoke candidly about the experience of the protest, acknowledged, however, the difficulty of talking or writing about it:

> In Ireland you don't speak about your period. You don't even mention the word. My mother hardly ever mentioned it to us and we were a family of eight girls and one boy. You get your period, but you just don't talk about it. It's a taboo. It can provoke great emotional stress especially during interrogation or in jail because it is used as a psychological weapon against you. It was very difficult at first among ourselves during the dirty protest. When you had your period you just tried to turn away. You were allowed sanitary towels but you were not allowed to dispose them. When the drinking water came in we would try to keep ourselves clean with it. I would stand by the window while my cellmate tried to wash herself the best she could. The window was boarded up but I would stand there until she had finished, and she did the same for me. But it was embarrassing at the same time. No wonder women don't want to talk about it. You are talking about sanitary towels wrapped in the cell with you and talking about it feels degrading. Visitors wouldn't mention it. Cardinal O'Daly and O'Fiaich visited the jail once and came into the cells with two women there and shit on the walls, piss on the floor and sanitary towels on the corner. They must have been gagging, and they were there sitting with a cup of tea that prison officers had provided them. They were there with a cup and saucer and the stench . . . and we were sitting there pretending we were just having a nice cup of tea with the local bishops! We got one visit a month and your mother or father, brother or sisters would come up and you tried to stand back from them. You were stinking, and you were aware of it. You tended to move very little. And your mother is trying to show how

much she loves you by pretending you don't smell at all. And you would
have preferred that she didn't do that, but they all pretended that you
didn't smell. We went through this farce for nine months!

One of the "no-wash" protesters publicly mentioned the isolation derived from the erasure of women's experience at a rally following her release: "I do get the impression that people outside don't fully realized
that there are actually women in Armagh. They don't understand what
the women are going through both physically and psychologically. You
go through a lot with your menstrual cycle." And she insisted: "There
should be a lot more publicity for the girls in Armagh, a lot more
protests. People are working for us, and we thank them from the heart,
but not as hard as they know they can, *maybe because they don't understand
how hard it is for us* [emphasis added]."[10] This was one of the rare occasions in which a suspicion of the incomprehensibility of their behavior
was openly admitted by a prisoner and publicly linked to a feeling of isolation. The shocking character of the imagery that the words of this released prisoner evoked was brought to my attention by Mary, a member
of the RAC:

> I remember one rally in which a girl released from Armagh spoke
> about what it was for them during their periods. It was very hard for her
> to talk about menstruation, to say that even during that time they could
> not get a change of clothes, could not get washed. And some people,
> including republican men, were saying, How can she talk about that?
> They did not want to hear that women were being mistreated in Ar-
> magh jail during their menstruation. And so, the republican movement
> did not talk about it. They only talked about the men, but they did not
> want to hear about girls. Some people just could not cope with that.

The nationalist community could neither understand nor cope with
women's suffering. This was not a mother's suffering, which ultimately
roused the emotions of nationalist people in support of the prisoners.
Nor was this the suffering of young men prisoners whose image, naked
and beaten, resembled that of Jesus Christ. Unintentionally, the women
prisoners in Armagh brought to the fore a different kind of suffering,
one systematically obscured in social life and cultural constructions and
devalued in Catholic religion and nationalist ideologies: women's suffering of which menstruation (the curse) is a sign and a symbol.

In her essay on abjection Julia Kristeva divides polluting objects into
two types: excremental and menstrual. "Excrement and its equivalents

(decay, infection, disease, corpse, etc.) stand from the danger to identity that comes from without: the ego threatened by the non-ego, society threaten by its outside, life by death. Menstrual blood, on the contrary, stands for the danger issuing from within identity (social or sexual); it threatens the relationship between the sexes within a social aggregate and, through internalization, the identity of each sex in the face of sexual difference." (1982, 71). It is precisely this threat to the boundaries and cultural construction of gender difference that provokes silence and horrified reactions among men, what Mary enunciates as an impossibility to cope.

Armagh's dirty protest encapsulated the negation of dominant models of femininity embedded in the idealized Catholic mother and elaborated in nationalist discourse around the image of Mother-Ireland. This model provokes high ambivalence in many nationalist women for whom motherhood is at once a source of comfort and support and a restrictive social role.[11] At the same time the women's dirty protest also represented a rejection of male violence fused, as noted below, with political dominance in colonial discourse and practice. In the prison context the visibility of menstrual blood can be read as a curse redirected from the bodies of women to the male "body politic" of colonialism.[12]

As symbol and weapon the dirty protest involved enormous suffering. The young women in Armagh conceptualized their physical and psychological pain within the parameters of a religious ethic of salvation acting in the political arena. Thus, at the level of consciousness they understood their pain as requisite to saving Ireland from colonization and reestablishing a just and equal society in a reunited Irish land. This ethic of salvation acted as an interpretive language for pain, which would otherwise be meaningless. Yet even if a religious-political frame could provide meaning to the women prisoners pain, it could not express it. Hidden by profound cultural taboos and submerged by the emotional economy of the prison, the experience of Armagh women eluded language. For Elaine Scarry (1985), inexpressibility characterizes pain, which must be objectified to be comprehended. Pain does not, however, operate in the same way for both women and men. In Armagh jail the prisoners' pain became objectified in the menstrual blood, a complex symbol that inscribed their suffering inside the contours of what Spivak has called "the space of what can only happen to a woman" (1988, 184). As this space had been actively silenced in the political culture of Northern Ireland, tensions were bound to arise on the different shades of the political horizon.

THE POWER OF TRANSGRESSION

The feminist movement in Ireland grew bitterly divided as the dirty protest continued.[13] Mainstream feminists were sharply critical of the male-dominated republican movement whose use of violence, they argued, divided women. At the head of these feminists was the Northern Ireland Women's Rights Movement (NIWRM), a broadly defined organization founded in 1975 and hostile to nationalism in general and republicanism in particular. Although the NIWRM had been actively breaking the silence on women's suffering, it had also actively criticized the republican movement for augmenting women's pain. NIWRM was the most qualified to understand the suffering of Armagh women, but it perceived the prisoners as followers of a male movement, the policies of which ultimately worked against women. Thus the NIWRM refused any support to Armagh prisoners on the grounds that they were aping their male comrades. Other women's groups such as the Socialist Women's Group and the Belfast Women's Collective quite literally agonized over the meaning and degree of support to the prisoners. The republican movement, however, was not less hostile to feminism, which its leaders easily dismissed as being pro-British. Preoccupied with the large number of male prisoners, republicans had largely ignored the existence of women in jail, saw them at best as an appendix to the men's protest. Was the Armagh women's protest a mimetic enactment? Yes and no. The women prisoners deny emphatically that they simply followed the men's lead, and indeed the circumstances that led women into the dirty protest differed from those of the men prisoners. Yet the Armagh women would not have embarked on such a protest had they not had the example of their male comrades. And in part they joined the dirty protest to underline their equal position as fighting political prisoners. Thus it is possible to argue a mimetic undercurrent instilling the Armagh protest, but one that had important political implications. Drucilla Cornell has argued that mimesis constitutes not a simple repetition but a reappropriation entailing a process of cultural refiguration (1991, 182; see also Taussig 1993). It is in this light that I interpret the Armagh protest.

When Armagh women demanded to be full militants of the IRA instead of members of Cuman na mBan—the IRA women's branch—they were criticizing a genderized system that held them as political subsidiaries. This critique already modified the terms of the system. Similarly, by mimetically reappropriating the dirty protest, the Armagh

143

women at first negated gender difference and stated that their struggle was the same as that of the men. Yet this attempt to transcend a gender-ized context by negating the feminine was negated in turn by the objec-tification of sexual difference that the menstrual blood represented. Thus the mimetic appropriation of the dirty protest entailed a process of rewriting a (hi)story of resistance, a rewriting that specified the femi-nine in its most transgressive form. It entailed a refiguration of the fem-inine inasmuch as it was affirmed not as a shared identity, as had been posited by mainstream feminism, but as existentially inseparable from class, ethnic, and political positions.

The rising tensions among feminist and republican organizations ex-ploded publicly when Nell McCafferty, a journalist from Derry city, wrote in the pages of the main Irish newspaper *The Irish Times*: "There is men-strual blood in the walls of Armagh prison in Northern Ireland."[14] Women's physiology acquired a new political meaning. McCafferty shouted aloud what a few republican feminists had been arguing for more than a year and what republicans and non-nationalist feminists had been refusing to hear: women's suffering was inextricably linked, al-though not reduced to, colonial oppression in Northern Ireland. Such a link was encapsulated in the menstrual blood as a symbol of an exis-tence, of a being-in-the-world that could not be represented by domi-nant feminist and nationalist discourses, even less by the discourse of the LAW. The menstrual blood stood as a symbol of that reality excluded from language. In so doing it acted as a catalyst of cultural change, a ve-hicle of reflection and discussion about the meanings of gender differ-ence in Northern Ireland. The most public manifestation of such—often bitter—debate was Nell McCafferty's article. As time went on Armagh prisoners began to inscribe their difference in language, translating the dirt and menstrual blood into a critique of a unitary feminist subject that failed to represent them. In a letter published in *The Irish Times* Armagh prisoners answered the Northern Ireland Women's Rights Movement, which had contended that the predicament of the prisoners did not con-cern feminists, with a demand for redefinition of feminism:

> It is our belief that not only is our plight a feminist issue, but a very fun-
> damental social and human issue. It is a feminist issue in so far as we
> are women, and the network of this jail is completely geared to male
> domination. The governor, the assistant governor, and the doctor are
> all males. We are subject to physical and mental abuse from male
> guards who patrol our wing daily, continually peeping into our cells. . . .

14. Falls Road. On the back, the building of the women's center the day after it was blasted by the IRA when attacking a British army patrol.

If this is not a feminist issue then we feel that the word feminist needs to be redefined.[15]

By the end of 1980, a policy document on women was for the first time adopted by Sinn Fein. Two years later, in 1982, a Women's Center was opened for the first time in the Falls Road amid discomfort and the protest of many nationalist men. Women flowed in with a hitherto muted knowledge. As one of the founders recalled: "There were battered women, incest, rape, appalling poverty. We had been too busy with the war and didn't realized until the Women's Center that all those problems were there too." Another kind of shit had surfaced. As it gained social visibility, the stinking reality of male violence against women deconstructed both Catholic models of gender and the nationalist heroic epic. In 1988 the Women's Center was accidentally destroyed during a failed IRA attack on the British army. The rocket left the army patrol unharmed and the Women's Center completely shattered. The center reopened a few months later on new premises farther up the road, not far from its former location. But for a while its ruins stood on Falls Road as an icon of the fractured and volatile nature of gender politics in Northern Ireland. The unfolding of the debate about the politics of gender among republicans and feminists is the issue I discuss next.

145

CHAPTER 7

En-Gendering a Nation

THE DEBATE ABOUT the politics of feminism and the gender politics of nationalism was greatly intensified by the dirty protest of Armagh. But some women within the republican movement had already started timidly to raise their voices, particularly during the late 1970s. Throughout the first half of the 1970s, the widely read republican weekly, *Republican News*, published occasional letters and articles on women's role in the nationalist struggle. These were little more than evocations of a wellknown list of nationalist heroines such as Countess Markievicz and Maud Gone (prominent feminist-nationalists such as Hanna Sheehy-Skeffington were mostly ignored) as role models for nationalist women. These few articles did, however, constitute an early attempt to recognize women's political presence in its own right. The reports on women's activities often shared the space of the paper with an old nationalist rhetoric in which suffering motherhood figured prominently as national allegory. This contraposition was not particularly awkward within the context of revolutionary nationalism in Ireland, which throughout its history had cultivated a model of womanhood that was militantly nationalist yet socially traditional (Ward 1983).

Nationalist women had not, of course, always followed this ideal. The most salient heroines of the period of Irish liberation from 1900 to 1920 had also been outspoken suffragists and labor organizers. But these early republican feminists were a definite minority and often had to wrestle with conflicting loyalties and political contradictions permeating the political struggles in which they took part (Ward 1983). The socially liberating current that these women represented within Irish nationalism was progressively suffocated during the decade that followed the signing of the treaty that granted home rule for Ireland in 1921. The treaty came at a heavy price: the trading of the Republic for a free state dependent on the British crown and the partition of the island. The agreement was unanimously rejected by republican women as well as socially radical tendencies within the republican movement. The defeat of the antitreaty side in the civil war that followed also ensured the elimination of socially progressive forces in Irish politics. When finally attained, the Republic did not offer a guaranty of civil rights to women. The Consti-

146

tution of 1937 that declared Ireland an independent republic also appealed to a national culture rooted in a rural Irish tradition. The constitution, deeply embedded in Catholic social doctrine, confined women to the role of mothers and enabled legislation curtailing the rights of working women. While various women's organizations rallied against this massive attack on women's rights, which made Irish women de facto second-class citizens, the organization of republican women, Cumman na mBann, dominated by its most conservative elements, remained silent (Ward 1983, 243–45).

The patriarchal ruralism through which Ireland was imagined in the Constitution of 1937 was the result of social processes that culminated in the cultural hegemony of Catholicism and the national leadership of the tenant-farmer class. These processes need to be contextualized within the history of political rhetoric that shaped Irish identity along shifting gender categories in colonial and postcolonial nationalist discourses. The most influential texts in the colonial construction of Irish identity were the studies on Celtic culture initiated by Ernst Renan and followed by Matthew Arnold. Drawing on the emerging sciences of philology, ethnology, and anthropology, as well as on the positivist discourse on sexuality, these intellectuals produced a discursive formation that Curtis (1968) has called *celticism*. Following a cue from Said (1978), Cairns and Richards (1988) have argued that celticism allowed England a position of superiority within a whole range of possible relationships with Ireland without ever losing the upper hand (Cairns and Richards 1988, 48).

In his influential essay *The Poetry of the Celtic Races* (1970[1896]) Renan defined the Celtic race along the lines of Victorian femininity—as sensitive, poetic, emotional, and spiritual—underlying his definition by directly invoking gender categories: "If it be permitted us to assign sex to nations as to individuals we should have to say without hesitance that the Celtic race ... is an essentially feminine race" (cited in Cairns and Richards 1988, 46). The feminine characteristic of the Celts did not imply for Renan, a Celt himself, a position of subsidiarity but one of complementariety. The superior spiritual qualities of the Celts made them an ideal complement to the rational, aggressive, warrior (that is masculine) character of the Teutons, of which the Anglo-Saxons formed a part. If Renan endowed the Celts, and therefore the Irish, with morally superior feminine qualities, this was, however, a double-edged argument given the contradictory and ambivalent character of Victorian notions of femininity.

147

The English intellectual Matthew Arnold, drawing on Renan's studies and the same gender discourse, produced an Irish identity characterized by political incapacity and emotional instability: "No doubt the sensibility of the Celtic nature, its nervous exaltation, have something feminine in them, and the Celt is particularly disposed to feel the spell of the feminine idiosyncrasy; he has an affinity to it" (cited in Cairns and Richards 1988, 48). This feminine affinity made the Irish—like women—simply incapable of government, a task for which the rational English with their masculine nature were perfectly suited. The irrationality of the Irish legitimized English political dominance under the guise of natural law, and often provided a convenient justification for the repression of peasant and nationalist rebellions in Ireland.[1] The strategic operations of gender and sexual categories in British colonial discourse have been amply discussed in the case of India (Chatterjee 1989, 1993; Mani 1990; Nandy 1980, 1983; Suleri 1992a), as well as other colonies (Comaroff and Comaroff 1991, 98–108; Jayawardena 1986). The emergence of an anticolonial nationalist discourse rested in no small measure on the negation of colonial cultural stereotypes. Yet such negation, as Chatterjee has pointed out, has the problem of locking the identity of the nation within the confines of the colonizers' imagination. In Ireland, Arnold's celticism was influential through the writers of the turn-of-the-century Irish renaissance in formulating an Irish identity rooted in a putative precolonial tradition. For the consciously nationalist writers of the revival, Arnold's feminization of the Irish was problematic inasmuch as it rendered Irish men politically impotent. Nationalist writers counteracted this subservient position by emphasizing a heroic tradition of Gaelic warriors and locating feminine traits of character in the imported follies of urban life. The extent to which national identity was tied to sexual identity becomes clear in this passage from Padraic Pearse: "A new education system in Ireland has to do more than restore a national culture. *It has to restore manhood to a race that has been deprived of it.* For this it must bring Ireland back to its Sagas" (Pearse 1916 in Deane 1991[2], 293). For Pearse the liberation of Ireland went far beyond physical force and far deeper than an independent political system. The Irish nation required a transformation of souls in the direction of masculinity. Once the discourse of dispossession was articulated in the language of castration, the political potency necessary to liberate Ireland required for Pearse a reversal of the process of emasculation that could restore national manhood. The production of mytho-poetics of Irish heroism as national representations of Irish identity was for Pearse a crucial task of the nationalist movement.

In addition to the heroic warriors of the sagas, the figure of the peasant and the romanticization of rural life became the embodiment of Irish identity and women became the highly idealized allegory of the nation. This shift of rhetoric allowed a powerful move. Ireland cast as a helpless woman—sometimes a young and beautiful maiden, sometimes a sorrowful mother—allowed the Irish the role of manly rescuers who would look at her sometimes with filial love like Padraic Pearse and sometimes with unabashed, and somewhat outdated, romantic love as represented by Joseph Plunkett:

> And we two lovers, long but one in mind
> and soul, are made only one flesh at length;
> praise god if this my blood fulfills the doom
> when you, dark rose, shall redden into bloom. (1916)

Yeats fused both images magnificently in his play *Cathleen Ni Houlihan* (1953) in which an old woman is transformed into a beautiful maiden after the men of the country go to fight for her. Such romantic imagery of old Ireland was very powerful and important in lending meaning to the failed rebellion of 1916. Increasingly, the romanticization of old Ireland was substituted by the romanticization of rural life, an imagery better suited to the political dominance of the Irish farmers' class. The defeat of the antitreaty faction during the civil war signified the triumph of pragmatic nationalism as represented by the conservatism of the farmers' class and the imposition of Catholic social policies fundamentally restrictive in matters of gender and sexuality. The dominant model of the nation emerging with the free state was patriarchal, rural, protectionist, and hostile to urban industrialism and foreign influence (Brown 1985). The model of Irish woman contained in this picture was an overt negation of modernity and unambiguously traditional.[2] Thus, the gender politics of Irish nationalism diverged substantially from those of other postcolonial nationalisms. The Indian case is a good example.

Scholars of Indian nationalism have noted that the model of woman to emerge within this movement was related to the function of women in colonialist discourse. The British critics, in asserting the barbaric character of native traditions, had persistently resorted to the oppression of women as a sign of cultural incivility (Chatterjee 1993, 115). The discussions about "the question of women" within Indian nationalism became in this way not so much debates about the position of women but about the status of native tradition vis-à-vis colonial power. This tradition, however, had already been overdetermined by the misrecognitions of colonialist's critics (Mani 1990). The nationalist response to the colonialist view of tradition included a particular model of national woman that "was not a dismissal of modernity but an attempt to make modernity consistent with the nationalist project" (Chatterjee 1993, 121). The "new woman" of Indian nationalism was educated and professionally competent—that is, modern—while she simultaneously upheld the standards of decorum prescribed by national tradition. This model, as Chatterjee has noted, suited the urban nationalist middle class that was concerned in India with the establishment of a differential national tradition that could coexist with the modernization of the country.

In Ireland the question of tradition was formulated in different terms. It was not the oppression of women that emerged as the salient sign of the barbarism of the Irish; rather, their feminine emotional instability rendered them politically impotent. The whole Irish culture was feminized in a way that made Irish men suspect of holding any control, whether social or sexual. The response of Irish nationalism was a fundamental negation of the colonialist discourse by, on the one hand, projecting the social malaise that colonialists associated with femininity into the domain of urban modernism and ejecting such domain outside the bounds of the Irish nation. On the other hand, Irish nationalists developed a discourse of nationality in which the masculinity of the people was underwritten by the idealization of traditional motherhood within the symbolic terrain of nationalist culture: the rural home. The national project, which materialized after 1921, was predicated on a rejection of modernity, not on its national adaptation; a return to an essentialized rural and mythical tradition, not on its modern reformulation. In so doing Irish nationalism, perhaps more than others, remained trapped within the framework of colonialist false essentialisms. The consequences were enormous for women who were erased from the professional and intellectual life of the country.

The conservative gender politics of the Irish nation made second-wave feminism in Ireland particularly suspicious of republican nationalism, which had historically demonstrated a fundamental disregard for the interests of women. This was also the case in the North, where the structures of inequality predicated on Protestant superiority had not impeded a substantial complicity between unionist and nationalist organizations in perpetuating the subordination of women. The question is: How did a new generation of republican women who became politically involved during the upheaval of the 1970s position themselves in this context? The varied and often conflicted voices of women were most clearly articulated in the pages of the weekly *Republican News*.

DEBATING GENDER, REIMAGINING THE NATION

The model of gender relations proposed from the republican ranks of the Provisional IRA in the first half of 1970s was tremendously conservative. If the male ideal was the republican martyr, then the female ideal was the devoted republican wife and mother.[3] The common analogies between country and family, mother and nation, were underpinned by the same strict Catholic moral discourse that permeated state politics in the South. This discourse rejected the use of contraception on the grounds that it "undermine[d] the dignity of women and the happiness of married life" and, most important, subverted "the values of the Irish people."[4] The dominant view of the role of women as faithful wives and mothers did not pass uncontested, however timidly, by republican women. Una O'Neill reminded republicans in 1973 that Irish women were much more than a holy ideal and expressed anger at the paternalist attitude "of some of our lordly menfolks." She recounted the participation of Irish women in politics and on the battlefield in an effort to claim for women an equal position with men in the fight for Ireland. Yet O'Neill demarcated herself from the feminist movement by asserting that women's liberation can only come from the struggle against British imperialism: "We have many valiant women and girls in our community now. They can be seen in many protest marches against injustice and British violence. This, to me, is the real Women's Lib."[5]

Una O'Neill's article is an early example of the difficult ideological and political position held by the few feminist-oriented republican women who were caught between a feminist movement fed up with Irish nationalism and a patriarchal republican movement that relegated women to the role of mothers, wives, and auxiliaries. The implications of this fragile but threatening political position appeared more clearly as the end of the 1970s approached, in conjunction with the republican prisoners' struggle and the rise of the feminist movement in Ireland. In the first half of the decade, voices like that of Una O'Neill were isolated in the republican movement.

The construction of women as allegory of the nation and the long establishment of sexuality as a battleground of political relations imposed serious constraints on the private life of individual women during those years of the early 1970s. Not only was sexual harassment of nationalist women frequently used by the British military to assert their dominant position in the Catholic community as a whole, but also after 1970 republicans punished women who dared to date British soldiers and kept tight surveillance on the sexual behavior of prisoners' wives. Women who transgressed the rigid lines of demarcation drawn by republicans between the nationalist community and state forces were treated as collaborators and shamed publicly by tarring and feathering or by shaving off all hair. Although silenced in republican narratives, this early nationalist violence against women has left a trace in the poetry and fiction of Northern Ireland. Jennifer Johnston narrates such an occurrence in her novel *Shadows On Our Skin* (1978), and Seamus Heaney (1975) ponders it in his poem "Punishment":

I can feel the tug
of the halter at the nape
of her neck, the wind
on her naked front.
It blows her nipples
to amber beads,
it shakes the frail rigging
of her ribs.

I can see her drowned
body in the bog,
the weighing stone,
the floating rods and boughs.

Under which at first
she was a barked sapling
that is dug up
oak-bone, brain-firkin:

her shaved head
like a stubble of black corn,
her blindfold a soiled bandage, her noose a ring

to store
the memories of love.
Little adulteress,
before they punished you

you were flaxen-haired,
undernourished, and your
tar-black face was beautiful.
My poor scapegoat,

I almost love you
but would have cast, I know,
the stones of silence.
I am the artful voyeur

of your brain's exposed
and darken combs,
your muscles' webbing
and all your numbered bones:

I who have stood dumb
when your betraying sisters,
cauled in tar,
wept by the railings,

who would connive
in civilized outrage
yet understand the exact
and tribal, intimate revenge.

I do not see tribal revenge in this violence, however, but the attempt to hold social control through the control of women's bodies; an attempt to dispel political ambiguity—the crossing of newly established, not fully recognized, political boundaries—through the tight control of women's sexuality. Women's sexuality becomes then a material and symbolic arena of political demarcation, and a political battleground itself. Republican women do not speak about this violence. They say that it serves to reinforce the stereotype of the Irish brute. For them it belongs to the past, to a particular moment when social structures were upturned and things were happening all too quickly. They do admit, however, the pressures to conform with sexual codes of behavior for married women whose husbands were in jail in those early days.

Foucault's thesis about sexuality is particularly relevant to understanding republican sexual politics. For him sexuality appears "as an especially dense transfer point for relations of power." "Sexuality," he says, "is not the most intractable element in power relations, but rather one of those endowed with the greatest instrumentality: useful for the greatest number of maneuvers and capable of serving as a point of support, as a linchpin, for the most varied strategies" (1978, 103). If discourses of sexuality had been deployed to articulate the violence of Anglo-Irish colonial relations, then it is not so surprising that sexual practices would become a strategic terrain wherein the fight for political hegemony between republicans and British forces was waged. Republicans' legitimacy rested on an unambiguous opposition of the nationalist community to the British army. In this sense, the familial metaphorics and the gender imagery of Mother-Ireland were instrumental in framing republican politics within a polarized social space. The flow of uncontrolled female sexuality manifested in dating British soldiers or the potential sexual affairs of prisoners' wives challenged both the fixed boundaries of British-Irish opposition and the pure, transcendental image of the nation represented by the virginal maiden and asexual mother. As symbols of the Irish nation, individual women were held responsible for maintaining its fiction. Yet, as individuals rarely conform to ideals, women represented also a major source of ambiguity that permanently threatened to disrupt the rigid construction of republican nationality. To eliminate such ambiguity was particularly important in the early 1970s because republicans were still struggling to establish moral and political legitimacy in Catholic communities. Before 1970, marriages between British soldiers and Northern Irish Catholic women were not unusual, and in 1969 flirting and dates between British soldiers and local young women in Belfast and Derry were commonplace. Sexual complicity signaled a form of political ambiguity that republicans were trying to erase, and which became intolerable after 1970.

Underpinned by Catholic imagery and misogynist perceptions of women, the gendered discourse of nationality furnished by republicanism reinforced a traditional ambivalence toward women. The idealized mother necessarily entailed the threatening whore (Loftus 1982). Women were far from passively accommodating of republican demands, as I showed in chapter 2, but not until the late 1970s did a public debate about women and gender relations take place in the republican movement.

In February 1978 the article "The Slaves of Slaves" criticized the complacency of the republican movement with the low participation of women in the struggle. The author asserted that the absence of women was a political problem and emphasized the urgent need to incorporate women in the movement: "Unless we are intending to build a dissatisfied section of people into Eire Nua [New Ireland] Sinn Fein must begin to find answers [to the obstacles for women's participation]. Remember that when we say victory to the PROVOS or the PEOPLE, half of them are women."[6] Publication of this article precipitated an intense debate about the role of women in Ireland, which was also a debate about the kind of nation republicans were imagining.[7] The discussion unfolded in a social context characterized by the rising political visibility of women. Women were demonstrating in favor of prisoners, female republican prisoners were on work strike, feminism was intensifying its voice in Ireland, and only two years earlier hundreds of women led by "Peace People" walked the streets of Belfast demanding peace. It was becoming clear that if women were ignored, silence would become embarrassingly conspicuous and politically dangerous.

The bulk of the debate among republicans on the question of women was held publicly in the Letters to the Editor of *Republican News*. In February 1978 Deirdre O'Neill urged the republican movement to consider the oppression of women seriously rather than relegating it to the struggle for independence, "for if women continue to be oppressed how can men ever be free?"[8] This position represented an important shift from that of Una O'Neill, who had portrayed nationalist women as already liberated. In June 1978 an article signed with the pseudonym Cen Chaoi advocated the drafting of a policy on women's rights. Criticizing the "paternalistic condescension" and neglect by the republican leadership of the social situation of women, the author expressed regret that the major policy document about the future Ireland, Eire Nua, did not even mention women: "We cannot wait any longer for an examination of women's role in society, there must be a coming together of women and true revolutionaries to work out the policy. We will not see our daughters who have fought as soldiers left behind when freedom is won, as often happens in many freedom struggles." In a familiar move, the author also attacked the "Women's movement," which "in this country offers no solution [to women's problems]," for being dominated by middle-class intellectuals, who are "too often British-oriented, so there is little the working-class republicans can relate to. This image of Irish Women Liberation has done more to harm women's equality than advance it and there is now the need for a true movement . . . and the lead must come from the revolutionary party, Sinn Fein."[9] The position taken by Cen Chaoi in relation to women's issues was related to an ongoing struggle for political legitimation at a more general level. The increased vocalism of Sinn Fein women on gender problems was a result of the conjunction of two relatively separate processes: on the one hand, the ongoing experience of political involvement for "ordinary" women had developed in them a new political consciousness; and, on the other, the rise of feminism in Ireland demanded a change in gender relations with increasing force by the late 1970s.

The feminist movement in Ireland, though diverse in its political orientations, was quite unanimous in its contempt for republicanism, which they perceived as a militaristic and male-dominated ideology and movement that had given rise in the South to a patriarchal, conservative government. Republican women in Northern Ireland needed to legitimize their political position vis-à-vis the feminist movement if they were to participate in the debate. They chose to do so by addressing the patriarchal ideology inside their movement while identifying the feminist movement as a whole in terms of class and British orientation. The working-class position of Northern republicans was an important dimension of women's political subjectivity, as I have discussed in the preceding chapters. This position marked a clear difference from the earlier nationalist-suffragist heroines, which Northern republicans so often invoked. The importance of class position interlocked with engrained ethnic discrimination in configuring the subjectivity of Northern republican women was misrecognized by feminists north and south of the Irish border as false consciousness—that is, the inability of nationalist women to see what their real interests as women were. However deep this misrecognition went, it must be admitted that the "middle class" and "Britishness," imputed sweepingly by republicans to the feminist movement as a whole, were also stereotypes that, as Margaret Ward has noted, all too often "conveniently ignored the root causes of women's oppression" (Ward 1983, 255). Women like Cen Chaoi hoped to open a political space for the interests of nationalist women, but the location of their critiques solely within Sinn Fein and the consequent demarcation from a stereotyped feminist movement ran the danger of political paralysis, a threat clearly perceived by some republican feminists outside the ranks of Sinn Fein.

Cen Chaoi's article was answered two weeks later by a newly formed feminist group called Women Against Imperialism (WAI), which argued against the monolithic characterization of the feminist movement as middle class and pro-British. While reminding Sinn Fein about the heterogeneity of the feminist movement, they defined themselves as an "anti-imperialist group, opposed to the British presence in Ireland and supporting the liberation struggle." They also affirmed that their base was "in the working-class areas of West Belfast." WAI firmly disagreed with the idea of Sinn Fein leading the banner to women's liberation: "the attitudes of Sinn Fein will not change overnight, and only constant pressure exerted by women themselves on their own behalf will effect change. An autonomous women's movement is a necessary element in safeguarding the advances made by women in the struggle for total liberation."[10] In contrast to the women in Sinn Fein, who raised their voices against the patriarchalism of the party, Women Against Imperialism located itself within the contours of both republicanism and feminism, but outside the constraints of existing organizations. In this way they were attempting to carve a space for an anticolonial feminism that could bridge the existing opposition between these movements. Such a project meant that not only did the republican movement have to incorporate feminist goals into the war of liberation, but also the feminist movement had to recognize the specific conditions of oppression that colonialism had created for women.

WAI was born in 1978 as a result of the tensions created in feminist groups such as the Belfast Women's Collective, a splinter of the Northern Ireland Women's Rights Movement, by the campaign of the Relatives Action Committees in favor of political prisoners. Disagreement over the degree of support given to the political campaign of the RAC split the Belfast Women's Collective into two groups. One formed the Socialist Women's Group, and the other formed WAI, which was composed of women from People's Democracy, the RAC, and the Irish Republican Socialist party (IRSP), a small leftist republican party. Large as it may sound, the core membership was only about twelve members, but this was not unusual for feminist organizations of that time in a place like Belfast. The organization operated from Catholic West Belfast, where most of its members lived. The location was in itself a political statement. Until then the existing feminist groups were located in the center of town: a neutral area. WAI was the first autonomous feminist group to operate in a working-class nationalist community and to support the republican struggle for a united Ireland. Although its members belonged to different republican persuasions, WAI did not align itself with any political party.[11]

In its two years of history, WAI played an important role in publicizing the protest of the Armagh women and bringing these women toward center stage of the political campaign. They also campaigned against restrictive republican policies that, for example, impeded women's access to republican social clubs. In a sense the political competition that WAI represented for Sinn Fein in the arena of women's rights was the outside challenge that Sinn Fein feminists needed to make their voices heard within their organization. The discussion in Sinn Fein about women's rights continued during 1979 and intensified during 1980, the year of the dirty protest in Armagh jail.

One thorny issue in the acrimonious exchanges between republican and nonrepublican feminist women was violence. Feminists, accusing republicans of contributing to the establishment of an "armed patriarchy" with their support of armed struggle were particularly critical of the punishment of women carried out on certain occasions by the republican movement. Republican women regarded the protests made by feminist groups against punishments of women as general attacks on republicanism and on the role of the IRA as an informal policing force within nationalist communities. Republican women often reacted defensively, in turn accusing their critics of being pro-British and ignoring the sexualized violence of state forces against nationalist women.

An example of the bitterness surrounding women's discussions of violence was the case of Dolours McGuigan. McGuigan was shot in Derry in the arms and legs as punishment for handing a gun belonging to the Irish National Liberation Army (INLA) to local, petty delinquent youths.[12] Some days later Women's Aid, a feminist group providing advice and refuge for battered women, staged a protest against the punishment. An argument ensued. Sinn Fein member Martha McClelland claimed in *Republican News* that "the protest was decidedly pro-Brit in intent" and that it was helping the forces of oppression.[13] WAI agreed with McClelland's accusation, but they were also aware that McClelland's argument reinforced the general stereotype that associated feminism and Britishness. Identifying themselves as both feminists and republicans, WAI members had a vested interest in breaking that association: "Women's Aid falsely align the women's struggle with the six county state and falsely pitted the women's struggle against the struggle for self-determination by the Irish people." Their attack on Women's Aid rested on not only republican grounds but, more important, feminist ones: "Would they [Women's Aid] want this woman to escape punishment altogether? In that case, Women's Aid would be furthering the oppression of women by perpetuating the age-old myth that women are irresponsible, irrational beings, less than full adults, who cannot reasonably be held accountable for their actions. . . . It is dishonest and hypocritical to condemn this act by the INLA simply because the person punished was a woman."[14] According to WAI, the public demonstration of Women's Aid against the violent punishment of McGuigan was not only pro-British but also anti-feminist. The WAI argument rested on the assumption that republican paramilitaries had the moral legitimacy to exercise authority in the nationalist communities. Women's Aid, of course, disagreed with this assumption: "We reject totally the suggestion put forward in the Women Against Imperialism statement that only those engaged in the national struggle can decide on what is the acceptable alternative to the present state [Northern Ireland]. Such a stand is at odds with any concept of democracy—a concept that the women's movement has always been conscious of."[15] Thus, they reinstated their rejection of any form of violence against women: "Women's Aid refuses to be drawn into moralizing over when the shooting and beating of women are acceptable and when they are not."[16] Women's Aid further expressed their anger at the fact "that so many organizations that claim to be revolutionary are male dominated in both their power structure and their use of women. It would appear to us that in terms of the feminist struggle for women's liberation such organizations need to examine and debate seriously rather than dismiss 'the women's question.'"[17]

Republican feminists could hardly dismiss the allegation that their organizations were dominated by men and disinterested in women's problems. Indeed they had already expressed concern about it. For Sinn Fein women representatives, the lack of an official policy on women's issues was a continuous embarrassment at a time when important debates about reproductive rights, family law, and equal opportunities in education and the workplace were taking place in Ireland. Without an official position Sinn Fein could not hope for any respect, let alone legitimacy, in the wide-ranging and increasingly influential circle of feminist women.

On November 17, 1979, after a meeting in Dublin, the most vocal women of Sinn Fein met in Belfast to discuss drafting a policy document on women. The report of the meeting reflects a rather conservative approach, given the general feminist tone in Ireland and in the rest of Europe, to the crucial issues of reproduction and family law. While acknowledging that contraception should be legalized, the problem of abortion was dismissed with an inadequate reference to the need for sexual education. Divorce was only recognized in tragic cases: "Divorce, like abortion, would not be necessary if there were good premarriage courses and if sex education was given to all children by their parents, backed up by their schools. Yet there would always be tragic cases in which divorce might be the only solution."[18] While abortion was opposed, divorce and contraception remained "a matter of personal conscience" rather than of social policy. As Margaret Ward observed (1983, 257), this was basically Catholic social teaching.

The resolutions that emerged from the Belfast meeting—timid as they were—proved, however, to be polemical within Sinn Fein. The debate, centering on morality, was characteristically framed in the discourse of British and Irish identities. The argument exploded publicly with a letter published in March 1980:

> I admire and agree with the ideals of Sinn Fein and what they are seeking to achieve for Ireland. Yet as I read about the women of Sinn Fein I become increasingly depressed. These ladies seem very eager to voice their opinions on contraception, divorce, etc. on which they obviously argue that both should be made available. I believe that the women in Sinn Fein should instead be assisting in the growth of Irish in the movement or in spreading the ideals of Sinn Fein. In this way they will be constructively useful. We are looking for an identity of our own as well as complete independence from Britain. We must repeatedly ask ourselves what are we fighting for. Without our language, culture, upkeep of our moral beliefs, we may as well rejoin Britain under a similar union as that of 1801. What is the point of seeking total freedom from England if we are just going to turn around and adopt BRITISH MORALITY?[19]

Irish identity had been imagined and reimagined through gender metaphors. Similarly Anglo-Irish colonial relations had been represented through the idiom of sexuality. Seamus Heaney provides a recent and most illustrious example. In *An Open Letter* (1983), for example, he represents Ulster as the darling of the South, raped by Britain who, "still imperially male," has produced bastard offspring by both:

> The hidden Ulster lies beneath
> A sudden blow, she collapsed with
> The other island; and the South's been made a cuckold.
> She has had family by them both,
> She is growing old
>
> And scared that both have turned against her.
> The cuckold's impotent in Leinster
> House. The party in Westminster,
> All passion spent,
> More down-and-out than sinister,
> Just pays the rent.

One could interpret the restrictive sexual and gender politics of postcolonial Ireland as an attempt to counteract what Seamus Heaney represents as a symbolic castration of the nation embodied in the partition that engendered Northern Ireland. This suggestive interpretation lies, of course, beyond orthodox codes of ethnographic and historical evidence. We should not be surprised, however, that, given the recurrent encoding of Anglo-Irish relations in the language of gender and sexuality, discussions about gender and sexuality would also be about national identity.

History, particularly precolonial history, was reinvented again to provide claims and counterclaims on gender and sexuality. Thus, Sinn Fein profeminist women argued that contraception and divorce had been widely available in Gaelic Ireland, while the rigid sexual morality that opposed contraception and divorce was part of the Victorian morality imported to Ireland. Furthermore, Gaelic society provided an example of "near equality between men and women" that "was to be broken down by colonialism."[20] More explicit in identifying feminism with genuine Irishness was a letter signed by Maire Ni Mhaoil Eoin:

> The morality that exists in Ireland at present, the morality which prevents women from expressing their individuality and leading independent lives, through non-availability of child-care facilities, un-equal pay, deliberate sex discrimination, the morality that dictates how a woman should dress in order to titillate when she is single, and how she should dress as an obedient wife and mother in order not to arouse desire because she is now owned by one man, the morality that allows her to be bound to that man for life despite battering, rape and constant dangerous child-bearing, the morality which dictates what her body is used for, and when, without her permission/feelings considered, is a morality that comes directly from Britain!
>
> Before the imperialist invasion by Britain, the ancient Irish Brehon laws in relation to women were probably the most advanced of any western country and will be difficult to surpass. . . . That is the true Irish morality which the women of Sinn Fein Women's Coordinating Committee seeks to reinstate in Eire Nua. Feminism as we know it today is not a British invention, it more than likely has its roots in the ancient laws of Brehon Ireland when women sat on war councils.[21]

This assertion of Gaelic gender equality had more to do with myth than with historical evidence. Margaret Ward has seen this argument as a form of making imperialism a convenient scapegoat for male domination (1983, 257). Yet in the context of the discourses that shaped Irish national identity, the argument of Ni Mhaoil Eoin constituted a subtle subversive maneuver. If the nationalist imagination of Gaelic Ireland

161

had been unambiguously patriarchal, then the Gaelic Ireland (and therefore the independent nation) envisioned by some republican women in 1980 was—if not feminist—at least egalitarian in its gender relations.[22] This reinvention of precolonial tradition did not constituted a discourse about the past as much as a political field for present gender battles.

The important point is that the model of gender relations upon which the Irish nation had been shaped was beginning to be challenged precisely with new constructions of nationality. This challenge was missed by mainstream feminist organizations such as the Northern Ireland Women's Rights Movement. In Northern Ireland, women's groups, like other political organizations, are sharply divided on the issue of nationalism. The contradictions that feminists face in confronting the issue of nationalism, became bitterly acute during the campaign in favor of Armagh republican prisoners.

The NIWRM, founded in Belfast in 1975, was the first and most significant feminist organization. Its strategy was oriented toward the implementation of a parity of rights with Britain, including the extension of British legislation on divorce and abortion to Northern Ireland. They opposed republicanism on the grounds that IRA violence was a permanent souce of tension and division between Protestant and Catholic women who otherwise had the same problems and needs. As I discussed in chapter 6, NIWRM refused to support the protesting women in Armagh by arguing that the republican movement was dominated by men and the Armagh women were merely "aping" their male comrades (Loughran 1986, 1987); other women's groups split over the meaning and degree of support to be given the prisoners.[23]

The hostility of the feminist movement toward nationalism and republican politics has impeded feminists to seriously explore the different meanings that violence has for unionist and nationalist women living in the working-class ghettos of Belfast. Their perception of republican women as puppets of a male war effectively obscured the complex social processes that lead women to take sides in a war. While feminist organizations in Britain and Ireland had no trouble recognizing male agency in the unfolding of political processes in Northern Ireland, they could not admit the same agency for republican women. Ironically, this position doubly alienated nationalist women and further estranged them from feminist organizations. Republican feminists, also forced to contend with the hostility toward feminism within the republican movement, found it increasingly frustrating that their feminist gains were systematically ignored by nonnationalist feminists. By the end of 1980, despite internal opposition and continuing discussion, a Department on Women's Affairs was created by Sinn Fein and a policy document on women was passed at the party's annual conference. The debate was far from over; built in the interstices of powerful and competing discourses, the project of a republican feminism was frail.

THE FRAILTY OF A PROJECT

Because discourses of gender are inseparable from nationalist and class discourses, the project of a working-class republican feminism is as frail at the political level as it is fraught with contradictions at the personal level. The first attempt at formulating such a project was Women Against Imperialism, which disintegrated in 1981. As the crisis in the prisons escalated into the hunger strikes, so too tensions rose in WAI. Disagreements between women belonging to different political parties became more prominent to the dynamic of the group. With the unfolding of the hunger strikes, social tension rose to a point that left little space for feminist campaigning. Not only did the hunger strikes take over politically, but the group itself was seriously hurt by assassination and imprisonment. Mary Daly, leader of the IRSP and member of WAI, was killed by a loyalist death squad in June 1980. Two other members had been imprisoned when they refused to pay court fines for demonstrating in front of Armagh jail during International Women's Day that same year. Another member lost her husband and brother; both were killed by loyalists in 1981. The losses were too massive for a group so small. After WAI's demise, most women who did not already belong to IRSP or PD (People's Democracy) joined Sinn Fein and began to work in the newly formed Women's Department.

The Department had been formed against the hostility of the traditionalist sector in Sinn Fein, which saw it as the crystallization of a critical ideological change in the organization. After the hunger strike Sinn Fein had taken a definite turn to the left and was invested in reorganizing into a revolutionary political party what had basically been until then a political cover for the IRA. Shortly after the formation of the Women's Department, tensions between feminist and more conservative women within Sinn Fein led to an irreconcilable conflict. The conflict escalated out of proportion into what former members described as "a very messy, very contentious split" that divided the whole organization into opposed camps. One former member of the Department explained what happened as "an attempt to infiltrate the Department by anti-feminist elements." The conflict started with an argument over the presence of men in the meetings of the Department: "The Department was officially open to women and men, but it was set in such a way that the door was closed after women. It was unofficially said that we wanted to keep it women's only. What happened was that men started to come into the Department and taking over the discussions supported by some of the women in it. Then it got very messy when the division unfolded along the lines of women in the IRA and women in Sinn Fein."

IRA women were not necessarily conservative; rather, they did not see the necessity for an organization of women within the republican movement. As I mentioned earlier, IRA women had fought to be admitted as full members into the IRA rather than remain in its feminine counterpart Cumman na mBan. They considered themselves equal to their male comrades, and the existence of an exclusively women's department was for them, as Margaret Ward has noted, a step backward (1983, 260). A women's department reintroduced an unwanted gender difference that singled them out as something apart from their male comrades; a difference IRA women wanted to transcend, not mark, independently of how conservative or liberating the terms of the marking were. For IRA women "the fight for women's rights cannot be separated in Ireland from the fight against imperialism."[24] This link, however, is understood only in one direction, that of participation in the republican struggle against imperialism: "Imperialism has generated the oppression of Irish women, it is part of the system of social domination we have inherited from a foreign enemy." It was "through the struggle [against British imperialism] that they [men] should overcome their sexist attitudes."[25] The problem, if there was a gender problem, was located by IRA women on men. They were the ones who had to change and would only do so through the realization that women were equal to men, which meant in this context no different from them. It was often in prison, as I have noted, that these women came to develop a more complex understanding of gender inequality.

Much of the opposition to the feminists in the Women's Department came, however, from conservative members who felt threatened by the new autonomy of women within the organization. For former members of the Women's Department the conflict was about power and the need to control women's lives. The conflict escalated out of any proportion to the issues involved. It divided families into bitterly opposed positions and terminated long-standing friendships. It became so irresolvable and demoralizing that the *Ard Chomhairle* (Sinn Fein executive committee) decided to suspend the department for a few months.

The resonances and consequences of the conflict, as well as the bitterness involved, can only be accounted for if we see gender relations as constituting a privileged terrain for a power struggle between traditionalist and leftist sectors in the republican movement. The Women's Department became a resonant space for this contest because gender is implicated in definitions of the nation as no other cultural construction is, articulating and deploying a multiplicity of control mechanisms. In the final analysis the split provoked by the conflict in the Women's Department was less about women than about the kind of nation imagined. Thus, as Lata Mani (1990) has shown in relation to the debate on *sati* in colonial India, the entanglement of gender and sexuality within colonialist and nationalist discourses of identity often makes women neither objects nor subjects of political dispute, but the actual terrain in which those disputes take place; in this context it is difficult for women to find a space from which to assert their own historical subjecthood. For a feminist member of the department the conflict questioned the "possibility of having a secure place for women in a male dominated political organization, or if the politics of feminism was not going to be overridden by the internal factionalism of the movement." The formation of the Women's Department had signaled the opening of a space of autonomous agency for women within the republican movement; its suspension represented a sober reminder of its limits.

The Women's Department survived the crisis, however, and started functioning again after a three-month suspension. Some of its feminist members left the department, demoralized; some abandoned the organization and remained republican outside Sinn Fein; and yet others stayed, trying to articulate again a semblance of republican feminism. The 1980s was, however, a time of backlash for feminism. Sinn Fein's refusal to take a position during the 1983 amendment referendum that made abortion unconstitutional in Ireland did not help to attract feminists to the republican movement. Nevertheless, the 1980s also saw the rise of articulate feminist-oriented women to positions of prominence within the republican movement. Many of these women had begun their political careers campaigning in the streets with the RAC.

Discussions about gender inequality and women's rights have remained a part, if small, of the republican agenda, although not without contradictions and constant tension. Sinn Fein's policy on women has been substantially updated to include issues of violence against women (rape, battered women, and pornography), calling for a dismissal of party members who abuse women. Contraception and divorce are unambiguously demanded as democratic rights; attacks by the Right on women's clinics are condemned: and in 1996 Sinn Fein's annual assembly adopted a policy of nondiscrimination in relation to sexual orientation. The very mention of gays and lesbians as specific minorities, subject to political rights, was a far cry from earlier republican ideology on issues of gender and sexuality. Abortion continues to be the most problematic issue within Sinn Fein; it is discussed every year at its annual congress. While still opposed, official rhetoric has been softened from the "we are totally opposed to abortion," which appeared in the first congressional document, to "we are opposed to abortion as a means of birth control." The Sinn Fein department began in 1988 to publish a women's pamphlet, *A Woman's Voice*, which is a far cry from the early discussions on women. Aimed at both Northern and Southern Ireland, the pamphlet includes discussion of women's poverty, women's prisoners, domestic violence, women's health, and International Women's Day, as well as a list of women's organizations throughout Ireland. Despite contradictions and constant tension the process of change unfolded during the 1970s by nationalist women has transformed the traditional discourse of republican nationalism. Mother-Ireland has given way to songs about Armagh women and images of women in revolutionary attitudes, which can be seen in the murals of West Belfast. Republican feminism, too, comprised of women both within and outside Sinn Fein, has become not a dominant, but certainly a stronger and more well-defined position within the politics of feminism. The emergence of a new organization of republican women Clar na mBan (Women's Agenda), independent of Sinn Fein, formed on the eve of the peace process to fully participate in it is a sign of this strength.

As republican women were articulating their own feminist politics, so, too, in the south of Ireland, different feminist groups at the end of the 1980s were reapproaching the inescapable question of nationalism and the legacy of British colonialism.

REPOSSESSING THE NATION

Problematizing the dominant gender politics of nationality while searching for new images and models to express the complex realities of Irish women has been a conflictive process, one that has torn women between different loyalties and left scars in the process. The need to find a creative space in a country where women had been made emblems of both a dispossessed people and a grieving history has forced Irish women in the South to rethink their relation to the nation. The dilemmas involved have been expressed by the well-known poet Eavan Boland in her essay *A Kind of a Scar*. For her, the nation, inscribed in the passivity of female images, simplifies both women and the nation. Seen only as signs of the nation, Boland argues, women were obscured as historical agents; at the same time that female images expressed the suffering of the country, women's own suffering, anger, and power remained invisible. Yet Eavan Boland cannot abandon the idea of the nation either. Born out of a colonial past, the nation is central to a history from which she cannot escape. Like republican feminists, Boland's dilemma stems from the necessity of opening a space of agency within a foreclosed male discourse, "from my own need to locate myself in a powerful literary tradition in which until then I had been an element of design rather than an agent of change" (1989, 14). Exposing the mechanisms of displacement that made women stand for the suffering of the nation is to place the essentialist discourse of nationalism within the arena of historical contingency and open thus a discursive gap through which to repossess the nation: "I thought it vital that women poets such as myself should establish a discourse with the idea of the nation. I felt sure that the most effective way to do this was by subverting the previous terms of that discourse. Rather than accept the nation as it appeared in Irish poetry, with its queens and muses, I felt the time had come to re-work those images by exploring the emblematic relation between my own feminine experience and a national past" (Boland 1989, 20).

The poet Máighréad Medbh produces a discursive gap by dislodging a female Ireland from masculinist nationalist projections and giving her a voice of her own. Her powerful poem "Easter 1991"—a day of nationalist celebration—begins with the demystifying words of the nation speaking in the first person:

I am Ireland and I'm sick
sick in the womb
sick in the head
and I'm sick of lying in this sick bed
and if the medical men don't stop operating
I'll die

I am Ireland and I'm silenced
I cannot tell my abortions
my divorces
my years of slavery
my fights for freedom
It's got to the stage I can hardly remember what I had to tell
and when I do
I speak in whispers

The disruption produced by the articulation of a woman's voice within the masculinist discourse of nationalism ends with defiance: "I am Ireland / and I am not waiting anymore" (Medbh 1993). But this defiance comes from an identification with the nation, not from disavowal of it—a nation, however, that speaks from the suppressed of nationalist discourse and thus subverts it.

Subverting the terms of the dominant nationalist discourse is also what women like Nuala Ni Dhomhnaill are doing. Nuala Ni Dhomhnaill, regarded as one of the finest contemporary poets in the Irish language, appropriates the discourse that feminized Irish language, and by extension Irish culture, from Spenser to Renan to undermine its very foundations. For Nuala Ni Dhomhnaill "Irish is the great mother tongue par excellence" that has been preserved (ironically by the avatars of colonial history) from "the masculinization that came upon all major European languages." The feminine character of the Irish language in the works of colonialist writers like Spenser and Arnold sanctioned its subaltern position. Now, that feminine character undergirds its subversive potential: "on a multiplicity of levels Irish is an excellent theoretical and practical weapon against patriarchal hegemony" (1989, 29).

Irish feminists have also turned to mythological sagas in search of female heroic images capable of providing women with empowering models of identification. In so doing they are reworking cultural models of heroism and changing a hitherto masculine imaginative space. For republicans, IRA woman Mairead Farrell, leader of the dirty protest in Armagh jail, who was killed in Gibraltar in 1988, has become the model of a new female nationalist hero. As a model she is particularly attractive to republican feminists for not only her leadership qualities but also her open rejection of traditional female images of nationality.[26] No other woman has become so popular in the pantheon of martyrs of northern nationalist culture. Martyrdom in the North has not only ceased to be a male monopoly—although that can hardly be considered an achievement—but with Mairead Farrell martyrdom has also changed its meaning: she fits the model of neither redemptive sacrifice nor Gaelic hero; indeed, she is remembered and mourned more as lost leader than as martyr. If the imaginings of the Irish nation displaced women to the margins of a subaltern position, women in turn began from the margins to disrupt the national narrative.

* Afterword *

WHEN I left Belfast in late December 1989, the Falls Women's Center was immersed in a battle against the City Council. As a community service, the Falls Women's Center, like other community organizations received municipal funding to cover basic expenses such as electricity and telephone. Toward the end of 1989, the corporation, dominated by unionist parties, decided to rescind the financial support allocated to Falls Women's Center on the grounds that the center was used by republican women and therefore had connections with terrorist activities. The argument was not new; it had been brandished often against community groups operating in nationalist areas. Most recently the accusation of terrorist connections had served to withdraw funding from Conway Mill, a popular educational center that has done much to promote open debate about the crucial questions of culture, identity, and politics. With a chronic shortage of money the Women's Center faced the all too real possibility of closure. The move against the Falls Women's Center provoked the outrage of all women's groups. When I returned to Belfast a year later, in October 1990, the Falls Women's Center was still embattled in a public campaign against the decision of the city council; yet the women involved in the campaign were radiant about a new development. The Women's Center in the staunchly loyalist Shankill Road had publicly expressed their outrage at the council's decision and had joined the women from the Falls in the battle against the closure of their center. Women's centers in other unionist areas also expressed their solidarity with the Falls women. For these women the council's allegations made no sense. The Shankill women made this clear by openly manifesting that serving a loyalist area, they could not restrict the access of loyalist women to their center any more than the Falls center could limit the access of republicans. Whether the women who seek the services of these centers belong to the IRA or to the UDA is simply impossible to determine in places like the Falls or the Shankill. Since the restriction of funding was unilaterally directed against the Falls Women's Center, it stood out as a sectarian decision. The significance of the campaign in solidarity with the Falls center resides on the fact that for the first time nationalist and unionist women were rallying together against a recognizable sectarian decision, one that directly attacked women. Furthermore, that alliance came from working-class groups and represented a

170

new approach to feminist politics. In confronting together the patriarchal politics of the City Council, nationalist and unionist women were defying the sectarian politics that had confined them to incommensurable worlds. This is not to say that women with strong republican or unionist sympathies abandoned their political identities in favor of an encompassing feminist one. Rather it meant that in allying in the common cause of working-class women, unionist and republican women were shifting their political positions, widening not only the restrictive space of feminist politics that demanded a primary loyalty to women, but also broadening the hitherto narrow conditions of possibility of ethnic politics.

The Falls Women's Center regained its funding and thus achieved what had at first seemed as an unlikely victory. The momentary alliance between nationalist and unionist women was formalized into a permanent coalition of working-class women's organizations: The Women's Support Network. The coalition gained notoriety and legitimacy in February 1992, when the president of the Republic of Ireland, Mary Robinson, visited Belfast at its invitation. It was the first time an Irish president had visited Belfast since the beginning of the current conflict, and a coalition of nationalist and unionist working-class women were the artificers of the historical occasion.

The Women's Support Network was formed on the basis of respect for difference rather than foregrounding of identity. Respect for difference meant in this case a recognition that women in Northern Ireland are divided about the national status of Northern Ireland and occupy different positions in the social field by virtue of belonging to the nationalist or unionist communities. Yet the group's existence is also an acknowledgment that, if this difference cannot be glossed over, neither can the common ground shared by working-class women be erased. This approach to politics has at its center a delicate balance between difference and sameness: difference is at the heart of what it means to be a woman in Northern Ireland; it must be faced rather than effaced. But difference is not incommensurable. A common ground among women is provided not just by virtue of gender—that is, by the fact of being subjected to a specific kind of second citizenship—but also by a shared class position. This is not a particularly abstract matter. It means that working-class women struggle with poverty, bad housing, inadequate services, and the social and political violence that affect their neighborhoods in ways that do not affect middle-class residential areas. Gender then is implicitly placed for the Women's Support Network as the terrain, the very matter where the lines of ethnic difference and class identity intersect and offer an Archimedean angle from which to look afresh to the political conflict in Northern Ireland. In managing to combine respect for each others' political views with a strong commitment to the needs of working-class women, the Women's Support Network has opened a successful model of dialogue in a social terrain marked by pervasive conflict. This dialogue did not come from the assumption of shared gender identity as the basis for women's unity, a view often heralded by mainstream feminist organizations. Rather, the dialogue sprang from the understanding that any form of common action had to depart from the acknowledgment of difference. Such understanding was not born from the manuals of conflict resolution but out of the hard lessons learned through embattled lives and articulated by "invisible" working-class women, living themselves in the political margins. The fact that this coalition of women's centers has solidified and strengthened throughout the perils of the intensified sectarian violence that preceded the cease-fires, the vicissitudes of the peace process itself, and its demoralizing breakdown constitutes a lesson from which those involved in the resolution of Northern Ireland conflict could well profit. For it seems to me that the end of the peace process was brought not by the military zeal of the IRA but by the British government's refusal to acknowledge that the IRA had a voice or, if you prefer, by the exclusion of republican nationalism from the sphere of legitimate discourse. It is significant that the impasse that dominated the peace process was provoked by the British unwillingness to hold all-inclusive talks. This rigid stand is all the more tragic because the talks represented nothing more (and nothing less) than a fresh attempt to explore political differences through dialogue. The insistence that the IRA should decommission its arms before the voice of Sinn Fein could be heard, a unilateral prerequisite that was not applied to the unionist parties associated with loyalist paramilitaries, constituted a disingenuous demand of the surrendering of republican voice and the abdication of political subjectivity. For it is precisely the IRA arms that give republican discourse political consistency in the same way that a state army gives the nation a forceful materiality. Without the arms that make the IRA a political force its voice can easily be dismissed; indeed, the very idea of talks is rendered irrelevant. In the contested arena of Northern Ireland the announced political talks represented what legal anthropologist Lawrence Rosen has felicitously called "bargaining for reality" (1984). But no bargaining takes place outside a relation of power. Without power there is no bargaining—only submission to other versions of reality.

It did not take a genius to see that the insistence on decommissioning of arms as a precondition for all-inclusive political talks was a recipe for failure. The president of Sinn Fein, Gerry Adams, had warned about a crisis of the peace process; so, too, did the representatives of the Irish government and the head of the independent commission Senator George Mitchell from the United States. As the impasse continued month after month for a long year, the tension in Northern Ireland also rose. In the nationalist areas the palpable frustration was reflected on the rise of Sinn Fein on the elections that followed the break of the cease-fire. At times it seemed like the "Cronical de Una Muerte Anunciada," Gabriel Garcia Marquez's story of a foretold death where everybody knows about the impending killing of one of the characters yet nobody wants to believe it will really happen until is too late; and then they encounter the news of the murder with shocking surprise. Sartre would have called the apparent shock with which politicians received the news of the IRA explosion that broke the cease-fire, bad faith, for indeed the possibility had been voiced for a long time.

I have heard many people, including republicans, reflect on the break of the peace process as a story about the impossibility of change in Northern Ireland. This is an understandable conclusion. Yet to adopt such narrative is to ignore the contingency of social processes, the multiple if not unlimited possibilities of the play of social forces. History is not so rigidly foreclosed. There was a time during the first five months when the conditions of possibility for a secession of violent conflict were ripe. It could have happened if the different parties would have initiated a process of talks. Rather than seeing it as a sign of a general state of affairs in Northern Ireland, I see the break of the peace process as an example of the fragility of social transformation, subject as it is to the contingencies of local, national, and territorial moves and countermoves. In itself the historical event of the cease fire was already an instance of change in the social and political life of Northern Ireland. It set in motion processes that cannot be just bracketed. Their failure does not imply a simple return to a former situation; the scene has already been transformed. There is no square one to return to; square one simply looks different now. The IRA knew this when it decided to hold a cease-fire. The impossibility to determine the outcome was the political risk involved in this decision. The consequences of the difference that the

173

peace process has made in the social and political field remain to be seen, but there is no question that the difference exists. This is also how I think of the transformations triggered by nationalist women during the first decade of the conflict that has constituted the bulk of this book. It is short sighted to say that women accomplished nothing because they have not radically transformed the structures of gender inequality that shape their lives. And it is equally naive to see these changes as stages in a progressive narrative of liberation. The post-structuralist challenge of grand historical narratives has made this claim rather difficult. But on the eve of the cease-fire the formation of an organization of republican women, Clar na mBan, to participate in the peace process on their own ground is a clear manifestation of a political subject that was nonexistent twenty-five years ago. So is it with the formation of a women's coalition capable of getting two representatives elected to the forum for peace and reconciliation during the elections held for that purpose.

I began this book by arguing that the critical attitude of republican women toward the cease-fire stems from recognizing the possibility of historical erasure. It seems to me that there is a parallel between the struggle of republican women for recognition and voice within the republican movement and the struggles of the republican movement for recognition and voice within the arena of Northern Irish politics. Both constitute specific social experiences that are left out of political representation: women moving against the grain of nationalist and mainstream feminist discourses; the republican movement steering against the grain of discourses of civility and terrorism. The obstacles faced by the republican movement to participate in all party talks, illustrate the difficulty of finding a space where its voice can be heard without the misappropriation and distortions of the discourse of terrorism, our contemporary discourse of savagery. Within this discourse that masquerades as common sense, the terrorist, like our former savage, must ultimately be tamed, defeated, and put in his or her place, before given a voice that can, thus effaced, be easily erased. Confronted with a simulacrum of speech, terrorism has ironically become for the IRA the only space from which to speak. It is ironic that after seventeen months of peaceful pleading for a beginning of talks the British government only provided a date for talks after the IRA explosion that broke the cease-fire; by then it was too late.

To find a space for their specific voice has also been the problem of republican women. It seems to me that the operations, mechanisms, and strategies undertaken by these women illuminate not only the possibilities of general political change in Northern Ireland but also its limits. Thus, the frailty of the feminist project of republican women illustrates the fragile character of the peace process, but the participation of republican feminists in broader networks of women's organizations points also to possible avenues for political dialogue. There is, of course, no natural end to social processes and the telling of them; the story must be left open, the future necessarily uncertain.

∗ *Notes* ∗

Chapter 1

OPENING THE SPACE OF INTERPRETATION

1. Such representations reached a high point in 1976, with the emergence of the Peace Women, an initially spontaneous gathering of Catholic and Protestant women against paramilitary violence. The Peace Women achieved international recognition with the awarding of the Nobel peace price to their founders Betty Corrigan and Mairead Maguire. They formed an organization named Peace People, soon undermined by lack of political direction and internal divisions. See McCafferty (1987).

2. Under the organization of Elizabeth Shannon, fifty-two Irish women north and south of the border encompassing different community organizations and professions gathered in Boston to discuss with American counterparts the peace process in Northern Ireland and women's part in it. Republican women were, however, absent from this conference that missed thus one of the most intriguing positionings in the peace process. For a report of this conference, see *Reaching Common Ground: A Conference of American and Irish Women*. Conference transcripts and workshop summaries. November 11–13, 1994.

3. *Clar na mBan* Women's Agenda for Peace, Conference Report, 1994. For a discussion of this report, see Connolly (1995). For an articulation of republican feminism within the political context of the peace process, see Hackett (1995).

4. See Rolston, *A Social Science Bibliography of Northern Ireland* (1983). Other helpful sources are Darby (1983) and Whyte (1990).

5. See also Montgomery and Davies (1990) for a compilation of publications and unpublished work about women in Northern Ireland.

6. For the development of debates in the feminist movement of Northern Ireland, see also *Women's News*, the only independent feminist magazine produced in Ireland, published in Belfast.

7. See also the reviews of Irish women writers by Donovan (1988) and Weekes (1995).

8. The question of colonialism has often been framed around the problematic issue of Irish identity. See, for example, the debates between nationalists and revisionist historians that have followed Connor Cruise O'Brian in downplaying the role of British colonialism in Ireland. See Boyce and O'Day (1996). See also the polemic sparked by Dean's anthology of Irish writing and *The Irish Review* (1992); its no. 12 issue is dedicated to this debate.

9. See, for example, Abu-Lughod (1993), Behar (1993), Kondo (1990), Shostak (1981), Strathern (1987), Visweswaran (1994).

10. See particularly *The History of Sexuality* (1978) and *Discipline and Punish* (1979).

CHAPTER 2
CATHOLIC WEST BELFAST: A SENSE OF PLACE

1. Ratepayers indicate those individuals who own a house or rent housing from the local council. An adult without a tenancy did not pay rates (non-ratepayer) and was not entitled to vote in local elections, according to the Northern Ireland legislation.

2. There was rioting and violence during the economic depression of the 1930s and again during the 1950s. The 1930s also witnessed a short-lived alliance between the Catholic and Protestant working classes in response to the terrible economic conditions. The brief coalescence, however, was dismantled by selective repression against Catholics and the instigation of Protestant supremacist ideology by the Unionist leaders and members of the government, who constituted the landowners and financial class of Northern Ireland. See Farrel, (1976).

3. The peace process initiated by the IRA cease-fire from September 1994 to February 1996 led to the withdrawal of the British army from the streets and sparked an important debate on the role of the police force. Since the breakdown of the cease-fire, British troops have returned to the streets.

4. The scholarship on colonialism has long noted the sexualization of domination through the metaphoric associations between landscape and the female body. See, for example, Bhabha (1994), Comaroff and Comaroff (1991), Said (1978), Suleri (1992a, 1992b). For the Irish case, see Herr (1990) and Jones and Stallybrass (1992).

5. This quote is taken from an interview with Mairead Farrell published in the political magazine *Magill* 1986.

CHAPTER 3
GENDER TROUBLE AND THE TRANSFORMATION OF CONSCIOUSNESS

1. It is typical of situations in which ethnic or state violence erupts with unforeseen intensity that an event, chain of events, or a period of time is condensed and isolated in the collective consciousness as temporal and symbolic marker. This is the case, for instance, with Soweto in South Africa, or *La Violencia* in Guatemala (Warren 1992).

2. Hurlic is a Gaelic game played with sticks similar to those of hockey.

3. For more information, see chapter 4.

4. Republican clubs acquired—and still maintain—tremendous significance in the life of Catholic working-class communities with the increased ghettoization that followed the disturbances of 1969. They are spaces of social meeting and entertainment that combine the characteristics of the pub, social center, and political club. Though clearly under republican control, they are open to all members of the community and provide a daily program of entertainment tailored to the interests of different groups of people (i.e., including folk music,

disco music, and bingo). The clubs play a crucial role in the production and re-production of republican ideology and culture.

5. This was not the first time that conflict had arisen between women and the male leadership of the IRA. In the early 1970s some young women had become militarily active in the IRA without, however, the status of full members. Cumann na mBan, the official women's organization, was subordinate to the IRA council. With the establishment of a new unit structure in the early 1970s, women were admitted into the IRA on an equal basis with men, leaving Cumann na mBan to operate with the most traditional women (Ward 1983).

6. In the recent Sinn Fein publication *Women in a War Zone; Twenty Years of Resistance*, which purports to be a history of women's resistance in Northern Ireland, the dimension of gender conflict is nonexistent.

Chapter 4
The Ritual Politics of Historical Legitimacy

1. The polyvalent meanings of the sacrifice model can be seen in the republican funerary memorials as well as in murals visible throughout the Catholic districts. The use of these mythical models, such as the Gaelic warrior Cuchulain and Jesus Christ, in the political arena has its main antecedent in Padraic Pearse, leader of the 1916 uprising.

2. The interpretation of Irish political hunger strikes in light of the ancient Gaelic practice of fasting is not idiosyncratic of republican nationalists. Researchers have often drawn this parallel in their analyses. See, for example, Beresford (1987), Fallon (1987), and O'Malley (1990).

3. These women must, no doubt, have been influenced by the history of political fasting in other parts of the British empire, especially in India and elsewhere overseas (Morris 1978). For the Irish suffragists, see Owens (1984), Fallon (1987), and Ward (1983).

4. He was a poet, playwright, and philosopher. The symbolism of the single, ultimate sacrifice is transparent in his writings. Like Pearse he believed a symbolic act would awaken the consciousness of Ireland.

5. The rebellion of Easter 1916 and its subsequent executions provided the prelude to the war of independence and the Anglo-Irish Treaty that gave rise to the Irish Free State and Northern Ireland.

6. For a recent exhaustive account of this process, see J. B. Bell (1993).

7. For detailed analyses of the blanket protest, see Coogan (1980b) and Feldman (1991). For an account of the experience of female relatives during the protest, see Fairweather et al. (1984).

8. The first hunger strike, begun in 1980, was led by Brendan Hughes and ended after fifty-three days when the British administration produced a document that seemed to concede implicitly to the prisoner's five demands. Once the hunger strike was abandoned, however, the British government claimed that the

document did not agree to the demands, a position that prompted the second hunger strike.

9. Historians Corrigan and Sayer (1985) have shown the centrality of the ideology of "the Law" in the development of the British nation and the role it has played in advancing upper-class and imperialist interests.

10. A multiplicity of sources explores the social experience of the young militants involved in the prison protest of the late 1970s and hunger strike. Among these sources, see Beresford (1987), Coogan (1980b), O'Malley (1990), and a variety of republican publications of the time, especially the *Republican News*.

11. "Taig" is a derogatory word for Catholic, equivalent to the term "nigger" used as a pejorative for African Americans in the United States.

12. This is not only reserved for nationalists. When it comes to British mainstream representations of Ireland, both Catholics and Protestants are frequently portrayed as brutish and irrational. See Curtis (1985) and Darby (1983).

13. Despite general perception that Mrs. Thatcher was the main obstacle to a political resolution, the leaders of the main political parties, including both the Liberal party and the Labour party, shared her position on the issue.

14. See Seamus Heaney "The Tollund Man" published in *North* (1975), and Nicholas McGuinn's *Seamus Heaney. A Student's Guide to the Selected Poems 1965–1975* (1986).

15. For the imagery of the 1916 uprising, see Thompson (1982). For an account of the 1916 rebellion in Ireland in the broader context of the British empire, see Morris (1978).

16. For an excellent biography of Padraic Pearse, see Edwards (1977).

17. The Penal Laws disenfranchised Catholic and Presbyterian religious practice. They denied Catholics and dissenting Protestants access to education, the right to vote, and government jobs. In the case of Catholics, the Penal Laws so drastically curtailed land rights that in 1775 Catholics held only 5 percent of the land. The Penal Laws must be understood in relation to the role of Protestantism in the formation of the English state. To Corrigan and Sayer, the establishment of a state church in the 1530s laid the ground for a potent fusion of Protestantism and [English] nationalism. "For 250 years Protestantism strengthened [English] patriotism, and the existence of an internal (papist) enemy as well as the neighboring popish Irish, help to bind Englishmen together in national unity" (Hill [1969] as quoted in Corrigan and Sayer [1985:46]; see also Colley [1992]).

18. The discussion of Sands's poetry within the larger cultural tradition of the Irish ballad falls outside the margins of this chapter. Suffice it to note the interesting resemblance between *The Crime of Castlereagh* and *The Ballad of Reading Gaol*, the celebrated work of that other great Irish poet, Oscar Wilde, also condemned to jail for being an outcast albeit of a different type by a British court.

19. For an account of the uncertainty and surrealism of the experience of in-

terrogation, see Timerman (1981). For an excellent interpretation of this experience, see Taussig (1987). The experience of living in a space between life and death, where the line between the real and the imagined blurs, has been exceptionally captured by Mexican writer Juan Rulfo, considered the father of magical realism, in his novel *Pedro Paramo* (1987).

20. The "supergrasses" trials, through which large numbers of people were sentenced on the sole evidence of the words of police informers, is perhaps the clearest and most chilling political expression of the truth-producing mechanisms utilized by the Northern Ireland state.

21. For the IRA leadership, priority had to be given to the military effort. A hunger strike was seen as divesting their resources by demanding attention to campaigns and propaganda in favor of the prisoners. In addition, the uncertain outcome of a hunger strike represented a high political risk.

22. Bernardette Devlin, elected member of Parliament in 1971 and forefront campaigner for the prisoners, was badly wounded, and several outspoken supporters were killed by Loyalist paramilitary organizations.

23. A key event in this sense is the Irish Famine of 1854 when English economic policies in Ireland allowed one million people to die of hunger. No doubt the fast of 1981 had deep historical resonance; many people in Ireland—although they disagreed with the hunger strikers—still thought the English were again starving Irish people.

24. The first hunger strike took the conventional form of a group fasting at the same time. The second, however, was orchestrated in a one-to-one sequential basis to prolong the duration of the protest and to add pressure to the action. This form, well suited to the large collective of male prisoners, could have much more devastating effects for the small collective of thirty women.

25. See also O'Malley (1990) and Vincent (n.d.).

Chapter 5
The Gendered Politics of Suffering: Women of the RAC

1. The Women's Peace movement, later called Peace People, was established in August 1976 as a response to the deaths of three children struck by an IRA car, whose driver had been shot by an army patrol. It was founded by Betty Williams, Mairead Corrigan, and Ciaran McKeown. For more information, see Flackes and Elliot (1989).

2. Sands's wife separated from her husband while he was in jail, and she was living in England at the time of the hunger strike.

3. See Coogan (1980b) and Feldman (1991) for extensive descriptions and analyses of men's use of their bodies to hold and smuggle a variety of forbidden objects.

4. *Republican News* (September 29, 1979).

CHAPTER 6
THE POWER OF SEXUAL DIFFERENCE: ARMAGH WOMEN

1. The events leading to the women's dirty protest are reconstructed from the early and excellent account of Nell McCafferty (1981), the archival sources housed in the political collection of the Linen Hall Library, and the accounts of the prisoners themselves.

2. Report of republican Eilis O'Connor smuggled out of Armagh prison and cited in Nell McCafferty (1981).

3. *Women Protest for Political Status in Armagh Gaol.* Report by Women Against Imperialism, April 9, 1980. I confirmed the statements made by prisoners in interviews with them during my fieldwork.

4. Ibid.

5. Ibid., 24.

6. There is a growing body of scholarship on the discourse of sexuality and power. See, for example, Comaroff and Comaroff (1991), Jordanova (1980), Stallybrass and White (1986), Stoler (1991), and Suleri (1992a). For more information on the sexualization of early colonial discourse in Ireland, see Jones and Stallybrass (1992).

7. As reported in *Women Protest for Political Status in Armagh Gaol* (1980, 25) and Coogan (1980b).

8. Ann Zell, *Banshee in the Office* (1990).

9. See reports of the successive court hearings in *Women's News* 1990, issues 47, 48; and reports of Falls Women's Center.

10. *Republican News,* September 27, 1980.

11. This ambivalence emerged in recurrent comments made by nationalist women during my fieldwork. Particularly important were the discussions following the screening in the nationalist districts of Belfast and Derry of the documentary *Mother-Ireland,* directed by Anne Crilly and produced by Derry Film and Video Company, and the play about the Armagh women, *Now and at the Hour of Our Death,* produced by the theater group Trouble and Strife.

12. In this sense the Armagh women's dirty protest is reminiscent of the kind of symbolic warfare enacted by women in some parts of Africa. Both Ardener (1975) and Ifeka-Moller (1975) have documented women's exposure of genitals as a powerful sexual insult used against men who violate women's dignity and rights. This display publicly states disrespect, denial of dominance, and non-recognition of authority.

13. In relation to the history and composition of the feminist movement in Northern Ireland, see Evason (1991), Loughran (1986), Ward (1987, 1991).

14. Nell McCafferty, "It is my belief that Armagh is a feminist issue," *The Irish Times,* June 17, 1980.

15. *The Irish Times* (1980) as quoted in Loughran (1986:64).

CHAPTER 7
EN-GENDERING A NATION

1. Gender could be bended, if you allow me the expression, to suit different political claims. Thus if the Irish were feminine in their emotionality and irrationality, they were also prone to violence and as often depicted as a base form of masculinity that threatened a vulnerable Hibernia in search of British protection. Both a masculine excess and a feminine irrationality were projected onto the Irish.

2. See, for example, female representations of Ireland in the work of national painters (e.g., McCurtain [1993:9–23]).

3. "Irish Womanhood," *Republican News*, September 15, 1972.

4. "Contraceptive Bill," *Republican News*, February 9, 1974. This article provoked such controversy that the IRA issued a statement saying that, as an organization, they did not have a fixed opinion about the issue of contraception.

5. "Is woman's lib. relevant for our readers?" *Republican News*, January 26, 1973.

6. "The slaves of the slaves," *Republican News*, February 2, 1978.

7. A major precedent of this debate occurred during the first quarter of the century when suffragists, labor activists, and nationalists engaged in a discussion about the new Ireland and the role of women in it; see Owens (1984) and Ward (1983). The attainment of partial independence meant different social realities for women in the North and the South. Nationalism also contained different meanings; for women in the South, it meant the state ideology that had sanctioned a patriarchal and restrictive legislation. For Catholic women in the North, nationalism (the imagining of a united Ireland) meant a future without sectarian (religious, ethnic) discrimination.

8. "Letters to the Editor," *Republican News*, February 25, 1978.

9. "Men's Irish republican movement?" *Republican News*, June 24, 1978.

10. "Post Bag," *Republican News*, July 8, 1978.

11. Women Against Imperialism was composed of women from the Irish Republican Socialist Party (IRSP), Sinn Fein, People's Democracy, and independent women involved in the Relatives Action Committees.

12. The Irish National Liberation Army (INLA) was born in 1975 as the military wing of the Irish Republican Socialist Party (IRSP), which formed in 1974 as a breakaway from official Sinn Fein. See Flackes and Elliot (1989).

13. *Republican News*, September 22, 1979.

14. Ibid.

15. *Republican News*, October 6, 1979.

16. Ibid.

17. Ibid.

18. *Republican News*, November 17, 1979.

19. *Republican News*, March 22, 1980.

20. *Republican News*, March 22, 1980; April 5, 1980.

21. *Republican News*, May 17, 1980.

22. Irish Gaelic society was in fact highly hierarchical. Men and women were far from being structurally equal. Women generally lacked independent legal capacity and existed under the authority of husband, father, or son—although their degree of influence varied with their social status. Divorce was permitted in Gaelic society, but so was polygamy. Early Irish marriage was highly complicated with nine forms of sexual union legally distinguished. For excellent sources, see Blinchy (1954) and F. Kelly (1988).

23. In relation to the history and composition of the feminist movement in Northern Ireland, see Evason (1991), Loughran (1986), and Ward (1987, 1991).

24. See *Irish*, no. 4, November 1982.

25. "A People's Army" (Interview with IRA women), *Irish*, no. 4 (November 1982). See also *Republican News*, May 20, 1982, where an IRA woman described the Women's Department as having "the job of politicising and educating women in the Movement on women's issues" and IRA women as fighting for a united socialist republic "only then will we ensure that we do not digress to the 'slaves of the slaves' status in Irish society."

26. See *Mother-Ireland* (i.e., video produced by Derry Film and Video and directed by Anne Crilly).

* References *

Abu-Lughod, L.
    1991   "The Romance of Resistance: Tracing Transformations of Power through Bedouin Women." In Peggy Reeves Sanday and Ruth Gallagher Goodenough, eds., *Beyond the Second Sex: New Directions in the Anthropology of Gender.* Philadelphia: University of Pennsylvania Press.
    1993   *Writing Women's Worlds: Bedouin Stories.* Berkeley: University of California Press.

Adams, Gerry
    1982   *Falls Memories.* Dingle, Kerry: Brandon.

Anderson, Benedict
    1983   *Imagined Communities: Reflections on the Origin and Spread of Nationalism.* London: Verso.

Appadurai, Arjun
    1986   "Theory in Anthropology: Center and Periphery." *Comparative Studies in Society and History* 28(2):357–61.
    1988   Introduction: Place and Voice in Anthropological Theory. Cultural Anthropology 3(1):16–20.

Ardener, Shirley
    1975   "Sexual Insult and Female Militancy." In Shirley Ardener, ed., *Perceiving Women*, pp. 29–54. London: Dent.

Aretxaga, Begoña
    1995   "Dirty Protest: Symbolic Overdetermination and Gender in Northern Ireland Ethnic Violence." *Ethos* 23(2):123–48.

Armstrong, D. L.
    1951   "Social and Economic Conditions in the Belfast Linen Industry 1850–1900." In *Irish Historical Studies* 7:235–69.

Bardon, Jonathan
    1982   *A History of Ulster.* Dundonald, Belfast: Blackstaff Press.

Beale, Jenny
    1986   *Women in Ireland: Voices of Change.* Basingstoke, U.K.: MacMillan.

Beall, Jo, Shireen Hassim, and Alison Todes
    1989   "A Bit on the Side?: Gender Struggles in the Politics of Transformation in South Africa." *Feminist Review* 33:30–57.

Beckett, James Camlin, et al., contributors
    1983   *Belfast: The Making of a City.* Belfast: Appletree Press.

Beckett, James Camlin, and Robin E. Glasscock, eds.
    1967   *Belfast: The Origin and Growth of an Industrial City.* London: British Broadcasting Corporation.

Beckett, Mary
    1980   *A Belfast Woman.* Dublin: Poolbeg Press.

Behar, Ruth
    1993   *Translated Woman: Crossing the Border with Esperanza's Story.* Boston: Beacon Press.

Bell, J. Bowyer
    1993   *The Irish Troubles: a Generation of Violence, 1967–1992.* Dublin: Gill and Macmillan.

Benjamin, Walter
    1978   "Critique of Violence." In *Reflections: Essays, Aphorisms, Autobiographical Writings,* pp. 277–300. New York: Harcourt Brace Jovanovich.

Beresford, David
    1987   *Ten Men Dead. The Story of the 1981 Irish Hunger Strike.* London: Grafton Books.

Bhabha, Homi
    1994   *The Location of Culture.* New York: Routledge.

Blinchy, D. A.
    1954   "Secular Institutions." In Myles Dillon, ed., *Early Irish Society.* Cork: Mercier Press.
    1973   "Distraint in Irish Law." *Celtica* 10:22–71.

Boal, Frederick, P. Doherty, and D. G. Pringle
    1974   *The Spatial Distribution of Some Social Problems in the Belfast Urban Area.* Belfast: Northern Ireland Community Relations Commision.

Boal, Frederick, and J. Neville Douglas
    1982   *Integration and Division: Geographical Perspectives on the Northern Ireland Problem.* New York: Academic Press.

Boal, Frederick, Russel Murray, and Michael Poole
    1976   "Belfast: The Urban Encapsulation of a National Conflict." In Susan E. Clarke and Jeffrey L. Obler, eds., *Urban Ethnic Conflict: A Comparative Perspective,* pp. 77–131. Chapel Hill: Institute for Research in Social Sciences, University of North Carolina.

Boland, Eavan
    1989   *A Kind of Scar: The Woman Poet in a National Tradition.* Dublin: Attic Press.

Bondi, Liz
    1990   "Feminism, Postmodernism and Geography: Space for Women?" *Antipode* 22:156–57.

Bourque, Susan C., and Kay B. Warren
    1981   *Women of the Andes: Patriarchy and Social Change in Two Peruvian Towns.* Ann Arbor: University of Michigan Press.

Boyce, D. George, and Alan O'Day
    1996   *Modern Irish History: Revisionism and the Revisionist Controversy.* London: Routledge.

Brasted, Howard
 1980 "Indian Nationalist Development and the Influence of Irish Home Rule, 1870–1886." *Modern Asian Studies* 14:37–63.

Brown, Terence
 1985 *Ireland: A Social and Cultural History, 1992–Present.* Ithaca, N.Y.: Cornell University Press.

Buckley, Anthony D., and Mary Catherine Kenney
 1995 *Negotiating Identity: Rhetoric, Metaphor, and Social Drama in Northern Ireland.* Washington, D.C.: Smithsonian Institution Press.

Buckley, Suzanne, and Pamela Lonergan
 1984 "Women and the Troubles, 1969–1980." In Yonah Alexander and Alan O'Day, eds., *Terrorism in Northern Ireland,* pp. 75–87. London: Croom Helm.

Budge, Ian, and Cornelius O'Leary
 1973 *Belfast: Approach to Crisis. A Study of Belfast Politics 1613–1970.* London: MacMillan.

Burton, Frank
 1978 *The Politics of Legitimacy: Struggles in a Belfast Community.* London: Routledge and Kegan Paul.

Butler, Judith P.
 1990 *Gender Trouble: Feminism and the Subversion of Identity.* New York: Routledge.

Butler, Judith, and Joan Scott, eds.
 1992 *Feminists Theorize the Political.* New York: Routledge.

Cairns, David, and Shaun Richards
 1988 *Writing Ireland: Colonialism, Nationalism and Culture.* Manchester: Manchester University Press.

Cameron Report
 1969 *Disturbances in Northern Ireland: Report of the Cameron Commission.* London: HMSO, Cmd. 532.

Canetti, Elias
 1978 *The Human Province: Notes 1942–1972.* New York: Seabury Press.

Canny, Nicholas P.
 1973 "The Ideology of English Colonization: From Ireland to America." *William and Mary Quarterly.* 30:575–98.

Chatterjee, Partha
 1986 *Nationalist Thought and the Colonial World. A Derivative Discourse?* London: Zed Books.
 1989 "Colonialism, Nationalism, and Colonized Women: The Contest in India." *American Ethnologist* 16:622–33.
 1993 *The Nation and Its Fragments: Colonial and Postcolonial Histories.* Princeton, N.J.: Princeton University Press.

Clifford, James

    1988   *The Predicament of Culture: Twentieth-Century Ethnography.* Cambridge: Harvard University Press.

Colley, Linda

    1992   *Britons: Forging the Nation 1707–1837.* New Haven, Conn.: Yale University Press.

Comaroff, Jean, and John Comaroff

    1991   *Of Revelation and Revolution: Christianity, Colonialism and Consciousness in South Africa, 1.* Chicago: University of Chicago Press.

Connolly, Clare

    1995   "Ourselves Alone? Clar na mBan Conference Report." *Feminist Review* 50:118–27.

Coogan, Tim Pat

    1980a   *The IRA.* London: Fontana Books.

    1980b   *On the Blanket: The H-Block Story.* Dublin: Ward River Press.

Cornell, Drucilla

    1991   *Beyond Accommodation: Ethical Feminism, Deconstruction, and the Law.* New York: Routledge.

    1993   *Transformations: Recollective Imagination and Sexual Difference.* New York: Routledge.

Corrigan, Philip, and Derek Sayer

    1985   *The Great Arch: English State Formation as Cultural Revolution.* New York: Basil Blackwell.

Coulter, Carol

    1990   *Ireland: Between the First and the Third Worlds.* Dublin: Attic Press.

    1993   *The Hidden Tradition: Feminism, Women, and Nationalism in Ireland.* Cork: Cork University Press.

Crapanzano, Vincent

    1985   *Waiting: The Whites of South Africa.* New York: Vintage Books.

Curtis, Lewis Perry

    1968   *Anglo-Saxons and Celts: A Study of Anti-Irish Prejudice in Victorian England.* New York: New York University Press.

Curtis, Liz

    1984   *Ireland: The Propaganda War. The British Media and the Battle for Hearts and Minds.* London: Pluto Press.

    1985   *Nothing But the Same Old Story: The Roots of Anti-Irish Racism.* London: Turnaround Distribution.

Dalton, G. F.

    1974   "The Tradition of Blood Sacrifice to the Goddess Eire." *Studies* 63(252):343–54.

Darby, John

    1983   *Northern Ireland: The Background to the Conflict.* Belfast: Appletree Press.

Das, Veena
   1995   *Critical Events: An Anthropological Perspective on Contemporary India.* New Delhi: Oxford University Press.
Das, Veena, and Ashis Nandy
   1985   "Violence, Victimhood, and the Language of Silence." *Contributions to Indian Sociology* 19(1):177–95.
Davis, Richard
   1986   "The Influence of the Irish Revolution on Indian Nationalism: The Evidence of the Indian Press, 1916–22." *South Asia: Journal of South Asian Studies* 9(2):55–69.
de Certeau, Michel
   1984   *The Practice of Everyday Life.* Steven F. Randall, trans. Berkeley: University of California Press.
   1986   *Heterologies: Discourse on the Other.* Minneapolis: University of Minnesota Press.
Deane, Seamus
   1983   *Civilians and Barbarians.* Derry: Field Day Theatre Company.
Deane, Seamus, ed.
   1991   *The Field Day Anthology of Irish Writing.* 3 vols. New York: Field Day Publications.
Devaney, Fran, Marie Mulholland, and Judith Willoughby, eds.
   1989   *Unfinished Revolution: Essays on the Irish Women's Movement.* Belfast: Meadbh Publishing.
Devlin, Anne
   1986   *Ourselves Alone.* London: Faber and Faber.
Dirks, Nicholas, ed.
   1992   *Colonialism and Culture.* Ann Arbor: University of Michigan Press.
Donovan, Katie
   1988   *Irish Women Writers, Marginalized by Whom?* Dublin: Raven Arts Press.
Douglass, Mary
   1966   *Purity and Danger: An Analysis of the Concepts of Pollution and Taboo.* London: Routledge and Kegan Paul.
Edgerton, Linda
   1986   "Public Protest, Domestic Acquiescence: Women in Northern Ireland." In Rosemary Ridd and Helen Callaway, eds., *Caught Up in Conflict: Women's Responses to Political Strife,* pp. 61–79. London: Macmillan.
Edwards, Ruth Dudley
   1977   *Patrick Pearse: The Triumph of Failure.* London: Gollancz.
Elshtain, Jean Bethke
   1987   *Women and War.* New York: Basic Books.
Etienne, Mona, and Eleanor Leacock, eds.
   1980   *Women and Colonization: Anthropological Perspectives.* New York: Praeger.

189

Evason, Eileen
  1980 *Ends that Won't Meet: A Study of Poverty in Belfast.* London: Child Poverty Action Group.
  1982 *Hidden Violence. Battered Women in Northern Ireland.* Belfast: Farset Co-operative Press.
  1991 *Against the Grain: The Contemporary Women's Movement in Northern Ireland.* Dublin: Attic Press.

Fairweather, Eileen, Roisín McDonough, and Melanie McFadyean
  1984 *Only the Rivers Run Free. Northern Ireland: The Women's War.* London: Pluto Press.

Faligot, Roger
  1983 *Britain's Military Strategy in Ireland. The Kitson Experiment.* London, Kerry: Zed, Brandon.

Fallon, Charlotte
  1987 "Civil War Hunger Strikes: Women and Men." *Eire-Ireland* 22(3):75–91.

Fanon, Frantz
  1967 *A Dying Colonialism.* Haakon Chev, trans. New York: Grove Press.

Farrell, Michael
  1976 *Northern Ireland: The Orange State.* London: Pluto Press.

Feldman, Allen
  1991 *Formations of Violence. The Narrative of the Body and Political Terror in Northern Ireland.* Chicago: Chicago University Press.

Ferguson, James, and Akhil Gupta
  1992 "Beyond Culture: Space, Identity, and the Politics of Difference." *Cultural Anthropology* 7(1):6–23.

Fernandez, James
  1974 "The Mission of Metaphor in Expressive Culture." *Current Anthropology* 15(2):119–46.
  1986 "Persuasions and Performances: Of the Beast in Everybody and the Metaphors of Everyman." In *Persuasions and Performances. The Play of Tropes in Culture,* pp. 3–27. Bloomington: Indiana University Press.

Fernández-Kelly, María Patricia
  1983 *For We Are Sold, I and My People: Women and Industry in Mexico's Frontier.* Albany: State University of New York Press.

Flackes, William D., and Sydney Elliot
  1989 *Northern Ireland: A Political Directory, 1968–1988.* Dublin: Gill and Macmillan.

Flax, Jane
  1992 "The End of Innocence." In Judith Butler and Joan Scott, eds., *Feminists Theorize the Political,* pp. 445–63. New York: Routledge.

Foster, John Wilson
  1991 *Colonial Consequences: Essays in Irish Literature and Culture.* Dublin: Lilliput Press.

Foster, Robert F.

    1988   *Modern Ireland 1600–1972.* London: A. Lane.

    1993   *Paddy and Mr. Punch: Connections in Irish and English History.* London: A. Lane.

Foucault, Michel

    1979   *The History of Sexuality.* Robert Hurley, trans. New York: Pantheon Books.

    1980   *Discipline and Punish.* New York: Vintage Books.

Garland, David

    1990   *Punishment and Modern Society: A Study in Social Theory.* Chicago: University of Chicago Press.

Geertz, Clifford

    1973   "Religion as a Cultural System." In *The Interpretation of Cultures*, pp. 87–125. New York: Basic Books.

Glassie, Henry

    1982   *Passing the Time in Ballymenone: Culture and History of an Ulster Community.* Philadelphia: University of Pennsylvania Press.

Gregory, Derek

    1994   *Geographical Imaginations.* Cambridge, Mass.: Blackwell.

Hackett, Claire

    1995   "Self-determination: The Republican Feminist Agenda." *Feminist Review* 50:11–118.

Haraway, Donna Jean

    1991   *Simians, Cyborgs, and Women: The Reinvention of Nature.* New York: Routledge.

Heaney, Seamus

    1975   *North.* London: Faber and Faber.

    1983   *An Open Letter.* Derry: Field Day Theater Pamphlets.

Herr, Cheryl

    1990   "The Erotics of Irishness." In *Critical Inquiry.* 17(1):1–34.

Herzfeld, Michael

    1992   *The Social Production of Indifference: Exploring the Symbolic Roots of Western Bureaucracy.* New York: Berg.

Hillyard, Paddy

    1983   "Law and Order." In John Darby, ed., *Northern Ireland: The Background to the Conflict*, pp. 32–60. Belfast: Appletree.

Ifeka-Moller, Caroline

    1975   "Female Militancy and Colonial Revolt: The Women's War of 1929, Eastern Nigeria. In Shirley Ardener, ed., *Perceiving Women*, pp. 127–59. London: Dent.

Jayawardena, Kumari

    1986   *Feminism and Nationalism in the Third World.* London: Zed Books.

Johnston, Jennifer

    1978   *Shadows on Our Skin.* New York: Doubleday.

Jones, Emrys
 1956 "The Distribution and Segregation of Roman Catholics in Belfast. *Sociological Review*, n.s. 4:169.
 1967 "Late Victorian Belfast: 1850–1900." In James C. Beckett and Robin E. Glasscock, eds., *Belfast: The Origin and Growth of an Industrial City*, pp. 109–19. London: British Broadcasting Corporation.
Jones, Ann R., and Peter Stallybrass
 1992 "Dismantling Irena: The Sexualization of Ireland in Early Modern England." In eds. Andrew Parker, Mary Russo, Doris Sommer, and Patricia Yaeger, eds., *Nationalisms and Sexualities*. New York: Routledge.
Jordanova, Ludmilla J.
 1980 "Natural Facts: A Historical Perspective on Science and Sexuality." In Carol MacCormack and Marilyn Strathern, eds., *Nature, Culture and Gender*, pp. 42–69. New York: Cambridge University Press.
Kearney, Richard
 1988 *Transitions. Narratives in Modern Irish Culture*. Manchester: Manchester University Press.
Kelly, Fergus
 1988 *A Guide to Early Irish Law*. Dublin: Institute for Advanced Studies.
Kelly, John
 1991 *A Politics of Virtue: Hinduism, Sexuality and Countercolonial Discourse in Fiji*. Chicago: University of Chicago Press.
Kelly, John, and Martha Kaplan
 1990 "History, Structure, and Ritual." *Annual Review of Anthropology* 19:119–50.
Kenney, Mary Catherine
 1991 "Neighborhoods and Parades: The Social and Symbolic Organization of Conflict in Northern Ireland." Ph.D. diss., University of Michigan.
Kleinman, Arthur, and Joan Kleinman
 1994 "How Bodies Remember: Social Memory and Bodily Experience of Criticism, Resistance, and Delegitimation Following China's Cultural Revolution." *New Literary History* 25(3):707–23.
Kondo, Dorinne K.
 1990 *Crafting Selves: Power, Gender, and Discourses of Identity in the Japanese Workplace*. Chicago: University of Chicago Press.
Kristeva, Julia
 1982 *Powers of Horror: An Essay on Abjection*. Leon S. Roudiez, trans. New York: Columbia University Press.
Lacan, Jacques
 1977 *Ecrits: A Selection*. Alan Sheridan, trans. New York: Norton.
Lederman, Rena
 1991 "Contested Order: Gender Constructions and Social Structure in the

Southern New Guinea Highlands." In Peggy Reeves Sanday and Ruth Gallagher Goodenough, eds., *Beyond the Second Sex: New Directions in the Anthropology of Gender,* pp. 59–80. Philadelphia: University of Pennsylvania Press.

Lloyd, David
    n.d.   "The Conflict of the Borders." Manuscript.
    1993   *Anomalous States: Irish Writing and the Postcolonial Moment.* Durham, N.C.: Duke University Press.

Loftus, Belinda
    1982   "Images in Conflict: Visual Images and the Troubles in Northern Ireland 1968–1981." Ph.D. diss., Keele University.
    1990   *Mirrors: William III and Mother Ireland.* Dundrum, N.I.: Picture Press.

Loughran, Christina
    1986   "Armagh and Feminist Strategy." *Feminist Review* 23:59–80.
    1987   "The Origins and Development of Feminist Groups in Northern Ireland." Ph.D. diss., Queen's University of Belfast.

MacBride, Sean
    1983   "Introduction." In Bobby Sands, *One Day in My Life,* pp. 7–22. London: Pluto.

MacCurtain, Margaret
    1982   "Towards an Appraisal of the Religious Image of Women." In Mark Patrick Hederman and Richard Kearney, eds., *The Crane Bag Book of Irish Studies (1977–1981),* pp. 539–43, Dublin: Blackwater Press.
    1993   "The Real Molly Macree." In Adele M. Dalsimer, ed., *Visualizing Ireland: National Identity and the Pictorial Tradition,* pp. 9–23. Boston: Faber and Faber.

Malinowski, Bronislaw
    1961[1922]   *Argonauts of the Western Pacific: an Account of Native Enterprise and Adventure in the Archipelagoes of Melanesian New Guinea.* New York: Dutton.

Mani, Lata
    1990   "Contentious Traditions: The Debate on *Sati* in Colonial India." In Kumkum Sangari and Sudesh Vaid, eds., *Recasting Women: Essays in Indian Colonial History,* pp. 88–125. New Brunswick, N.J.: Rutgers University Press.

McAteer, Geraldine
    1983   *Down the Falls.* Belfast: Falls Community Council.

McAuley, Chrissie
    1989   *Women in a War Zone: Twenty Years of Resistance.* Dublin: Republican Publication.

McCafferty, Nell
    1981   *The Armagh Women.* Dublin: Co-Op Books.

McCafferty, Nell
  1987 *Good Night Sisters: Selectie Writings.* Vol. 2. Dublin: Attic Press.
  1989 *Peggy Deery: A Deery Family at War.* London: Virago.
McCann, Eamon
  1980 *War and an Irish Town.* London: Pluto.
McCann, Mary
  1985 "The Past in the Present: A Study of Some Aspects of the Politics of
        Music in Belfast." Ph.D. diss., Queen's University.
McGuinn, Nicholas
  1986 *Seamus Heaney: A Student's Guide to the Selected Poems.* Leeds: Arnold-
        Wheaton.
McLaverty, Michael
  1939 *Call My Brother Back.* London: Longmans.
McVeigh, Robbie
  1994 *"It's Part of Life Here . . . ": The Security Forces and Harrassment in Northern
        Ireland.* Belfast: Committee on the Administration of Justice.
Meaney, Gerardine
  1991 *Sex and Nation: Women in Irish Culture and Politics.* Dublin: Attic
        Press.
Medbh, Máighréad
  1993 Nationalism and National Identities. *Feminist Review* 44.
Memmi, Albert
  1965 *The Colonizer and the Colonized.* Boston: Beacon Press.
Messenger, Betty
  1975 *Picking Up the Linen Threads.* Belfast: Blackstaff Press.
Mohanty, Chandra Talpade, Ann Russo, and Lourdes Torres, eds.
  1991 *Third World Women and the Politics of Feminism.* Bloomington: Indiana
        University Press.
Montgomery, Pamela, and Celia Davies
  1990 *Women's Lives in Northern Ireland Today: A Guide to Reading.* Coleraine:
        University of Ulster.
Moore, Ruth
  1993 "Proper Wives, Orange Maidens or Disloyal Subjets: Situating the
        Equality Concerns of Protestant Women in Northern Ireland." M.A.
        thesis, University College Dublin.
Moore, Sally
  1987 "Explaining the Present: Theoretical Dilemmas in Processual Ethnog-
        raphy." *American Ethnologist* 14(4):727–751.
Morris, James
  1978 *Farewell the Trumpets: An Imperial Retreat.* London: Faber and Faber.
Murphy, Brenda
  1989 "A Curse." In Louis DeSalvo, Kathleen Walsh D'Arcy, and Katherine
        Hogan, eds., *Territories of the Voice. Contemporary Stories by Irish Women
        Writers,* pp. 226–227. Boston: Beacon Press.

Nandy, Ashis
   1980   *At the Edge of Psychology: Essays in Politics and Culture.* Delhi: Oxford University Press.
   1983   *The Intimate Enemy: Loss and Recovery of Self under Colonialism.* Delhi: Oxford University Press.
Nash, Catherine
   1993   "Remapping and Renaming: New Cartographies of Identity, Gender and Landscape in Ireland." *Feminist Review* 44:39–58.
Nash, June, and María Patricia Fernández-Kelly, eds.
   1983   *Women, Men, and the International Division of Labor.* Albany: State University of New York Press.
Ni Dhomhnaill, Nuala
   1989   "Ghaeilge as a Feminist Weapon/An Ghaeilge Mar Uirlis Fheiminteach." In Fran Devaney, Marie Mullholland, and Judith Willoughby, eds., *Unfinished Revolution: Essays on the Irish Women's Movement,* 22–23. Belfast: Meadbh Publishing.
Nordstrom, Carolyn, and JoAnn Martin, eds.
   1992   *The Paths to Domination, Reistance, and Terror.* Berkeley: University of California Press.
O'Dowd, Liam
   1987   "Church, State and Women: The Aftermath of Partition." In Chris Curtin, Pauline Jackson, Barbara O'Connor eds., *Gender in Irish Society,* pp. 3–36. Galway: Galway University Press.
O'Hogain, Daithi
   1985   *The Hero in Irish Folk History.* Dublin: Gill and Macmillan.
O'Malley, Padraig
   1990   *Biting at the Grave. The Irish Hunger-Strikes and the Politics of Despair.* Boston: Beacon Press.
Obeyesekere, Gananath
   1975   "Sinhalese-Buddhist Identity in Ceylon." In George De Vos and Lola Romanucci-Ross, eds., *Ethnic Identity, Cultural Continuities, and Change,* pp. 231–259. Palo Alto, Calif.: Mayfield Publishing.
   1990   *The Work of Culture: Symbolic Transformation in Psychoanalysis and Anthropology.* Chicago: University of Chicago Press.
Ong, Aihwa
   1983   "Global Industries and Malay Peasants in Peninsular Malaysia." In June Nash and María Patricia Fernández-Kelly, eds., *Women, Men and the International Division of Labor,* pp. 426–39. New York: State University of New York.
Ortner, Sherry
   1984   "Theory in Anthropology in the Sixties." *Comparative Studies in Society and History* 26(1):126–66.
   1995   "Resistance and the Problem of Ethnographic Refusal." *Comparative Studies in Society and History* 37(1):173–93.

Owens, Rosemary Cullen
  1984   *Smashing Times: A History of the Irish Women's Movement 1889–1922.*
         Dublin: Attic Press.

Pathak, Zakia, and Rajeswari Sunder Rajan
  1992   "Shahbano." In Judith Butler and Joan Scott, eds., *Feminists Theorize the
         Political,* pp. 257–79. New York: Routledge.

Pearse, Padraic
  1917   *Collected Works of Padraic Pearse: Plays, Stories, Poems.* Dublin: Phoenix
         Publishing.

Peteet, Julie Marie
  1991   *Gender in Crisis: Women and the Palestinian Resistance Movement.* New
         York: Columbia University Press.

Plunkett, Joseph
  1916   *The Poems of Joseph Mary Plunkett.* Dublin: Talbot.

Renan, Ernest
  1970 [1896]   *The Poetry of the Celtic Races: And Other Studies.* William G. Hutchin-
         son, trans. Port Washington, N.Y.: Kennikat Press.

Ridd, Rosemary, and Helen Callaway
  1986   *Caught Up in Conflict: Women Responses to Political Strife.* London: MacMillan.

Rolston, Bill
  1983   *A Social Science Bibliography of Northern Ireland.* Belfast: Queen's University.
  1987   "Politics, Painting and Popular Culture: The Political Wall Murals of
         Northern Ireland." *Media, Culture and Society* 9:5–28.
  1989   "Mothers, Whores and Villains: Images of Women in Novels of the
         Nothern Ireland Conflict." *Race and Class* 31(1):41–58.

Rolston Bill, and Mike Tomlinson
  1988   *Unemployment in West Belfst: The OBAIR Report.* Belfast: Beyond the Pale
         Publications.

Rosaldo, Renato
  1989   *Culture and Truth. The Remaking of Social Analysis.* Boston: Beacon
         Press.

Rosen, Lawrence
  1984   *Bargaining For Reality: The Construction of Social Relations in a Muslim
         Community.* Chicago: University of Chicago Press.

Rowthorn, Bob, and Naomi Wayne
  1988   *Northern Ireland: The Political Economy of the Conflict.* Cambridge: Polity
         Press.

Rulfo, Juan
  1987   *Pedro Paramo.* Mexico: Fondo de Cultura Economica.

Said, Edward
  1978   *Orientalism.* New York: Pantheon Books.

Sands, Bobby
  1982   *Skylark Sing Your Lonely Song. An Anthology of the Writings of Bobby Sands.*
         Cork and Dublin: Mercier Press.

1983   *One Day in My Life.* London: Pluto Press.

Sangari, Kumkum, and Sudesh Vaid

1990   *Recasting Women: Essays in Indian Colonial History.* New Brunswick, N.J.: Rutgers University Press.

Scarry, Elaine

1985   *The Body in Pain: The Making and Unmaking of the World.* New York: Oxford University Press.

Scheper-Hughes, Nancy

1992   *Death without Weeping: The Violence of Everyday Life in Brazil.* Berkeley: University of California Press.

Scott, James C.

1985   *Weapons of the Weak: Everyday Forms of Peasant Resistance.* New Haven, Conn.: Yale University Press.

Scott, Joan

1988   *Gender and the Politics of History.* New York: Columbia University Press.

1991   "The Evidence of Experience." *Critical Inquiry* 17(4):773–97.

Shannon, Elizabeth

1989   *I Am of Ireland: Women of the North Speak Out.* Boston: Little, Brown and Company.

Shostak, Marjorie

1981   *Nisa, the Life and Words of a !Kung Woman.* Cambridge, Mass.: Harvard University Press.

Silverblatt, Irene

1987   *Moon, Sun and Witches: Gender Ideologies and Class in Inca and Colonial Peru.* Princeton, N.J.: Princeton University Press.

Sluka, Jeffrey

1989   *Hearts and Minds, Water and Fish. Support for the INLA in a Northern Irish Ghetto.* Greenwich, Conn.: AI Press.

1992   "The Politics of Painting." In Carolyn Nordstrom and JoAnn Martin, eds., *The Paths to Domination, Resistance, and Terror,* pp. 190–218. Berkeley: University of California Press.

Spenser, Edmund

1970 [1633]   *A View of the Present State of Ireland.* Oxford: Clarendon Press.

Spivak, Gayatri

1988   "Introduction to Draupadi by Mahasweti Devi." In *In Other Worlds: Essays in Cultural Politics.* New York: Routledge.

1988   "Can the Subaltern Speak?" In Cary Nelson and Lawrence Grossberg, eds., *Marxism and the Interpretation of Cultures,* pp. 271–316. Urbana: University of Illinois Press.

Stallybrass, Peter, and Allon White

1986   *The Politics and Poetics of Transgression.* Ithaca, N.Y.: Cornell University Press.

Steedly, Mary Margaret

1993   *Hanging Without a Rope: Narrative Experience in Colonial and Postcolonial Karoland.* Princeton, N.J.: Princeton University Press.

Steedman, Carolyn
  1987   *Landscape for a Good Woman: A Story of Two Lives.* New Brunswick, N.J.:
          Rutgers University Press.
Steward, Anthony Terence Quincy
  1986   *The Narrow Ground. Patterns of Ulster History.* Belfast: Pretani Press.
Stoler, Ann Laura
  1991   "Carnal Knowledge and Imperial Power: Gender, Race and Morality in
          Colonial Asia." In Micaela De Leonardo, ed., *Gender at the Crossroads of
          Knowledge: Feminist Anthropology in the Postmodern Era,* pp. 51–101.
          Berkeley: University of California Press.
Strathern, Marilyn
  1986   "Concrete Topographies." *Cultural Anthropology* 3(1):88–96.
  1987   "An Awkward Relationship: The Case of Feminism and Anthropology."
          Signs 12(2):276–92.
Suarez-Orozco, Marcelo
  1992   "A Grammar of Terror: Psychocultural Responses to State Terrorism in
          Dirty War and Post-Dirty War Argentina." In Carolyn Nordstrom and
          Jo Ann Martin, eds., *The Paths to Domination, Resistance and Terror,*
          pp. 219–60. Berkeley: University of California Press.
Suleri, Sara
  1992a   *The Rhetoric of English India.* Chicago: University of Chicago Press.
  1992b   "Women Skin Deep." *Critical Inquiry* 18(4):756–69.
Sunday Times Insight Team [STIT]
  1972   *Ulster.* London: Andre Deutsch.
Tambiah, Stanley Jeyaraja
  1985   *Culture, Thought, and Social Action: An Anthropological Perspective.* Cam-
          bridge, Mass.: Harvard University Press.
Taussig, Michael
  1987   *Shamanism, Colonialism, and the Wild Man: A Study in Terror and Healing.*
          Chicago: University of Chicago Press.
Thompson, William I.
  1982   *The Imagination of an Insurrection. Dublin, Easter 1916: A Study of an Ide-
          ological Movement.* West Stockbridge, Mass.: Lindistarne Press.
Timerman, Jacobo
  1981   *Prisoner without A Name, Cell without A Number.* New York: Knopf.
Toibin, Colm
  1987   *Martyrs and Metaphors.* Dublin: Raven Art Press.
Vincent, Joan
  n.d.   "Fasting to Death: The Poetic and Politics of the Irish Hunger Strike of
          1981." Manuscript.
Visweswaran, Kamala
  1994   *Fictions of Feminist Ethnography.* Minneapolis: University of Minnesota
          Press.

Ward, Margaret, ed.
  1983   *Unmanageable Revolutionaries. Women and Irish Nationalism.* London: Pluto Press.
  1987   *A Difficult, Dangerous Honesty. Ten Years of Feminism in Northern Ireland. A Discussion.* Belfast: Women's News.
  1991   "The Women's Movement in the North of Ireland: Twenty Years On." In S. Hutton and P. Steward, eds., *Ireland's Histories: Aspects of State, Society and Ideology,* pp. 149–63. London: Routledge.
Ward, Margaret, and Marie-Therese McGivern
  1980   "Images of Women in Northern Ireland." In Mark Patrick Hederman and Richard Kearney, eds., *The Crane Bag Book of Irish Studies,* pp. 579–85. Dublin: Blackwater Press.
Warner, Marina
  1983   *Alone of All Her Sex: The Myth and Cult of the Virgin Mary.* New York: Vintage.
Warren, Kay
  1989   *The Symbolism of Subordiantion: Indian Identity in a Guatemalan Town.* Austin: University of Texas Press.
  1992   "Interpreting *La Violencia* in Guatemala: The Many Shapes of Mayan Silence and Resistance in the 1970s and 1980s." In Kay Warren, ed., *The Violence within: Cultural and Political Opposition in Divided Nations.* pp. 25–56. Boulder, Colo.: Westview Press.
Weber, Max
  1949   *On the Methodology of the Social Sciences.* Edward A. Shils and Henry A. Finch, eds. Glencoe, Ill.: Free Press.
  1978   "The Sociology of Religion." In *Economy and Society,* 1:399–634. Berkeley: University of California Press.
Weekes, Ann Owens
  1995   "Ordinary Women: Themes in Contemporary Fiction by Irish Women." *Colby Quarterly* 31(1):88–99.
Whyte, John
  1990   *Interpreting Northern Ireland.* New York: Oxford University Press.
Wilde, Oscar
  1982 [1898]   "The Ballad of Reading Gaol." In H. Montgomery Hyde, ed., *The Annotated Oscar Wilde: Poems, Fiction, Plays, Lectures, Essays, and Letters,* pp. 60–74. New York: Clarkson N. Potter.
Williams, Raymond
  1977   *Marxism and Literature.* London: Oxford University Press.
  1983   *Keywords: A Vocabulary of Culture and Society.* London: Fontana Paperbacks.
Wilson, Basil C. S.
  1967   "The Birth of Belfast." In James Beckett and Robin Glasscock, eds., *Belfast: The Origin and Growth of an Industrial City,* pp. 14–25. London: British Broadcasting Corporation.

Women Against Imperialism
   1980   *Women Protest for Political Status in Armagh Gaol.*
Yeats, William Butler
   1937 [1904] *The King's Threshold.* London: Macmillan.
   1953   *Collected Plays.* New York: Macmillan.
Zell, Ann
   1990   *Banshee in the Office.* Belfast: Falls Women's Center.
Zimmerman, Georges Denis
   1966   *Irish Political Street Ballads and Rebel Songs.* Geneva: Impr. La Sirene.
Zulaika, Joseba
   1988   *Basque Violence: Metaphor and Sacrament.* Reno: University of Nevada Press.

* Index *

abjection, 20
abortion, 162, 165, 166, 168
Abu-DLughod, Lila, 19, 101, 177n.9
Adams, Gerry, 3, 173
agency, 8, 16–17, 38, 162–63, 165, 167
allegory, 70, 74, 151
Algerian war of liberation, 66
Amnesty International, 102
Anderson, Benedict, xii, 15
Anglo-Irish Treaty, 15, 95, 179n.5
anticolonial nationalist discourse, 148
Antigone, 5
anthropological location, 25–26
Appadurai, Arjun, 25, 26
Ard Chomhairle, 165
Ardner, Shirley, 182n.12
Aretxaga, Begoña, 136
Armagh dirty protest. *See* dirty protest
Armagh prison, 76; "A" wing, 125, 137; "B" wing, 123
Armagh women, beatings of, 123–24; and gender, 138; and feminism, 144; and IRA, 122, 143–44; and language, 144; and mimesis, 126, 144, 162; and NIWRM, 143–44, 162; and pain, 134–35; play produced about, 182n.11; political interest in, 126; and popular consciousness, 137; protest of treatment of, 125; and sexual violation, 51; work strike of, 122
"the armalite and the ballot box," 93
Armstrong, D. L., 29
Arnold, Matthew, 147, 148, 168
Ashe, Tomas, 83
Association for Legal Justice, 132

"B Specials," 31, 56
ballads and songs, 108
Ballymurphy, 35
Bardon, Jonathan, 28, 51
Basque country, 21–22
Basque nationalism, 22
Bateson, Ann, 123–24
Beale, Jenny, 129

Beall, Jo, Shireen Hassim, and Alison Todes, 78
Beckett, James Camlin, and Robin E. Glasscock, eds., 26, 27
Beckett, Mary, 10
Beechmount, 36, 72 fig. 10
Behar, Ruth, 177n.9
Belfast, 24–29; and geography, 92–93; ghettoes in, 61, 88–89; ghettoization of, 42–43, 178–79n.4; and identity, 41–42; landscape of, 92; and military surveillance, 43; street names, 42; and territoriality, 41–42; topography of, 32. *See also* East Belfast; West Belfast
Belfast neighborhoods, 32–37
Belfast Women's Center, ix
Belfast Women's Collective, 143, 157
Bell, J. Bowyer, 179n.6
belonging, 40–42
Benjamin, Walter, 94
Beresford, David, 90, 126, 179n.2, 180n.10
Bhabha, Homi, 12, 66, 67, 178n.4
"Black and Tans," 40, 58–59
"black taxis," 33–34
blanket protest, 84, 179n.7
Blinchy, D. A., 82
Boal, Frederick, and J. Neville Douglas, 32, 41, 42
Boal, Frederick, Russel Murray, and Michael Poole, 32
body. *See* hunger strike; men's bodies; women's bodies
body searches, 112–14; of women, 66–67, 132
Boland, Eavan, 167
Bondi, Liz, 24
border zone, 36–37
Bourdieu, Pierre, 8
Bourque, Susan C., and Kay B. Warren, 17
Brasted, Howard, 13
Brehon Law. *See* Gaelic Brehon Law
British Army, 67–68; and occupation, 43, 70, 89, 92; and sexual harassment, 70, 151–52